Perspectives on the Architecture and Acquisition of Syntax

Gautam Sengupta · Shruti Sircar
Madhavi Gayathri Raman
Rahul Balusu
Editors

Perspectives on the Architecture and Acquisition of Syntax

Essays in Honor of R. Amritavalli

Springer

Editors
Gautam Sengupta
Center for Applied Linguistics
and Translation Studies
University of Hyderabad
Hyderabad, Telangana
India

Madhavi Gayathri Raman
Department of Materials Development,
Testing and Evaluation
The English and Foreign Languages
University
Hyderabad, Telangana
India

Shruti Sircar
Department of Linguistics and
Contemporary English
The English and Foreign Languages
University
Hyderabad, Telangana
India

Rahul Balusu
Department of Computational Linguistics
The English and Foreign Languages
University
Hyderabad, Telangana
India

ISBN 978-981-10-4294-2 ISBN 978-981-10-4295-9 (eBook)
DOI 10.1007/978-981-10-4295-9

Library of Congress Control Number: 2017939307

Printed on acid-free paper

This Springer imprint is published by Springer Nature
The registered company is Springer Nature Singapore Pte Ltd.
The registered company address is: 152 Beach Road, #21-01/04 Gateway East, Singapore 189721, Singapore

Foreword

Raghavachari Amritavalli has made outstanding contributions to syntactic theory, the study of the interfaces, and the analysis of South Asian languages. She also focused on the acquisition of morpho-syntax and on language-related developmental pathologies, as well as on language teaching and education curricula.

This volume honors Amritavalli's contribution to the field through a collection of cutting-edge research papers ranging from syntactic theory and the morpho-syntax of South and East Asian languages, to the syntax–semantics interface, and the acquisition of syntax. This impressive collection mirrors Amritavalli's wide range of interests and reflects the need to extend the empirical coverage of syntactic theorizing to new empirical domains, such as the study of language acquisition, a need that many syntacticians now consider a priority for the field.

Why is this aspect so important? In these introductory remarks, I would like to briefly dwell on the reasons which lead many of us to consider different kinds of enrichment of the empirical domains of our formal models. One motivation finds its roots in the very nature of formal linguistic theoretical work (and, in fact, in any form of abstract modeling). Theoreticians are typically confronted with a proliferation of analytic options, consistent with the available empirical data and inconsistent with each other. One reasonable tack to reduce the explosion of possible analytic paths is to severely constrain the technical apparatus, our "bag of tricks," trying to admit only the bare minimum required to meet empirical adequacy. This is the tack adopted by minimalism. One difficulty that this research strategy is confronted with is to agree on what the "bare minimum" is: Different concepts of simplicity may give conflicting results on what is the minimal specification of analytic tools. For instance, if we understand "simplest" as "least constrained," we may be led to assume n-ary merge as the optimal form of the operation: The least constrained formulation of merge is one which does not specify the number of elements undergoing the operation, hence n-ary merge, for n = 1, 2, 3,…. On the other hand, if we understand "simplest" as "requiring minimal computational resources," we may be led to assume binary merge: Unary merge is too weak in expressive power to capture the properties of natural languages, and ternary merge (and, a fortiori, merge of 4 elements, 5 elements, etc.) requires more resources than binary merge, as all the elements to be merged together must be held simultaneously in operative memory. In this case, much evidence in favor of binary branching syntactic structures, ever since Richard Kayne's classical contributions in the 1980s, supports the conception of simplicity qua "requirement of minimal computational resources," which selects binary merge.

This leads us to the second strategy to limit the proliferation of analytic paths, which can fruitfully integrate the minimalist strategy. If the empirical coverage of theoretical models is extended to new domains, it is to be hoped that new kinds of evidence will emerge which will favor certain analytic paths over others. Over the last quarter of century, much work on the theory-guided study of language acquisition has nourished formal theoretical work in important ways, and the same is to be expected from the theory-guided experimental study of production and comprehension, of language-related pathologies, and, through brain imaging techniques, of the concrete expression in neural circuitry of our linguistic capacities, among other research directions.

Reciprocally, richly structured theoretical analyses are of fundamental importance for all kinds of experimental work on language, with the role of generators of precise predictions identifying interesting research questions. Otherwise, there is a concrete risk that a sophisticated methodological apparatus may be used by experimental approaches to merely test commonsense ideas on language. Clearly, experimental approaches must be based on structured theories of the fundamental capacities under investigation, rather than on mere commonsense ideas, if the potential of an extraordinary investment in methodology, a characteristic of experimental psycholinguistics, is to be fully exploited.

Another important reason favoring the extension of formal syntactic approaches to new testing grounds has to do with the image and role of syntactic theory in the larger scientific context of cognitive and brain studies, and of its applications in clinical work and education. It is of decisive importance for the future of our discipline that it will not be perceived as an exoteric, self-centered domain, but as a fundamental research direction capable of offering insights on language to neighboring disciplines and generating a wealth of applicative studies on linguistic capacities broadly construed. This is essential if formal linguistics wants to maintain the central role that it had from the outset of the cognitive revolution.

Amritavalli's work has always aimed at such a breadth of range, without sacrificing the necessary depth of formal analysis of such phenomena as ergativity, finiteness, argument structure and the nature and properties of thematic roles, and the other phenomena addressed in her scientific production. This volume, through its joint focus on theoretical architecture and language acquisition in chapters written by major figures in the field, pays a well-deserved tribute to Amritavalli's influential contribution to linguistic studies, in Asia and in the world.

Geneva, Switzerland
December 2016

Luigi Rizzi
Professor of Linguistics, University of Geneva

Contents

Editors and Contributors

About the Editors

Gautam Sengupta received his Ph.D. in linguistics from the University of Massachusetts at Amherst in 1990 and is currently Professor at the Center for Applied Linguistics and Translation Studies, University of Hyderabad. He has also taught at the Jawaharlal Nehru University, New Delhi, and Jadavpur University, Kolkata. His areas of interest are syntax, semantics, and language processing.

Shruti Sircar teaches at the Department of Linguistics and Contemporary English, EFL University, as a Professor. Her major areas of interest are first- and second-language acquisition, psycholinguistics, reading development, and disorders.

Madhavi Gayathri Raman teaches at the Department of Materials Development, Testing and Evaluation, EFL University. Her research interests are Specific Language Impairment and Dyslexia in the ESL context, curriculum development, materials design and cognitive linguistics.

Rahul Balusu teaches at the Department of Computational Linguistics, EFL University. He received a Ph.D. in linguistics at NYU in 2009. His areas of interest are syntax and semantics, focusing on Dravidian languages.

Contributors

Josef Bayer is professor of linguistics at the University of Konstanz. Before 2000, he held a professor's position at the University of Jena and various research positions. His interest focuses on syntax and its interfaces as well its relation to language processing. He has worked on Germanic (mainly German and its dialects) and on Indo-Aryan (Bangla). For a number of years, the proper syntactic representation of focus, as well as discourse particles, has been central to his work. Josef Bayer's research was funded by a number of grants from the Deutsche Forschungsgesellschaft (DFG) (German Research Counsil). He is author or coauthor of two monographs and seventy six articles, and editor or coeditor of eight volumes.

Rajesh Bhatt received his Ph.D. in Linguistics from the University of Pennsylvania in 1999 and is currently Professor in the Department of Linguistics at the University of Massachusetts Amherst. He has also taught at UT Austin and MIT. His work focuses on syntax and its interfaces with semantics and on the Modern Indo-Aryan languages.

Fanyin Cheng is a graduate student at the University of Colorado at Boulder. She is interested in speech and language processing of bilinguals. Her current project examines the language processing of Mandarin–English bilinguals.

Probal Dasgupta Ph.D. (Linguistics), 1980, New York University, has taught in New York, San Francisco, Melbourne, Barlaston, Kolkata, Pune, Hyderabad and is presently based at the Indian Statistical Institute, Kolkata, since 2006. His editorial work includes *Indian Linguistics* (1982–87), *Language Problems and Language Planning* (with Humphrey Tonkin, Tim Reagan 1990–), *Beletra Almanako* (with Jorge Camacho, Istvan Ertl, Tim Westover, Jesper Jacobsen, Suso Moinhos, 2007–), book series *Language and Development* (with Udaya Narayana Singh, 1993–2004), and *Yearbook of South Asian Languages and Linguistics* (with Rajendra Singh, 1998–06).

He is Member of the Akademio de Esperanto since 1983 [on account of translation of 50 poems by Tagore into Esperanto, published as *Primico*, Antwerp: TK/Stafeto, 1977], its Vice-President 2001–15, and now its President (2016–). He is an honorary member of the Linguistic Society of America (2004–) and was President of the World Esperanto Association, *Universala Esperanto-Asocio* (2007–2013). He was awarded the Annual Visiting Lectureship in Philosophy 2008–09 by the Indian Council of Philosophical Research.

He has over 400 other publications in Bangla, English, Esperanto, in the domains of linguistics, literature, translation, philosophy. Book-length publications in English include *The Otherness of English: India's Auntie Tongue* Syndrome, New Delhi: Sage, 1993; *Inhabiting Human Languages*: The *Substantivist Visualization*, Delhi: Samskriti, on behalf of the Indian Council of Philosophical Research. Books in Bangla include: *Kathaar Kriyaakarmo* (Dey's 1987), *Chinno Kathaae Shaajaaye Taroni* (Gangchil 2011), *Bhaashaar Bindubishargo* (Gangchil 2013), *Merur Praarthonaa*: *Bishuber Uttor* (Abhijan 2015). Books translated into Bangla: *Hlaapicer Kaando* by Ivana Brlić-Mažuranić (Samatat 2006); *Nemesis* by Alfred Nobel (M.C. Sarkar 2014).

Patricia Davidson is a graduate student in Linguistics at Syracuse University with a concentration in Information Representation and Retrieval, as well as a Certificate of Advanced Study in Data Science. Research interests include Language Acquisition and Natural Language Processing, with a particular interest in text mining and machine translation.

K.A. Jayaseelan obtained an M.A. in Linguistics from Lancaster University. He was at that time employed at the Central Institute of English and Foreign Languages (CIEFL) in Hyderabad. Further interest in linguistics ensued, and at Simon Fraser University in Canada he completed a Ph.D in 1980, the dissertation being on Deletion and Interpretation in Comparatives. He returned to CIEFL and was able to create a unique atmosphere for generative linguistics at CIEFL which had a lasting impact for years to come. Jayaseelan held the chair of the School of Language Sciences until his retirement in the year 2002 and trained an impressive number of students up to the level of Ph.D.

Pui Fong Kan is an Associate Professor in the Department of Speech, Language, and Hearing Sciences of the University of Colorado at Boulder. Her research examines the effects of language experience on bilinguals' language learning across the life span. Her current projects investigate the developmental trajectory of the language learning in typically developing bilingual children and bilingual children with language impairments.

Richard S. Kayne is currently Silver Professor of Linguistics at New York University. He previously taught at the CUNY Graduate Center, at MIT and at the University of Paris VIII. He has a Docteur ès Lettres degree in linguistics from Paris VIII (1976) and a Ph.D. in linguistics from MIT (1969). He also has three honorary degrees: Laurea honoris causa 2015 Venice, Doctorate honoris causa 2011 Bucharest, Doctorate honoris causa 1995 Leiden.

Stefan Keine received his Ph.D. in Linguistics from the University of Massachusetts Amherst in 2016 and is currently Assistant Professor in the Department of Linguistics at the University of Southern California. His work focuses on syntax and its interfaces with morphology, semantics, and sentence processing.

Hilda Koopman is Professor of Linguistics at the University of California at Los Angeles. She works in formal syntax and comparative (morpho-) syntax. As a fieldworker and theoretician, her descriptive and theoretical interests interact closely in her research. She brings data from typologically diverse languages to bear on issues of a highly theoretical nature, and conversely, she applies abstract and complex theoretical concepts to their analysis. Her current research explores the idea that syntactic properties of individual languages fall out from the way surface constituency is built by merge from minute atomic parts that underlie morphological and syntactic constituency, with linear order mapping onto asymmetric c-command. Her publications include several books such as *The Syntax of Verbs From V Movement in the KRU Languages to Universal Grammar* (1983), *The Syntax of Specifiers and Heads* (2000), *Verbal Complexes* (2000, with Anna Szabolcsi), and *Introduction to Linguistic Analysis and Syntactic Theory* (2013, with Dominique Sportiche and Edward Stabler), and numerous articles. Since 2013, she has been in charge of the development of SSWL Syntactic Structure of the World's Languages, a community database for the (morpho-)syntactic properties of the world's languages.

Utpal Lahiri is an Associate Professor at the Department of Linguistics and Contemporary English, EFL University, Hyderabad. His research interests are primarily in semantic theory, with its interfaces with syntax and other areas of theoretical linguistics. He has published widely on the semantics of questions, polarity, scalar particles and on their relevance to semantic theory in general and is currently involved in research on modals.

Keiko Murasugi is Professor at Nanzan University. Her research interests are syntax and psycholinguistics, in particular, grammar acquisition. She was born in Nagano Prefecture, Japan and holds a Ph.D. in Linguistics from the University of Connecticut (1991).

Bhuvana Narasimhan is an Associate Professor of Linguistics at the University of Colorado, Boulder. She conducts research on argument structure and verb meaning, the language–cognition interface, and first language acquisition. Her specific interests include cross-linguistic and developmental studies of lexical semantics, verb argument structure, information structure, and morpho-syntax.

Mamoru Saito after completing his Ph.D. at MIT in 1985 taught at USC, University of Tsukuba, and University of Connecticut. He has been Professor of Linguistics at Nanzan University since 1995. His main research interest is in Japanese syntax and syntactic theory. Among his recent articles are "Sentence Types and the Japanese Right Periphery" (in Günther Grewendorf and Thomas Ede Zimmermann, eds., *Discourse and Grammar*, de Gruyter, 2012), "Selection and Incorporation in Complex Predicate Formation" (in Audrey Li, Andrew Simpson, and Wei-Tien Dylan Tsai, eds., *Chinese Syntax in a Cross-Linguistic Perspective*, Oxford University Press, 2014), "Cartography and Selection: Case Studies in Japanese" (in Ur Shlonsky, ed., *Beyond Functional Sequence*, Oxford University Press, 2015), "Remnant Movement, Radical Reconstruction, and Binding Relations" (in Günther Grewendorf, ed., *Remnant Movement*, de Gruyter, 2015), and "(A) Case for Labeling: Labeling in Languages without ϕ-feature Agreement" (*The Linguistic Review* 33.1, 2016). He has been a coeditor of *Journal of East Asian Linguistics* since 1995 and edited a few books, the most recent being *Japanese Syntax in Comparative Perspective* (Oxford University Press, 2014).

William Snyder is Professor of Linguistics at the University of Connecticut. His work examines the time course of child language acquisition as a source of insight into what exactly the child is acquiring, and how exactly the child is doing it.

Specific research topics include argument structure (datives, resultatives, particles, path phrases), A- and A-bar movement (passives, reflexive-clitic constructions, P-stranding, comparatives), compound words, and syllable structure. Snyder completed his S.B. and Ph.D. degrees at the MIT. He is past editor of the journal *Language Acquisition: A Journal of Developmental Linguistics,* and he is the author of *Child Language: The Parametric Approach,* and coeditor of *The Oxford Handbook of Developmental Linguistics.*

Wei-Tien Dylan Tsai received his Ph.D. degree in linguistics from MIT in 1994 and is currently Professor at the Graduate Institute of Linguistics, National Tsing Hua University, Taiwan. His recent research explores issues on the syntax-semantics interface under the cartographic approach, with an emphasis on Chinese, Austronesian, and Slavic languages from a comparative point of view. These studies lead to a series of publications on the inner-outer dichotomy of *wh*-adverbials, reflexive adverbials, affectives, and light verbs, which is shown to encode comitativity in the *v*P periphery and causality in the left periphery. Furthermore, he proposes a formal analysis of the grammaticalization of conjunctions/linkers across languages, based upon the notion of "conjunctive reduction." He serves as Editor of *International Journal of Chinese Linguistics* (with Hongming Zhang and Ning Yu) since 2013.

Madison Wagner is an undergraduate student at Scripps College. She is studying Gender Studies, French, and Linguistics. Her research interests include reproductive justice and linguistic relativity.

Chapter 1
A Life in Linguistics

Gautam Sengupta, Shruti Sircar, Madhavi Gayathri Raman and Rahul Balusu

Raghavachari Amritavalli was born in Bangalore and obtained an M.A in English from Bangalore University in 1972, before finding employment at the Central Institute of English and Foreign Languages (CIEFL) in the Department of Media and Television. This department had the distinction of being the pioneer (in India) of the use of radio and television for educational purposes—specifically English Language Teaching. Her work here involved making English lessons for All India Radio (AIR), the state-run national radio channel, and producing TV programs for English teaching that combined game, drama, and documentary-style narrative. This was the background to her abiding interest in the language curriculum: she would eventually play a pivotal role in developing a national curriculum for English in Indian schools. She has also written books in this field such as *English in Deprived Circumstances: Maximizing Learner Autonomy* (Cambridge University Press, 2007) and *Language as a Dynamic Text: Essays on Language, Cognition and Communication* in the CIEFL Akshara series in 2000. Her interest in English

G. Sengupta
Center for Applied Linguistics and Translation Studies, University of Hyderabad, Hyderabad, Telangana, India
e-mail: gsghyd@gmail.com

S. Sircar
Department of Linguistics and Contemporary English, The English and Foreign Languages University, Hyderabad 500007, Telangana, India
e-mail: shrutisircar@gmail.com

M.G. Raman
Department of Materials Development, Testing and Evaluation, The English and Foreign Languages University, Hyderabad 500007, Telangana, India
e-mail: gayathriraman@yahoo.com

R. Balusu (✉)
Department of Computational Linguistics, The English and Foreign Languages University, Hyderabad 500007, Telangana, India
e-mail: kodiguddu@gmail.com

G. Sengupta et al. (eds.), *Perspectives on the Architecture and Acquisition of Syntax*, DOI 10.1007/978-981-10-4295-9_1

language learning and the role of language in society and education has led to such output as "Teaching Language and Achieving Literacy: Interfering with Learning or Guiding It?" (Amritavalli 2014a); "An English for Every Schoolchild in India" (Amritavalli 2013a); "Helping Children Become Readers" (Amritavalli 2012a); "Visible and Invisible Aspects of Language Ability" (Amritavalli 2012b); "Media Work: An Authentic Context for Developing Communication Skills in English" (Amritavalli 2008a,b); "Students' Understanding of Dictionary Entries: A Study with Respect to Four Learners' Dictionaries" (Amritavalli et al. 2003); "Pictured Realities and Pictures of Reality: Cross-cultural Intelligibility of the Visual in Television" (Amritavalli 1997a); "Communication, technology, and the evolution of systems of knowledge and education" (Amritavalli 1996); "Audio Versions of Textbook Materials: A Tryout" (Amritavalli and Visalakshy 1992); "Understanding English by Radio" (Amritavalli 1988a); and "The role of audio-visual aids in distance education" (Amritavalli 1988b).

Her fascination for the cognitive and scientific underpinnings of natural language took her to the linguistics department of Simon Fraser University, from where she obtained a Ph.D. in linguistics in 1980. She came back to CIEFL to teach and do cutting-edge research in theoretical linguistics, before retiring a few years after holding the post of vice-chancellor's at EFLU (CIEFL had been made a university and renamed the English and Foreign Languages University some years previously), one of India's largest public universities specialized in humanities and languages. In CIEFL and EFLU, she epitomized an intellectual life that was as honest as it was creative and balanced. She was the chairperson of the English Focus Group of the committee that formulated the National Curriculum Framework (NFC) (2005) of the National Council of Educational Research and Training (NCERT); a member of National Assessment and Accreditation Council for Universities, University Grants Commission, India; and a member of the National Knowledge Commission, Working Group on Languages. She is currently a member of the Task Force, Cognitive Science Research Initiative, Ministry of Science and Technology, Government of India (GOI).

She views "India as a laboratory for language and cognitive science" (Amritavalli 2015). Her academic career over four decades involved sharing her passion for generative linguistics and language acquisition through both highly original papers and innovative teaching. Her research interests span a broad gamut of topics in Cognitive Science—Theoretical linguistics (morphology, syntax); acquisition/teaching of first and second languages in natural and instructional settings; and the psychology of perception, especially in media and education, and reading research. Her broad spectrum of interests culminated in her founding and editing *The EFL Journal*, a peer-reviewed journal published twice a year, that includes articles from both young and established researchers internationally in the areas of literature, language learning and teaching, and linguistics pertaining to English and foreign languages such as Arabic, Chinese, French, German, Japanese, Russian, and Spanish; this journal has been publishing now for over seven years (2010–2017) (www.openhumanitiesalliance.org/journals/eflj).

She has worked on a wide range of significant empirical phenomena in South Asian languages that have broadly impacted syntactic theory, including ergativity, non-nominative subjects, causatives, argument structure, case assignment and agreement processes, number and gender, and finiteness.

Her landmark paper, "The genesis of syntactic categories and parametric variation," with K. A. Jayaseelan (Amritavalli and Jayaseelan 2003) argues from a crosslinguistic perspective that the dative case on experiencers and inalienable possessors is tied to an absence, or at least impoverishment, of the category of adjectives, which is true of Dravidian languages. The dative experiencer construction has three properties that are pursued in quite a few of her research papers. The experiencer dative is the focus on some of her works where she argues that it is in the result projection of the verb, and is thus actually a resultative, which starts in the lowest projection in the verb phase and moves out of this low PP and gets dative case in the Spec of a P/Kdat. The dative case on the experience-theme noun, an instance of the dative case floating onto this argument, a unique property of Kannada among the Dravidian languages, is capitalized on in another strand of her work, which leads her to conclude that the possessive dative case adjectivalizes the noun. In languages like English, Jayaseelan and Amritavalli posit that this case is absorbed by the experience noun to yield an adjective. This completes the paradigm where the dative case appears on either the subject, the predicate noun, or the copula which then gets realized as *have* (Kayne 1993, following the analysis of the Hungarian possessive construction in Szabolcsi 1983), all three constructions being derived from the same underlying thematic structure according to them. In a third strand, she examines the verb in the predicate beyond the copula, to other light verbs, and concludes that the experiencer and the experience nouns occur in the result projection of the verb under a first-phase approach, thus giving it a rich result structure and depleting the process projection.

Another major focus of her work is finiteness in Dravidian. Recent theories of finiteness, looking crosslinguistically, arguing against a universal instantiation of TenseP and reducing finiteness to a property of Tense, propose finite vs. nonfinite contrasts even without the realization of Tense, in languages that lack morpho-syntactic realization of contrastive tense marking. Rizzi (1997) proposes that clausal finiteness is the function of a dedicated Fin head in a low CP layer of the clause. Ritter and Wiltschko (2014) propose that finiteness is a property of INFL. Amritavalli, in her most recent work on finiteness, "Separating Tense and Finiteness: Anchoring in Dravidian," published in 2014 in *Natural Language and Linguistic Theory* (Amritavalli 2014b), and also her earlier paper co-authored with K. A. Jayaseelan, "Finiteness and Negation in Dravidian," in 2008 in the *Oxford Handbook of Comparative Syntax* (edited by G. Cinque and R. Kayne) (Amritavalli and Jayaseelan 2005), proposes that finiteness in Dravidian is a property of MoodP. She further examines how negative sentences are formed in Kannada and Malayalam and shows how their tense interpretations arise from aspectual properties of nonfinite heads. Finiteness on the other hand is claimed to be anchored by a finite negative element, or agreement, or modals. Thus, negation is argued to contribute finiteness features, and what is currently understood as Tense is broken down into a complex of finiteness features and temporal aspect features. *Neg*, *Agr*, or modals, which are all in complementary distribution with each other, Amritavalli claims, are the heads that instantiate the markers of finiteness in MoodP in Dravidian languages. The temporal aspectual features are located in an Aspect projection. The Dravidian verb in negative sentences, it is argued, first adjoins to the negative auxiliary in MoodP and then moves to AspP.

In her 2003 paper, "Question and Negative Polarity in the Disjunction Phrase," published in *Syntax* (Amritavalli 2003), she discusses in detail how Kannada very interestingly instantiates in the same language two forms of disjunction, inclusive and exclusive, that are each common typologically, but separately in various languages. Russian, Hungarian, French, and others have *or* preceding each disjunct to yield an exhaustive disjunction interpretation. Kannada instantiates this with the *illa….illa* disjunction marker. Sinhala, Japanese, and Malayalam have iterated versions of *or* on each disjunct, but the interpretation is not exhaustive but inclusive, like the plain noniterated English *or* Kannada instantiates this with the *oo…oo* disjunction marker. She also shows how when finite clauses in Kannada are coordinated by the disjunction marker, the coordinated clauses are interpreted as questions.

Her work on resultatives—"Rich Results" (Amritavalli 2014c) and "Result Phrases and Dative Experiencers in Kannada" (Amritavalli 2013b)—examines the achievement resultatives found in this language, and argues that the dative experiencer construction is also an achievement resultative.

A large body of her linguistics research is on Kannada, with output such as "Nominal and Interrogative Complements in Kannada" (Amritavalli 2013c), where she examines the right periphery in Kannada, and draws parallels to Japanese complementizers. In "Parts, Axial Parts and Next Parts in Kannada" (Amritavalli 2007), she explores the function of the dative case in Kannada in forming structures that denote a place or a region, called "axial parts" by Svenonius (2006) like *in front of*, from part-denoting nouns or stems like *the front of*. Other oeuvre include "Some Developments in the Functional Architecture of the Kannada Clause" (Amritavalli 2004a), "Experiencer Datives in Kannada" (Amritavalli 2004b), "Lexical anaphors and pronouns in Kannada" (Amritavalli 2000a), "Result Clauses in Kannada" (Amritavalli 2000b), "A Kannada perspective on morphological causatives" (Amritavalli 1997b), "Case and Theta-role Absorption in Kannada" (Amritavalli 1988c), and "Anaphorization in Dravidian" (Amritavalli 1984).

In Hindi, her work has included a detailed analysis of its person-split ergativity, where she argues that the ergative appears where nominative fails, due to the absence of Person checking. Ergative she argues is a participial case, and Person checking is essential for nominative case to obtain. Languages do not differ in case "alignment," i.e., there are no "ergative alignment" languages such that intransitive subjects and transitive objects pattern together for case. Rather, ergative languages differ from nominative languages in the ways in which they allow or disallow person checking (and therefore nominative case). In Hindi/Urdu, these differences she observes are seen between imperfective and perfective aspect. In person-split ergative languages, they are seen between [+Person] and [−Person] or [0Person] arguments.

Her research in theoretical linguistics makes specific reference to Kannada and Hindi, but she has made forays into Dakkhani ("Tense and the Epistemic Modal in Dakkhani and Hindi-Urdu," with Naila Iffat; Amritavalli and Iffat 2012), Tamil ("The Acquisition of Functional Categories in Tamil with special reference to Negation," with Deepti Ramadoss; Ramadoss and Amritavalli 2007), and Assamese ("A Case Distinction between Unaccusative and Unergative Subjects in Assamese" with Partha Protim Sarmah; Amritavalli and Sarmah 2002) in collaboration with students whom she guided in finding and situating theoretically interesting and challenging data from languages of which they are native speakers.

Her acquisition work includes "Inflection in Specific Language Impairment (SLI) and Second Language Acquisition" (Raman and Amritavalli 2007); and "The Acquisition of Functional Categories in Tamil with Special Reference to Negation" (Ramadoss and Amritavalli 2007), among others.

An early paper of hers "Addressee markers on verbs: a form of agreement?" (Amritavalli 1992) looked at addressee agreement before its time, when it was not the rage yet as it is now. She has even made forays into pragmatics with a paper "The Pragmatic Underpinnings of Syntactic Competences" (Amritavalli 1998).

She has also tried her hand at creative writing with a short story "Past Indefinite" in *Indian Literature* published by the Sahitya Akademi in 2006, and a translation of her grandfather Masti Venkatesa Iyengar's "Venkatiga's wife," in Yatra One: Writings from the Indian Subcontinent, edited by Alok Bhalla, Nirmal Verma, and U.R. Anantamurthy, brought out by HarperCollins in 1993.

We would like to end this brief sketch of her academic enterprise by thanking Amritavalli for her spirited interest and generosity in engaging with topics and researchers in linguistics that have come her way, and for inspiring generations of South Asian linguists with her out-of-the-box thinking which has always been true to the language even if at the cost of breaking the theoretical tools that try to analyze it.

The present volume contains 12 essays written in honor of R. Amritavalli's lifelong work. The themes of these essays, broadly divided into four parts—*Architecture of Syntax: The engines of Syntax*, *Architecture of Syntax: Focus and the VP domain*, *Architecture of Syntax: The Syntax-Semantics Interface*, and *Acquisition of Syntax*—are related to her work—crosslinguistic syntax and its acquisition, with state-of-the-art linguistic theorizing.

Hilda Koopman's chapter (Chap. 2), "A Note on Huave Morpheme Ordering: Local Dislocation or Generalized U20?" addresses the question whether postsyntactic ordering mechanisms that rearrange morpheme orders as in frameworks like distributed morphology (DM) can be dispensed with, thus making syntax and morphology of one piece, a desirable goal a priori. To this end, it takes the famous Huave dataset of Embick and Noyer (2007) which led to the proposal for post-syntactic local dislocation in the first place, and attempts to implement it in an antisymmetric framework with no postsyntactic rules. The author shows that not only can this be done, but also it better accounts for the dataset and the typological patterns for such data based on Cinque's (2009) pioneering model for U20 patterns. The local dislocation analysis, on the other hand, it is shown, needs a syntax that is as a matter of fact unworkable. U20 patterns have generalized to many syntactic domains and the Huave data too falls within the U20 typology, including variation between different Huave dialects. The author leverages a lot on the U20 pattern of invariant prenominal patterns and very variable postnominal patterns, derived by pied-piping and variation in the height of movement. U20 patterns by now have been shown to exist not only in the DP, but also for adverbs; for tense, mood, aspect and V; and verbal complexes. This paper is one of the first to study U20 patterns with respect to morpheme orders.

The antisymmetric model that the author assumes has only phrasal movement, no complex feature bundles or fully inflected items entering the numeration, prefixes and suffixes as heads (with an extra EPP feature on suffixes to pull up the stem to its left) and of course, no postsyntactic morpheme order readjustment mechanisms. DM, on the other hand, allows only semantically contentful items to project in syntax and all semantically vacuous but phonologically active items to merge postsyntactically which has its own structure building, structure reducing, and readjustment mechanisms.

In Huave, the postverbal alignment of affixes is a puzzle. The order Refl-1 is excluded in the context of a plural, and the order 1-Refl is obligatory in the context of a plural. Embick and Noyer (2007) capture this by ordering Refl directly before the final verbal affix, if any, with local dislocation to adjust any mismatches, basically achieving a second position effect from the right edge of the verb. So when PL is present, it is the last morpheme and Refl is ordered before it. When PL is absent, -1 is the last morpheme and Refl is ordered before it. The author shows that this, however, is a very problematic assumption as the syntax it needs is highly implausible. For this to work, Refl has to be peripheral to inflection, but Refl affixes are closer to the verb, both typologically, and in Huave as well, when checked in transitive verb data. So even within a DM syntax, this assumption is unviable.

The author then carefully and convincingly demonstrates that a U20 account derives the possible and impossible morpheme orders in Huave. -1 must be merged highest given the person hierarchy. The relative order of PL and Refl is unclear and treated as two hypotheses: Refl > Pl and Pl > Refl. The verb is at the bottom. Taking -1 Refl Pl V as 1 2 3 4; and -1 Refl V as 1 2 3, the attested morpheme orders 1423, and 4123; and 132, 321 are possible U20 patterns. 4213 is not generated and also ungrammatical. But the order 4231 or 312 is generated which should be ungrammatical. A combination of pied-piping and stranding is exploited to rule it out. Unexpectedly, the 4213 pattern, which is a U20 violation, is found in a dialect of Huave. Here, the author appeals to the variable relative order of Pl and Refl, and the relative order Pl > Refl now derives the otherwise excluded dialect pattern of V Refl 1 Pl as 4 3 1 2, a U20 pattern. Interestingly, neither of the relative orders generates any other variation, thus closing the space for variation. The data falls exactly into this grid. Variation is thus at the level of the indeterminacy in the order of merge, which makes specific predictions about patterns of dialectal variation. Thus, the author shows there is no motivation to adopt Local dislocation for Huave. The antisymmetric U20 account delivers and more.

In their chapter "Tense and the Realization of the Feminine Plural in Hindi-Urdu" (Chap. 3), Rajesh Bhatt and Stefan Keine develop a structured representation of tense and the neutralization of the number feature in the feminine and show a range and types of interactions among them. Plural is neutralized in the feminine in Hindi-Urdu—a phenomenon that patterns with Gujarati, and contrary to Punjabi, Sindhi, and Kashmiri where the plural and the feminine are encoded with two separate morphemes. The neutralization is shown to disappear in freestanding participles, negative triggered auxiliary deletion, counterfactuals, and past habituals, where the plural feature is realized as nasalization.

What Bhatt and Keine quite convincingly claim is that this neutralization is a property of agreement and finiteness rather than of morphological feature bundles. The plural feature is neutralized in the feminine when it is not a sister of TP, and is realized as nasalization when it is a sister of TP, i.e., in freestanding participles. This agreement-based neutralization is, however, called into question in the second person context, where number neutralization in the feminine is seen in freestanding participles that are sisters of TP.

To sort this confusion, the authors claim that freestanding participles have a covert auxiliary, and that if the covert tensed auxiliary has nasalization, then the freestanding participle also has nasalization. The present auxiliary "hE/ho" shows nasalization in first and third person in the feminine but not in second person, while the past auxiliary shows nasalization only in the feminine plural. In order to represent a covert feature that determines spell-out, the authors present two explanations: a morphological and a syntactic one. In the first, the realization of nasalization depends on the internal morphological complexity and grouping of the person and plural features. When the agreement controller has feminine plural features and the participle has a [PL] feature that has not been spelled out, then it is realized via nasalization. In the second person, since there is only a [2, PL] feature and no distinct [PL] feature, it results in a silent T[PL]. In the syntactic explanation, the burden of realization/neutralization is simply shifted from the morphological grouping to the syntactic features of the auxiliary.

Both explanations in a way try to bring syntax and morphology under the same roof, and do away with a distributed morphology account. What remains further to be brought under this proposal are the morpho-syntactic properties of the free-standing past participle and the [PL] feature on the second person singular pronoun *tum*, which apparently poses a potential threat to this agreement-based explanation for nasalization/neutralization.

Richard S. Kayne's chapter (Chap. 4), "English *One* and *Ones* as Complex Determiners," is a *tour de force* with silent nouns and adjectives. It proposes that all instances of the English *one* (and *ones*, with the plural-*s*) are complex determiners, that have a bimorphemic internal structure of a classifier plus an indefinite article, which the author glosses as *w* + *an*. This central claim of the chapter that *one* is an indefinite article (plus classifier), the author observes, nicely complements Postal (1966) who proposes that pronouns are definite articles, with both items (*one* and pronouns) resisting compounds. The differences in the distribution of *one* and *an* (which Perlmutter 1970; Barbiers 2005 have tried to unify) can now be accounted for in terms of the classifier on *one*, which among other things prevents it from occurring with *few* (because the silent noun NUMBER accompanying *few* resists the classifier on *one*, as it itself is classifier-like). Similarly, the classifier on *one* blocks the preposing of degree phrases with *one*.

The chapter starts with Perlmutter's (1970) attempt at unifying non-numeral pre-N *one* and numeral *one*, and finds this line promising by noting that they pattern together in being incompatible with plural nouns and mass nouns. The author then takes on the tough task of unifying into this *one*, the anaphoric *one* that seems like a noun "I have a red pen and you have a blue one." The author marshals a number of data points against a nominal and in favor of a determiner analysis for this *one*, beginning with the inability to be a bare plural, followed by close parallels between English *ones*, and French *uns*, and a milder similarity with Spanish *unos*, in that they are all not nouns but have determiner properties. A possible significant objection that the noun-like *one(s)* cannot take an overt noun, as in "blue ones cars," is defused by noting a parallel to French *lesquels* (clearly a complex determiner) which again disallows an overt N.

Then, the author tackles the question of how these complex determiner DPs are derived. Basing himself on his earlier proposal (Kayne 2006) that a silent noun is not in the same position as its pronounced counterpart, the author proposes that *lesquels* starts off as quel [les NOUN] and "blue ones" as [one [blue PEN-s]]. The -*s* of *ones* the author asserts actually follows the silent noun here, rather than *one* itself. The relation with the antecedent is mediated by the silent noun, and not directly by *one*. The antecedent-(pro)noun relation is thus in all cases (following Kayne 2002) mediated by movement, is another strong claim that the author makes in this paper, with the only recourse to co-indexing that derivational syntax has is via internal merger.

The author then observes that not all adjectives are good with *ones*. *Few*, for example, is not, contends the author, because it comes with NUMBER, which is incompatible with the classifier of *one*. But when *few* occurs not by itself but as a modifier of another adjective, then suddenly it is compatible with *ones*, thus supporting the author's claims. The licensing role of the pre-*ones* adjective is thus important, and a parallel between prenominal adjective/reduced relative licensing in colloquial Slovenian is drawn (Marušič and Žaucer 2006; Leu 2015). Another licensing requirement similar to that of *ones* the author notes is the *the* of "the very poor" which also needs an adjective in the context of a silent noun PEOPLE, though here the adjective is a postdeterminer.

The author now comes back to numeral *one*, which seems to need no adjective even with a silent noun "Here are three books. Only one is worth reading." The special status of numeral *one* is extended from Barbiers (2007), and the author analyzes this numeral *one* as coming with a silent adjective SINGLE, or sometimes silent ONLY. Ordinals cannot be formed with this *one* it is claimed because the ordinal *-th* resists either the complex determiner or the silent SINGLE.

The ability of demonstratives to license *one* is then noted. This, the author shows, is not surprising since demonstratives are significantly like adjectives. However, the ability of plural demonstratives to license *ones* is more variable, and its unacceptability for a set of speakers is left as an open question. Possessors on the other hand uniformly do not license *one* or *ones*.

Finally, human *one* as in *someone* is examined, and the author establishes that this *one* is also the same *one*, only differing in its syntactic context and thus distribution, by having a silent PERSON. The difference between *someone* and *somebody* it is claimed is due to *somebody* being underlyingly [some ONE body].

K.A. Jayaseelan's contribution (Chap. 5), "Parallel Work Spaces in Syntax and the Inexistence of Internal Merge," explores and explodes an assumption in the generative syntactic framework that till now has not been given its rightful scrutiny, though works such as Koster (2007), Epstein et al. (2014) have recognized it—the ephemeral nature of nonmain workspaces. External merge assumes that the external argument is merged into Spec, vP from a different workspace where it is built up. Once this phrase is merged into the main derivation, the parallel workspace is supposed to perish. The author makes a radical and far-reaching proposal that the parallel workspaces where arguments and adjunct phrases are built up and then merged into the main derivation do not disappear after merge but persist and sourced for further merges of the phrases built up in them for later merge into the main derivation, thus leading to multi-dominance of the phrase here by multiple mother nodes in the main derivation. This was otherwise the work of internal merge, which now is done away with. The consequences of this main thesis of the paper that there is always and only external merge have manifold significance. The closest that previous literature comes to this idea is the "survive minimalism" proposal of Putnam and Stroik (2010), but that does not push the idea to its logical conclusion.

The first the author considers is pied-piping. Subextraction does not exist as all arguments of arguments have their own workspace and are directly sourced from into the main derivation. This avoids the problem of feature percolation. The most problematic part of feature percolation is that it must jump over VP and TP to CP. In this proposal, since only arguments/adjuncts get a parallel workspace from which they can be remerged, functional projections on the clausal spine of the main derivation are fixed at merge and cannot move. This includes VP and TP. They cannot thus be pied-piped. CPs on the other hand are arguments, and therefore have their own workspaces, and as a consequence can be remerged. Significantly, this account is the only one in the market that can predict this difference between CPs and VP/TPs with respect to pied-piping. All other analyses of pied-piping have to stipulate it.

The second is the problem of labeling that still persists in current theory and receives ad hoc solutions in the likes of Chomsky (2008). This is nicely solved in the current proposal as only elements in the main derivation project and determine labels. Phrases brought in from parallel workspaces are inert.

A third ramification of this proposal is on successive-cyclic movement. Since there is no internal move and no need for phase edges to which a phrase has to move to survive spell-out and be accessible to higher derivation, the existence of intermediate landing sites would seem like a problem for this proposal. But the author makes interesting use of a third-factor explanation of keeping a phrase active in derivational memory by constantly remerging it as the reason for intermediate remerges.

Finally, the author considers extraction islands, and accounts for them in terms of late insertion and postcyclic derivational timing. This also buys the author an explanation for parasitic gaps, as the gap in the adjunct is now parasitic on the gap in the main derivation, due to the fact that the arguments in the main derivation are already built up when the adjunct is being built up (which happens late in the derivation). The author, however, remains silent about remnant movement, which if it exists has to be an operation of internal merge, which thus cannot be completely banned from syntax.

Argument doubling is ubiquitous in Japanese. On the basis of this evidence, Kuroda (1988) concluded that the standard version of the θ-criterion was untenable. Taking Kuroda's work as his point of departure, Mamoru Saito in his chapter (Chap. 6), "Argument Doubling in Japanese with VP-Internal Focus," argues that "although the θ-criterion seems untenable, there may be a more general requirement that each argument plays a unique role in semantic interpretation." On the basis of extensive data, Saito shows that subjects, dative and accusative objects, as well as prepositional phrases can be doubled under certain conditions. While in the case of subject doubling—in the so-called major subject constructions—the two arguments do not bear the same thematic relation with the predicate, in instances of VP-internal argument doubling they must. The latter, then, appear to be clear counterexamples to the θ-criterion.

Saito demonstrates that the argument doubled constructions are degraded unless the second argument is extraposed to a focus position or the first is topicalized. It is also shown that these constructions are felicitous only if a certain semantic relationship obtains between the two arguments: The first must specify the set of alternatives for the focus indicated by the second. Predictably, the constructions turn infelicitous if the first argument is focused. Each of the two elements of the doubled argument thus plays a unique role in semantic interpretation, suggesting that the θ-criterion may need to be reformulated along these lines.

Wei-Tien Dylan Tsai's chapter (Chap. 7), "*Self* and *Only*: A Comparative Study of Reflexive Adverbials in Squliq Atayal and Mandarin Chinese," investigates the syntax and semantics of *nanak* in Squliq Atayal in a crosslinguistic context. When construed as an adverbial, *nanak* very often gets a focus reading, akin to *only* in English, and its distribution is relatively free. By contrast, when attached to an argument, *nanak* has a much restricted distribution, and its reading is distinctively reflexive. However, there is a gray area in between the two construals, where *nanak* occupies an adjunct position, though interpreted with a variety of reflexive readings shown below.

Tsai's chapter tries to find out whether there is a conceptual connection between *only* and *self*, especially in view of a strong resemblance from Chinese *ziji* "self," which behaves much like an intensifier before negation while serving as a reflexive adverbial after negation. In Squliq Atayal, when *nanak* is associated with an external argument, it is interpreted as "only," and when the focus is only a peripheral argument, it is interpreted as self and results in the inner-outer dichotomy. Reflexive adverbials show a far greater range of interpretative possibilities closely associated with their syntactic distributions, and the syntax-semantics correspondence strictly observes an inner-outer dichotomy of adverbials also observed across languages, i.e., inner Self expresses comitativity, whereas outer Self expresses causality. The inner self is consistently blocked when the subject is not an agent, as in passives, unaccusatives, and psyche verbs; however, agentive subjects allow outer and inner reflexive interpretations. This hybrid structure of adverbial reflexives, he argues, can be accommodated by a general theory of reflexivity along the line of Reinhart and Reuland (1993).

In the latter part of this chapter, Tsai attempts an interpretive procedure which aims to capture the generalization behind various construals of *nanak* and *ziji*. Tsai builds upon Horn's (1969) classic analysis of *only*, and characterizes reflexive adverbials as focus operators involving negation over an alternative set, thus presenting a unified account of *only* and *self* in the following manner:

$$F(x) \,\&\, \sim (\$y) \quad \left(y^1 x \,\&\, F(y)\right)$$

which explains away the spectrum of "selfhood" readings across Squliq Atayal and Mandarin Chinese. The chapter will lead to a deeper understanding of how focus semantics interacts with reflexivity in natural languages.

Bangla sentences that instantiate the structure [...[V_1*te*] V_2*te*] (where V_1 and V_2 are verbs bearing the infinitival suffix *-te* and $V_1 = V_2$) appear to be hard to comprehend. In his chapter, "Getting the Identical Infinitives Filter in Bangla Under Control" (Chap. 8), Probal Dasgupta sets out to situate this observed phenomenon "on the map of familiar processes in grammar and in psycholinguistics." Until a descriptively adequate account of the phenomenon is available, he proposes to encode this observation in the form of a filter, the Identical Infinitives Filter, and mark the sentences filtered out by it with the double ampersand notation "&&." It is demonstrated on the basis of uncontroversial data that the filter does not apply unless V_1 and V_2 are identical. It is further argued, albeit on the basis of not-so-uncontroversial data that the filter effect is also absent unless the V*te* V*te* sequence doubles as a progressive participle in other sentential contexts. For instance, when the V in the V*te* V*te* sequence is a multi-word, "composite" verb, the participial reading is unavailable and according to the author, so is the filter effect. Similarly, if a focus particle intervenes between the two elements of a V*te* V*te* sequence, the progressive participial reading is precluded and the filter effect is absent. Dasgupta notes that native speakers respond differently to these sentences depending on whether they are presented with written or spoken stimuli. The progressive participial construal is preferred, but this effect can be offset by intonation in an ambiguous spoken stimulus. Parallels are drawn between these and adjectival constructions in Bangla with reduplicated adjectives.

It would appear that the observed phenomena lend themselves to a processing account, while a grammatical account remains somewhat elusive. However, after providing a meticulous description of the phenomena to be accounted for and the patterns that emerge from them, the author stops short of taking a decisive stance on whether the effect of the proposed filter is due to grammatical or processing factors, leaving it open to further inquiry within a paradigm rooted in whole word morphology and a substantivist approach to grammar.

Utpal Lahiri's contribution (Chap. 9), "Binding Theory, Scope Reconstruction, and NPI Licensing Under Scrambling in Hindi," uncovers some novel facts and makes an important addition to the discussion of reconstruction and presents very interesting data on reconstruction. The author sets up his discussion in the context of two generalizations about the interaction of binding theory reconstruction and scope reconstruction, namely generalizations A and C. Simply put both these generalizations make the point that binding theory and semantic scope go hand in hand. The author clearly and convincingly shows that these generalizations do not hold in Hindi. This is a clear contribution of major theoretical import. The reconstruction required for NPI licensing is different. Following an extensive line of research in the literature (Romero 1998; Fox 2000; Fox and Nissenbaum 2004, among many others), the chapter assumes that syntactic reconstruction (SynR) exists in the grammar. With this background, the chapter presents data on scrambled NPIs in Hindi that "seem to suggest that semantic reconstruction [SemR] should be an available, though possibly marked, option." The upshot is that, once we leave out cases that do not have the adequate test configuration (examples [19]–[22], [28]), the NPI examples in the text are best explained if the mandatory scope reconstruction of the scrambled NPIs is done not through SynR but through SemR. More concretely:

(a) Simple scope reconstruction: (16) can be done equally by SynR or by SemR.
(b) Scope reconstruction plus Principle C: (23), (24), and (26) have mandatory scope reconstruction but no Principle C violation. This contradicts the prediction of SynR and matches the expectation of SymR.
(c) Scope reconstruction plus Principle A: (33)–(35) have mandatory scope reconstruction. (33)–(34) could be accounted equally with SynR or with SemR. But the (local) binding of the reciprocal in (35) seems to be performed not from the reconstructed position but from the surface position. Again, this contradicts the prediction of SynR and matches the expectation of SemR.

Josef Bayer's chapter (Chap. 10), "Prima La Musica, Dopo Le Parole? A Small Note on a Big Topic," uses five interesting crosslinguistic datasets to show that the semantic system prefers alternatives, but when a feature is used merely to satisfy certain formal constraints, the semantic distinction is suspended or underspecified.

In German, for instance, indefinites such as *etwas* "something", *nicts* "nothing" and feminine substance nouns such as *kalter* "coldness", *hitze* "heat" are bare in structural case and get a definite reading with a definite determiner (which is case marked). The distinctive semantic effect disappears between use and nonuse of definite determiner when a lexical case is used, suggesting that there is a semantically interpretable D1 and an underdetermined D2. Similarly, in Turkish, an interpretive effect comes along with the accusative case morpheme—*y*(*I*) which is typically specific, and nonapplication of—*y*(*I*)—yields a nonspecific interpretation.

However, it fails to be a reliable marker of specificity when the accusative marker is required for formal reasons. Bangla case-particle *-ke* marks specificity, and a zero particle nonspecificity. Again, this specificity effect is suspended when the ECM (Exceptional Case Marking) requires marking of overt and distinctive case in the Romanian example, *-L-* marks definiteness when it is used as a determiner as opposed to *–un* which marks indefiniteness. When *-L-* is used in its default form, i.e., as the sole assigner of genitive case, it is free of any definiteness implication. Bayer moves away from the case and definiteness/specificity concerns and looks at the verb *tun* "do" in German which introduces an agentive semantics. However, in V(P)-topicalization, *tun* is chosen as a default form to carry φ and *T*, and it loses its original semantics, posing no clash with the semantics of the VP.

Bayer ties in these datasets beautifully with the title by showing that like music, which is a purely formal system and lacks intentional meaning, aptly provided by "word/*le parole,*" natural language syntax gives primacy to a pure form of constraint satisfaction. If the constraint satisfaction is met by a set of semantic alternatives, the semantic system enables it. But when there are no alternatives, semantics leaves its work to be done by other extra syntactic factors or just circumvents it by underspecification or suspended specification, thus making the formal system primary, like music in the title.

In an experimental study (Chap. 11), "The Influence of Visual, Auditory, and Linguistic Cues on Children's Novel Verb Generalization," aimed at examining whether young children attend to perceptual cues over linguistic cues in novel verb learning, Narasimhan and her colleagues use the tested nonce word paradigm to study verb production in 4-year-olds. Drawing on the theory of Golinkoff and Hirsh-Pasek (2007), which holds that "children are sensitive to multiple cues in word learning," and that certain cues are weighted over others at different points in time as word learning progresses, the authors set out to determine which of three cues—visual, auditory, or linguistic—children rely on when they are asked to produce nonce verbs presented in novel sentential contexts and in conflicting cue conditions.

In a carefully setup experiment, 16 children, seven female, and nine male, between the ages of 3;5 to 4;10, were taught two verb labels—*wug* and *meek*—for two action standards associated with different properties, i.e., each of the nonce verbs had a set of visual, auditory, and linguistic features associated with it. After a training phase, the participants were presented with test items which consisted of 16 pairs of video clips in which two puppets performed action on four toys in two conditions—"simple cue" and "conflicting cue" conditions. Twelve video clips consisted of the novel test stimuli. Of these, six were "simple cue" stimuli which provided visual, auditory, or linguistic information associated with the verb, while the other six video clips presented stimuli in the three "cue-competition" conditions. "4 control" clips were also presented to the participants.

An analysis of the results revealed that in the "simple cue" condition, children were more likely to rely on perceptual—both visual and auditory—rather than on linguistic cues, with a greater preference for visual over auditory cues. In "competing" conditions too, children showed an overwhelming tendency to rely on visual cues while generalizing a verb label to an unknown action. It appears then that different kinds of cues play different roles in influencing verb extensions. This seems to be in line with Golinkoff and Hirsch-Pasek (2007), who suggest that even when a range of cues are available, not all of them are used equally during the task of word learning. Furthermore, the strength of the association of a cue with the verb when it occurs in the "simple cue" condition does not appear to be a predictor of its preference in the "competition condition." The authors suggest that a number of factors might contribute to this. They also suggest that the over-reliance on visual cues (even as late as at age 4) could be due to the kind of linguistic context provided and the lack of temporal overlap between the sentences uttered and actions shown. While it would be worthwhile investigating what cues take precedence in later stages of vocabulary learning and in exactly what kinds of contexts, what does seem certain is that word-world mapping in the initial stages, and perhaps even later, depends on the concreteness and imageability of its referents, an idea seminal to work in vocabulary acquisition.

William Snyder's "On the Child's Role in Syntactic Change" (Chap. 12), discusses the phenomenon of "Survival versus Obsolescence" in the context of child language acquisition and language change. Using evidence from Lightfoot and Westergaard (2007) and the *do*-support in English as starting points for demonstrating why certain aspects of language survive as marginal forms while others disappear altogether, he advances a revised version of his original Grammatical Conservatism thesis with a view to offering a more robust account of this phenomenon.

In his initial version of the "Grammatical Conservatism" (GC) (2011) thesis, Snyder suggested that children made productive, spontaneous use of a new syntactic structure only after they had "both determined that the structure is permitted in the adult language, and identified the adults' grammatical basis for it." This 2011 thesis was supported by evidence gathered from a number of languages and across a range of syntactic structures. However, morpho-syntactic changes that occurred in English from Late Middle English (LME) to Early Modern English (EME) (Lightfoot and Westergaard 2007), suggest that children do not always wait for evidence from adult grammars, leading the author to revise his GC thesis.

The revised GCr attempts to accommodate children's ability to adopt a form that is not present in parental grammar while at the same time choosing, to a large extent, grammatical options used by their parents. It does so by suggesting that rather than depending on quantity of evidence before choosing an option, children rely on quality of evidence; a limited input with extremely specific features could lead to the choice of a particular grammatical option. Drawing upon the analogy of a lock and key, the author suggests that UG serves as the lock and the characteristic features in the input are the keys that help "unlock" the correct grammatical option. The use of third-person-singular *their* in a sentence like *Every doctor treated their patients* is one such example of the (extended) use of the pronoun by young children even when such a form was not prevalent in adult grammar. Drawing on examples from Germanic languages in general and Norwegian in particular, the author illustrates how syntactic forms appear to require different minimum input frequencies to survive. In English, for instance, V-to-I movement appeared to exist alongside the *do*-support until the former fell below the minimum threshold for it to survive in the language.

Using the revised GCr thesis to explain the SvO puzzle, the author goes on to examine how the child recognizes certain specific features (the key) of a particular grammatical operation before adopting it into its own grammar. Snyder suggests that when two bits of competing data are present in the input, the child, driven by GCr, chooses the first type of evidence encountered and which is accessible, thereby blocking the alternative option. In most cases, the first type of evidence is likely to be higher in caretaker speech. This leads to the lower frequency option becoming obsolete. In cases where there is no conflict, the low-frequency form stays on as it is presented only rarely to the learner.

That children acquiring a language produce erroneous sentences that do not match the target adult-like forms is a well-attested fact in acquisition. One such typical verbal error is the production of Root infinitives (RI), a phenomenon observed across a variety of languages. In her chapter titled "Root Infinitive Analogues: Evidence from Tamil, Korean, and Japanese" (Chap. 13), Keiko Murasugi provides evidence for this phenomenon from three Asian languages—Tamil, Korean, and Japanese.

Root infinitives, attested frequently as infinitival verbal forms, appear in child language until approximately the age of 2 years, across a number of languages. In morphologically rich languages, children optionally use the infinitival forms of inflection on the verbs (e.g., Dutch, French), whereas in morphologically poor languages, RIs appear in finite contexts as bare verbs (e.g., English, Chinese). In languages where verbs do not form well-formed words if they are uninflected, then children use a default affix or the surrogate infinitive form (e.g., Japanese, Korean, and Turkish). The author outlines a set of six salient morpho-syntactic and semantic properties common to RIs crosslinguistically to argue her case.

Using examples from research on young Tamil-speaking children to show that the inflection phrase and complementizer phrase as well as inflection associated with finite verbs are missing in children's language until almost age 2, she suggests that these errors could be indicative of an RI stage.

Gathering longitudinal data from a Korean-acquiring child over a five-month period, Kim and Phillips (1998) showed that the child tended to use the default mood inflection *-e* in contexts where it was correct as well as in contexts that required other forms. This V-*e* form is seen as an RI analogue form as it possesses some of the properties typical of RIs. Similar is the case with Japanese, where past-tense form (V-*ta*), mimetics (*-ta/-sita*), and mood form (*-na*) correspond to the RI analogue. One reason advanced by the author for this is that all three types are possible imperatives in adult Japanese. The author uses examples to show how *-na* functions as a negative marker or mood marker depending on the verbal form that it is attached to and then goes on to demonstrate that "sentence-ending" mood marking property of Japanese allows the existence of a truncated RI structure.

Attempting to establish that RI analogues are comparable in child Tamil, child Korean, and child Japanese, Murasagi points out that in the early stages when verbs are wrongly associated with the mood markers, case marking on the subject and conjugation with tense on verbs is also absent. It appears that a finiteness head in the mood phrase assigns finiteness to the child RI analog. This is seen in Dravidian languages such as Kannada and Malayalam and provides further support for a proposal advanced by Amritavalli and Jayaseelan (2005).

The chapter concludes with the observation that child grammar though different in some ways from adult grammars is bound by the same universal constraints. During the process of acquisition, the child grammar of one language could have a correlate with other possible adult languages making a strong case for Universal Grammar.

References

Amritavalli, R. 2015. India as a laboratory for language and cognitive science. Keynote address at *International Conference of the Linguistic Society of India*, JNU, Delhi, October 15–17, 2015.

Amritavalli, R. 2014a. Teaching language and achieving literacy: Interfering with learning, or guiding it? In *Innovations in the language classroom*, eds. Rama Kant Agnihotri, A. L. Khanna, and Anju Sahgal Gupta. New Delhi: Orient BlackSwan.

Amritavalli, R. 2014b. Separating tense and finiteness: Anchoring in Dravidian. *Natural Language & Linguistic Theory* 32: 283–306.

Amritavalli, R. 2014c. Rich results. In *The lexicon-syntax interface: Perspectives from South Asian languages*, ed. Pritha Chandra, and Richa Srishti, 71–100. Amsterdam: John Benjamins.

Amritavalli, R. 2013a. An English for every schoolchild in India. In *English impact report: Investigating English language learning outcomes at the primary school level in rural India*, ed. Vivien Berry. Kolkata: British Council and ASER, Pratham.

Amritavalli, R. 2013b. Nominal and interrogative complements in Kannada. In *Deep insights, broad perspectives: Essays in honor of Mamoru Saito*, eds. Yoichi Miyamoto, Daiko Takahashi, Hideki Maki, Masao Ochi, Koji Sugisaki, and Asako Uchibori, 1–21. Tokyo: Kaitakusha.

Amritavalli, R. 2013c. Result phrases and dative experiencers in Kannada. 19th ICL (International Congress of Linguists), Geneva. Published and distributed by: Département de Linguistique de l'Université de Genève, www.cil19.org/. Accessed March 21, 2016.

Amritavalli, R. 2012a. Helping children become readers. *Language and Language Teaching* 1 (1): 1–4.

Amritavalli, R. 2012b. Visible and invisible aspects of language ability. In *Indian English: Towards a new paradigm*, eds. Rama Kant Agnihotri and Rajendra Singh, pp. 49–62. New Delhi: Orient Blackswan.

Amritavalli, R. 2008a. Media work: An authentic context for developing communication skills in English. *TESL EJ* 12 (3).

Amritavalli, R. 2008b. The origins of functional and lexical categories: Tense-aspect and adjectives in Dravidian. *Nanzan Linguistics* 4: 1–20. Centre for Linguistics, Nanzan University.

Amritavalli, R. 2007. Parts, axial parts and next parts in Kannada. *Tromso Working Papers on Language & Linguistics*: Nordlyd 34.2, special issue on *Space and scalar structure*, eds. Monika Basic, Marina Pantcheva, Minjeong Son, and Peter Svenonius, 1–16. CASTL, Tromso.

Amritavalli, R. 2004a. Some Developments in the functional architecture of the Kannada clause. In *Clause Structure in South Asian Languages*, eds. Veneeta Dayal, and Anoop Mahajan, 13–38. Kluwer: Boston (Studies in Natural Language and Linguistic Theory).

Amritavalli, R. 2004b. Experiencer datives in Kannada," In *Non-nominative subjects,* Vol. 1, eds. Peri Bhaskararao and Karumuri Venkata Subbarao, 1–24. John Benjamins: Amsterdam.
Amritavalli, R. 2003. Question and negative polarity in the disjunction phrase. *Syntax* 6 (1): 1–18.
Amritavalli, R. 2000a. Lexical anaphors and pronouns in Kannada. In *Lexical anaphors and pronouns in selected South Asian languages: A principled typology*, eds. Barbara Lust, Kashi Wali, James Gair, and K.V. Subbarao, 49–112. The Hague: Mouton.
Amritavalli, R. 2000b. Result clauses in Kannada. In *Linguisticoliterary: A Festschrift for Professor D.S. Dwivedi*, eds. R.E. Asher and Roy Harris, 51–59. New Delhi: Pilgrims Books.
Amritavalli, R. 1998. Is language acquisition a behavioural issue? Review (invited) of *Language behaviour: Acquisition and evolutionary history* by R. Narasimhan, *The Book Review* XXII:12, Delhi.
Amritavalli, R. 1997a. Pictured realities and pictures of reality: Cross-cultural intelligibility of the visual in television. In *Contemporary television: Eastern perspectives*, eds. Michael Richards and David French, 246–261. New Delhi: Sage Publications.
Amritavalli, R. 1997b. A Kannada perspective on morphological causatives. In *Phases and interfaces of morphology*, Vol. 2, eds. M. Hariprasad, Hemalatha Nagarajan, P. Madhavan, and K. G. Vijayakrishnan, 180–205. Hyderabad: CIEFL.
Amritavalli, R. 1996. Communication, technology, and the evolution of systems of knowledge and education. In *Distance education: Theory and practice*, G. Ram Reddy commemorative Volume 2, ed. K. Murali Manohar, 1–15. Hyderabad: Open Learning Society.
Amritavalli, R. 1992. Addressee markers on verbs: A form of agreement? In *Linguistics at large*, eds. V. Prakasam, and S.V. Parasher, 38–51. Booklinks: Hyderabad.
Amritavalli, R. 1988a. Understanding English by Radio. *Journal of English & Foreign Languages* 2: 34–51. Hyderabad: CIEFL.
Amritavalli, R. 1988b. The role of audio-visual aids in distance education. In *Studies in distance education*, eds. B.N. Kaul, et al. New Delhi: Association of Indian Universities and IGNOU.
Amritavalli, R. 1988c. Case and theta-role absorption in Kannada. *CIEFL Working Papers in Linguistics* 5 (1): 66–76. Hyderabad: CIEFL.
Amritavalli, R. 1984. Anaphorization in Dravidian. *CIEFL Working Papers in Linguistics* 1 (1): 1–31. Hyderabad: CIEFL.
Amritavalli, R., and N. Iffat. 2012. Tense and the epistemic modal in Dakkhani and Hindi-Urdu. *EFLJ* 3 (1): 47–74.
Amritavalli, R., A. Jana, and Vijaya. 2003. Students' understanding of dictionary entries: a study with respect to four learners' dictionaries. *Indian Journal of Applied Linguistics* 29 (1): 5–20.
Amritavalli, R., and K.A. Jayaseelan. 2003. The genesis of syntactic categories and parametric variation. In *Generative grammar in a broader perspective: Proceedings of the 4th GLOW in Asia*, ed. Hang-Jin Yoon, 19–41. Seoul: Hancook.
Amritavalli, R., and K.A. Jayaseelan. 2005. Finiteness and negation in Dravidian. In *The Oxford handbook of comparative syntax*, eds. Guglielmo Cinque, and Richard S. Kayne, 178–220. New York: Oxford University Press.
Amritavalli, R., and P.P. Sarmah. 2002. A case distinction between unaccusative and unergative subjects in Assamese. *Snippets*.
Amritavalli, R., and K. Visalakshy. 1992. Audio versions of textbook materials: A tryout. *Journal of English & Foreign Languages* 7. Hyderabad: CIEFL.
Barbiers, S. 2007. Indefinite numerals one and many and the cause of ordinal suppletion. *Lingua* 117: 859–880.
Barbiers, S. 2005. Variation in the morphosyntax of one. *Journal of Comparative Germanic Linguistics* 8: 159–183.
Chomsky, N. 2008. On phases. In *Foundational issues in linguistic theory*, eds. R. Freidin, C.P. Otero, and M.L. Zubizarreta, 133–166. Cambridge, MA: MIT Press.
Cinque, G. 2009. The fundamental left-right asymmetry of natural languages. In *Universals of language today*, 165–184. Springer, Berlin.
Embick, D., and R. Noyer. 2007. Distributed morphology and the syntax/morphology interface. In *The Oxford handbook of linguistic interfaces*, 289–324.

Epstein, S.D., H. Kitahara, and T.D. Seely. 2014. Labeling by minimal search: Implications for successive-cyclic A-movement and the conception of the postulate 'phase.' *Linguistic Inquiry* 45 (3): 463–481.
Fox, D., and J. Nissenbaum. 2004. Condition A and scope reconstruction, *Linguistic Inquiry* 35: 475–485.
Fox, D. 2000. *Economy and semantic interpretation*. Cambridge: MIT Press.
Golinkoff, R.M., & K. Hirsh-Pasek. 2007. Language development: The view from the radical middle. [Keynote address.] In *Proceedings of the 31st Annual Boston University Conference on Language Development*, ed. H. Caunt-Nulton, S. Kulatilake, and I. Woo, 1–25. Somerville, MA: Cascadilla Press.
Horn, L. 1969. A presuppositional theory of only and even. CLS 5, Chicago Linguistic Society.
Kayne, R.S. 2006. On parameters and on principles of pronunciation. In *Organizing grammar. Linguistic studies in Honor of Henk van Riemsdijk*, eds. H. Broekhuis, N. Corver, R. Huybregts, U. Kleinhenz and J. Koster. Berlin: Mouton de Gruyter, 289–299 (reprinted in (2010c) *Comparisons and Contrasts*).
Kayne, R.S. 2002. On some prepositions that look DP-internal: English of and French de. *Catalan Journal of Linguistics* 1: 71–115 (reprinted in *Movement and Silence*).
Kayne, R.S. 1993. Toward a modular theory of auxiliary selection. *Studia Linguistica* 47 (1): 3–31.
Kim, M., and C. Phillips. 1998. Complex verb constructions in child Korean: Overt markers of covert functional structure. In *Proceedings of the 20th Annual Boston University Conference on Language Development* (BUCLD 22), 430–441.
Koster, J. 2007. Structure preservingness, internal merge, and the strict locality of triads. In *Phrasal and clausal architecture: Syntactic derivation and interpretation (Linguistik Aktuell/ Linguistics Today 101)*, eds. Simin Karimi, Vida Samiian, and Wendy K. Wilkins, 188–205. Amsterdam: John Benjamins.
Kuroda, S.-Y. 1988. Whether we agree or not: A comparative syntax of English and Japanese. *Linguisticae Investigationes* 12: 1–47.
Lightfoot, D., and M. Westergaard. 2007. Language acquisition and language change: Inter-relationships. *Language and Linguistics Compass*, 1 (5): 396–415.
Leu, T. 2015. *The architecture of determiners*. New York: Oxford University Press.
Marušič, F., and R. Žaucer. 2006. The 'definite article' TA in colloquial Slovenian. *Formal Approaches to Slavic Linguistics*, 14: 189–204.
Perlmutter, D.M. 1970. On the article in English. In *Progress in linguistics*, eds. M. Bierwisch and K.E. Heidolph. The Hague: Mouton, 233–248.
Postal, P.M. 1966. On so-called 'pronouns' in English. In *Report of the Seventeenth Annual Roundtable Meeting on Linguistics and Language Studies*, ed. F.P. Dineen. Georgetown University Press, Washington, D.C., 177–206 (reprinted in Reibel, D.A., and S.A. Schane (eds.). 1969. *Modern studies in English*. New Jersey: Prentice-Hall, Englewood Cliffs.)
Putnam, M., and T. Stroik. 2010. Syntactic relations in survive-minimalism. In *Exploring crash-proof grammars*, ed. M. Putnam, 143–166. Amsterdam: John Benjamins.
Ramadoss, D., and R. Amritavalli. 2007. The acquisition of functional categories in Tamil with special reference to negation. In *Nanzan linguistics special issue 1: papers from the consortium workshops on linguistic theory*, 67–84. Nanzan University: Graduate Program in Linguistic Science.
Raman, M.G., and R. Amritavalli. 2007. Inflection in specific language impairment (SLI) and second language acquisition. In *Nanzan linguistics special issue 1: papers from the consortium workshops on linguistic theory*, 85–104. Nanzan University: Graduate Program in Linguistic Science.
Reinhart, T., and E. Reuland. 1993. Reflexivity. *Linguistic Inquiry* 24: 657–720.
Ritter, E., and M. Wiltschko. 2014. The composition of INFL. *Natural Language & Linguistic Theory* 32 (4): 1331–1386.

Rizzi, L. 1997. The fine structure of the left periphery. In *Elements of grammar*, 281–337. Netherlands: Springer.

Romero, M. 1998. *Focus and reconstruction effects in Wh-phrases*. Doctoral Dissertation, University of Massachusetts at Amherst, Amherst.

Svenonius, P. 2006. The emergence of axial parts. Nordlyd: Tromsø Working Papers in Language & Linguistics 33 (1): 49–77.

Szabolcsi, A. 1983. The possessor that ran away from home. *The Linguistic Review* 3 (1): 89–102.

Part I
Architecture of Syntax: The Engines of Syntax

Chapter 2
A Note on Huave Morpheme Ordering: Local Dislocation or Generalized U20?

Hilda Koopman

Introduction

In the past few decades, different frameworks have emerged which claim that a single computational engine drives both syntactic and morphological composition, either to a large extent, as in Distributed Morphology (DM), or entirely, as in frameworks based on Antisymmetry (Kayne 1994).

Where morpheme order is concerned, Distributed Morphology (DM) attributes a major, but not exclusive, role to the syntax (see among others, Halle and Marantz (1993); Embick and Noyer (2007); Bobaljik (2012; 2015) and Harley (2012)). Mismatches may arise between the output of the syntax and the actual morpheme order, in which case postsyntactic readjustment rules (Lowering and Local Dislocation) apply to generate the observed linear orders.

In Minimalist frameworks based on Antisymmetry, the linear order in syntax and morphology is read off the syntactic output directly; hence, there is or can be no need for lowering or local dislocation postsyntactically (see among others, Kayne (1994; 2005; 2010); Julien (2002), my own work Koopman and Szabolcsi (2000); Koopman (2005; 2014; 2015), and work in Nanosyntax Starke (2010); Caha (2009); Muriungi (2009)).

The question whether postsyntactic ordering mechanisms that rearrange morpheme orders can be dispensed with or not depends on the syntactic framework one adopts.

How do we decide between these two (broad) syntactic frameworks? Joshi (1985) proposes that the class of possible human languages is properly included in the class of Mildly Context-sensitive grammars. As Stabler and his colleagues have shown, frameworks with right adjunction and without, with head movement or without, with antisymmetry or without, etc., all fall within the class of Mildly

H. Koopman (✉)
Department of Linguistics, UCLA, 3125 Campbell Hall, Los Angeles, CA 90095-1543, USA
e-mail: koopman@ucla.edu

G. Sengupta et al. (eds.), *Perspectives on the Architecture and Acquisition of Syntax*, DOI 10.1007/978-981-10-4295-9_2

Context-sensitive grammars Stabler (2011), and Sportiche et al. (2013, Chap. 12). An intuitive notion of syntactic complexity or whether head movement is better than phrasal movement will not decide which framework to adopt.

What matters is how well the frameworks account for the empirical data, not just for individual languages but for human languages in general, whether they generate predictions that can be verified, and how appropriate they are for the interfaces with phonology and semantics. This is what the discussion will focus on.

To make the question of whether we need postsyntactic reordering or not tractable, and test it on Huave morpheme orders that have been argued to illustrate the need for the postsyntactic reordering of **Local Dislocation**, a powerful post-syntactic reordering process that applies to linear (not hierarchical) orders discussed in Embick and Noyer (2001), as well as in their handbook article (Embick and Noyer 2007), this chapter will start laying out the two frameworks, DM and (my version of) the minimalist antisymmetry approach to morphology will be detailed in Section "Two Frameworks".

It develops an expected typology of morpheme orders, based on Cinque's inspiring paper that models the possible and impossible syntactic word order patterns known as Greenberg's 1963 Universal 20 (U20) (Greenberg 1963; Cinque 2005), discussed in Section "Syntax: Universal 20".

Universal 20 word order patterns turn out to generalize to many other syntactic hierarchies as well (see, for example, Cinque (2009)) (Section "Syntax: U20 Patterns Generalize"). This provides important information about the framework needed to account for typology of word order patterns.

This generalized U20 syntactic word order typology leads to a concrete hypothesis about a crosslinguistic typology of morpheme orders (Section "Morphology: Morphology Tracks U20 Patterns"). If there is one syntactic engine for syntax and morphology, the same ordering patterns *and* restrictions should be found in morphology as well. If postsyntactic reordering is not unavailable in UG, orders that require postsyntactic reordering in DM must be accounted for by the generalized U20 framework, with possible morpheme orders falling within the U20 typology.

The frameworks are put to the test in Section "Huave Morpheme Ordering: Local Dislocation or U20?" on a puzzling morpheme order paradigm from Huave, which is taken to illustrate the need for **Local Dislocation** (see Embick and Noyer (2001), and their handbook article (Embick and Noyer, 2007).

The local dislocation analysis is discussed in Section "A Puzzle: Huave Morpheme Order". It falls short because the underlying syntactic structure, on which local dislocation is supposed to operate given the DM framework, cannot be adopted. In Section "A Sketch of a Syntactic Analysis", the U20 approach to the Huave data is worked out and evaluated. The data patterns fall within the expected U20 typology. Some ungrammatical morpheme orders fall outside the typology, and their ungrammaticality is thereby fully expected, as such orders simply cannot be derived. Other ungrammatical patterns can be related to general syntactic problems, as expected under a single computational engine. Lastly, the syntactic account extends to capture variation in morpheme orders between different Huave dialects, and in fact predicts the possible space of variation.

Overall, there is no motivation to adopt Local dislocation for Huave, not even within DM. A syntactic account can in fact be constructed, based on a direct interface between the syntax and phonology, and the similarity of the typology of word order patterns in syntax *and* morphology.

Two Frameworks

Here, I briefly spell out the assumptions that underly the two frameworks.

Distributed Morphology DM

DM in practice is in essence a (narrow) syntax → "morphology" → phonology model. I present here the assumptions that many seem to share. Narrow syntax and morphology use different atoms, and rules. Only semantically meaningful atoms are hypothesized to project in "narrow syntax," which feeds into compositional semantics. Semantically vacuous,[1] but phonologically meaningful atoms (case, agreement, linkers, theme vowels, etc.) are hypothesized to be merged in the (postsyntactic) morphological component, which interfaces with spell-out/ phonology.

The syntax in practice is a standard Minimalist one (without antisymmetry), with head (not phrasal) movement responsible for creating the skeleton of word structure. The syntax can generate only the possible morpheme orders that derive by head movement: Any "unusual" linear orders (unusual w.r.t. the syntactic expectations) must be dealt with by additional operations in the postsyntactic morphology module, which thus has its own structural atoms, structure building and reducing mechanisms, and readjustment rules/realization rules. These further adjust and modify the syntactic structures for linearization and prepare for vocabulary insertion and the interface with phonology.

A Single Computational Engine: Antisymmetry, Minimalism, and Phrasal Movement

Antisymmetry is a syntax → phonology model, with the syntax of natural languages showing a fundamental left right asymmetry (cf. starting from Kayne (1994)) There is a single syntactic component: There is no distinction between "narrow" syntax (semantically interpretable), and postsyntactic syntax. Syntactic

[1]Deciding if some element is semantically vacuous or not is more challenging than often assumed.

structures are strongly decompositional, with small atoms (most probably single features) and their associated lexical properties driving the derivation. Neither complex feature bundles, nor fully inflected lexical items are selected from the lexicon as input to merge, with feature checking from the inside out mirroring the syntactic hierarchy (Chomsky 1992). Traditional verb placement or noun placement results from Internal merge (feature-driven (remnant) phrasal movement, not head movement). Under a single computational engine, this holds for morpheme ordering as well. Since there is no syntax/structure building postsyntactically, there should be no postsyntactic adjustment rules for morpheme orders either.

So as to be able to talk about morphology, I assume that affixes (prefixes, suffixes) have the following lexical specifications.[2] With DM, I assume late spell-out: This is by no means a shared assumption.[3]

(1) a. Prefixes are heads (or perhaps specifiers of silent heads) merging with a complement.
    b. Suffixes are heads. In addition to merging with a complement, they carry an *EPP* feature may be further specified for category (Koopman 2005) or not. This triggers Internal merge to satisfy the *EPP*, and yields the surface head final property of English morphology, for example. Head finality is a derived surface property, not a special property of the morphological component.
    c. Interface properties with the phonology may be further specified on *EPP* features (and by hypothesis, these are the only place where these may be so specified.)[4]

Finally, lexical properties must be locally satisfied, i.e., checked under sisterhood. This means that prefixes are syntactically head complement structures which simply happen to align in a head complement configuration. There is no need to be a X^0 constituent.

Deciding Between Frameworks

The two frameworks assume quite different syntactic derivations. We decide between frameworks in how well the frameworks account for the empirical data, not just for individual languages but for human languages in general, whether they

---

[2]The following are close to traditional assumptions about lexical entries. This is probably the major difference with nanosyntax.

[3]Chris Collins and Richard Kayne (p.c).

[4]See Koopman (2014) for "size" restrictions imposed by ph. These properties range from "no bigger than a light foot," to no bigger than "root", or "no bigger than phrases of size x derived through pied-piping", to specifications how deeply embedded in the syntactic structure phonological material is allowed to occur. They can be directly read off from the output of the syntactic derivation (cf. the complexity filters in Koopman and Szabolcsi (2000), and "grafts" on structure building EPP features in Koopman (2014)).

generate predictions that can be verified, and how appropriate they are for the interface with the phonology and semantics.

In Koopman (2015), building on earlier work,[5] I present a novel argument in favor of a single computational engine for syntax and morphology. This argument builds on the research that has emerged around Cinque's (2005) modeling of U20,[6] and is quite simple. If there is one syntactic engine which covers both syntax and morphology, we should find the exact same ordering patterns and restrictions in syntax and morphology. This approach provides us with a typology of possible and impossible morpheme orders, and initial exploration about what is found and what is not is quite promising.

Syntax: Universal 20

Cinque (2005) lists and models the attested and unattested word order patterns of Dem, Num, A, and N, known as Universal 20 (U20) patterns (Greenberg 1963). The orders reveal a fundamental asymmetry of human languages: Prenominally, the order appears to be invariant, but postnominally, many more orders are attested.

As Cinque (2005) shows, only 14 out of the 4!=24 logically possible word order patterns are attested,[7] as summarized in Table 2.1.[8] The numbers 1, 2, 3, 4 in the tables represent an independently established syntactic/scopal hierarchy where 1 c-commands 2, 2 c-commands 3, etc.). The patterns in the gray shaded cells do not occur. Cinque asks why we find these particular orders, and why certain orders are not found. Cinque's provides an answer to these questions: Only orders that can be generated by UG can surface. Orders that are not found cannot arise, and are thus excluded in principle. His proposed account reduces to antisymmetry, a characteristic of human languages, and properties of Merge (External Merge: a fixed universal hierarchy), and Internal Merge (properties of movement). Well-motivated independent parameters related to Merge capture the variation in orders.[9]

(2) a. Antisymmetry (Kayne 1994).
b. An independently motivated universal syntactic/semantic hierarchy:

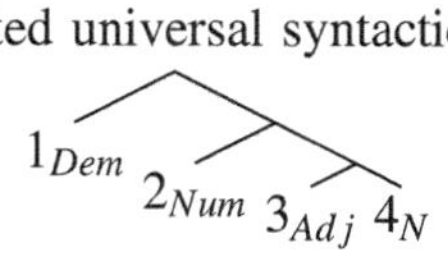

[5]In particular, Koopman and Szabolcsi (2000), Koopman (2005), and Koopman (2014).

[6]Universal 20 also plays a central role in Nanosyntax.

[7]The generalizations hold up in Cinque's own now quite extensive database of 1535 languages as of April 30, 2015. Of the potential counterexamples, Cinque (pers. com.), only one could perhaps be qualified as a genuine counterexample.

[8]Frequency of patterns is omitted from Table 2.1.

[9]Abels and Neeleman (2009) propose an analysis without the LCA/ antisymmetry, which permits right and left adjunction, but restricts movement to leftward movement.

Table 2.1 Universal 20 patterns (*1* Dem, *2* Num, *3* Adj, and *4* N)

Attested: ✓ Un-attested: 0

1234 ✓	1324 0
1243 ✓	1342 ✓
1423 ✓	1432 ✓
4123 ✓	4132 ✓ or 0?
2134 0	2314 0
2143 0	2341 ✓
2413 0	2431 ✓
4213 0	4231 ✓
3124 0	3214 0
3142 0	3241 0
3412 ✓	3421 ✓
4312 ✓	4321 ✓

c. Different surface orders (in neutral orders) are derived from this hierarchy by (leftward) Movement (Internal Merge) of (i) a *phrase* that (ii) must contain the lexical noun.

Variation (language internal or crosslinguistic) is due to two different types of parameters:

1. **height of movement** parameters[10] capture how high the subtree with the noun moves up in the hierarchy (if at all). This captures well-established empirical generalizations about variation, starting with Pollock (1989) study of the distribution of verbal forms in English and French.
2. **pied-piping** parameters determine whether the nominal constituent pied-pipes Adjectives, or Numerals, etc. on its journey up into the hierarchy.

Because of (2-c), there is no crosslinguistic order variability prenominally: 123 can only be reordered by pied-piping with the Np,[11,12] 1243, 1423, and 4123 orders correspond to derivations with the (phrasal) nominal constituent halting at different heights, stranding adjectives, numerals, and demonstratives. Remaining orders correspond to height of movement and pied-piping possibilities, yielding greater order variability in linear orders postnominally. Finally, unattested orders, i.e., gaps, fall out in a principled fashion: *2134, *3124, etc. cannot arise in neutral contexts, because it would require a numeral or an adjective to move without the nominal constituent: This is illegal.

---

[10]I am not concerned here with the question of how this is achieved technically.

[11]Here and below, I use small caps p to remind the reader of the phrasal nature of the moved constituent.

[12]It remains to be seen to what extent prenominal order can also be the effect of Internal merge (movement). See Koopman and Szabolcsi (2000: 24–25) for arguments that a 1 2 3 4 order in verbal complexes in Hungarian must be the result of internal merge, i.e., movement.

The statement in (2-c) is the modern incarnation of head movement, with broader and better empirical coverage. The 1243, 1423, and 4123 orders are traditionally dealt with by head movement, which is part of the standard toolbox in syntax. Why then depart from this assumption? Why phrasal movement, not head movement? The problem is not that these particular orders cannot be so derived in individual languages, but rather that a head movement analysis (as Cinque et al. (1994) himself proposed in his earlier work on the Romance noun phrase) cannot capture the crosslinguistic generalizations from a fixed syntactic/semantic hierarchy (cf. Cinque 2010). This is also an important argument in Koopman and Szabolcsi (2000), where we show that a head movement analysis for verbal complexes in Hungarian does not allow for a unified account underlying the different orders of the same verbal complexes in different environments, whereas a phrasal movement account does. The support for phrasal movement analysis thus comes (in part) from the unification it allows, with comparative syntax playing a central role.[13]

Syntax: U20 Patterns Generalize

Since 2005, U20 patterns have been shown to be much more general. Cinque (2009) details similar left right asymmetries (order before the noun or the verb is invariant, postnominal or postverbal order is more variable) and gaps for many different syntactic domains.[14]

This line of research, while still in its infancy, is exciting. It leads to the question what sequences form U20 hierarchies and why. It also leads to the question if the typology of morpheme orders tracks U20 patterns as well. Indeed, if there is a single computational system for syntax and morphology, and if that computational system yields syntactic U20 patterns, we expect the typology of morpheme orders to do so as well (Koopman 2015).

[13]The failure of nominal complements to pied-pipe with the N is often taken to be problematic for phrasal movement, and support head movement. This presupposes that nouns do take complements, or/and that complements can remain in their thematic positions. Neither assumption has empirical support (Kayne (1994); Kayne (2000, Chaps. 14, 15), Kayne (2005, Chap. 7), and Hoekstra (1999) among others). This means that a N is both a N and an NP, compatible with either a head movement or a phrasal movement analysis.

[14]See Cinque (2009) for examples and references of relative orders of attributive adjectives, relative orders of different types of adverbs, the order of tense, mood, aspect and V, Directional Locative P NP, clitic complexes preverbally or postverbally, verbal complexes in Germanic (cf. Koopman and Szabolcsi (2000) on verb clusters in Hungarian, Dutch, and German; Barbiers (2005), Wurmbrand (2006), and Abels (2011), who is the first to demonstrate that the hierarchy/order relations four-membered Germanic verb clusters track the U20 patterns in the noun phrase.

Table 2.2 Morphological patterns and gaps for any hierarchy of 123: English

123 ✓	[re [de [activate]]]	
132 ✓	[un [lock able]]	*not able to be locked*
312 ✓	[madonna [wanna [be]]]	
321 ✓	[[[[nation] al] iz] e]	
231 ✓	[[un [lock]] able]	*able to be unlocked*
213	* ?0	

Morphology: Morphology Tracks U20 Patterns

What do we expect to find if morpheme orders track syntactic U20 patterns? We should observe left right asymmetries, and all and only possible U20 patterns. U20 patterns that cannot be generated should never occur. For an independently motivated fixed (scope) hierarchy of three elements, two affixes, and a lexical category, we expect to find at most five patterns within a single language, with one gap *213. At most, because which patterns occur depends on the morpheme inventory in the language, and their specific lexical properties. In a language like English, which has prefixes and suffixes, all five expected patterns appear to be attested, as shown in Table 2.2.

123 (stacked prefixes), 132, 321 (mirror orders), and perhaps 231, with right-branching structures before the head,[15] are expected under any syntactic theory of morphology. 312 orders, however, *are* expected in the U20 approach, but not by syntactic theories based on head movement, which will assume postsyntactic movement for such orders. 312 will be briefly discussed in the next section. Evaluating gaps is difficult. However, 213 orders in English seem to be excluded: *de-re-activate* in so far as possible only corresponds to *de* scoping over *reactivate* (123), not to a reading where *de* is interpreted in the scope of *re* (*231). *Unrelockable* can only correspond to a reading where *un* takes scope over *re*, not a reading where *un* has undergone raising, and is interpreted in the scope of *re* (see Koopman (2015) for further discussion).

For a fixed hierarchy of four elements, we should find the 14 patterns presented in Table 2.1.

312 Orders

312 orders are also known as Scope violations or Mirror order violations. These orders are expected to arise under generalized U20 through phrasal movements

[15]These orders are ruled out by the Final over Final constraint of Biberauer et al. (2014). Since such orders are clearly attested, a different account is needed for the dislike languages often have for right-branching structures before a head.

(i.e., spec to spec movements). They occur in Korean and Japanese (Koopman 2005), Quechua (Muysken 1981; Myler 2013), Bantu (Hyman 2003; Muriungi 2009; Buell 2005; Ryan 2010), and Wolof (Torrence 2003; Buell 2005), among many languages, and, as we will see below, also in Huave.

Chichewa

Here, we discuss some examples from Chichewa, so as to familiarize the reader with the framework, and show how to proceed building up the syntactic analysis.[16]

A linear *V Caus Inst* order in Chichewa is structurally ambiguous Hyman (2003), reflecting two different Merge (=scope) hierarchies, as indicated in the examples. (3) is derived by the (remnant) Vp pied-piping Caus, yielding a regular 321 mirror order: Caus

(3) $1_{Ins} > 2_{Caus} > 3_V$ 321

íl- íts- il- a
cry Caus- Ins- FV
'..use an instrument to make x cry'

The example in (4), however, is derived by the subtree containing Vp stranding the Ins. This is a 312 order, where the head complement merge order surfaces after verb.

(4) $1_{Caus} > 2_{Ins} > 3_V$ 312

takas- its- il- a
stir- Caus- Ins- FV
'.. cause [to stir with]'

Apart from cases where a linear order corresponds to two different hierarchies, there are also cases where two different linear orders map onto a single merge hierarchy, recalling the variable orders of verbal complexes in Hungarian and Dutch (Koopman and Szabolcsi 2000). This depends, however, on the order in which the suffixes are merged. This can be illustrated with different combinations of Rec, Caus, and V.

The reciprocal suffix −*an* (Caus) can merge either with Caus or with V, yielding two different syntactic hierarchies with different semantic interpretations.

[16] I make no attempt here to contrast this approach to the account in Hyman (2003).

(5) a. $1_{Caus} > 2_{Rec} > 3_V$ (..cause reciprocal Ving)
b. $1_{Rec} > 2_{Caus} > 3_V$ (.. reciprocal causing to V)

The hierarchy in (5-a) yields two different linear orders with the same meaning:

(6) Two linear orders (312 and 321) from the fixed hierarchy $1_{Caus} > 2_{Rec} > 3_V$:
a. a- ku- máng- íts- an- a [312]
3Pl- PROG-tie- Caus- Rec- FV
b. a- ku- máng- án- its- a [321]
3Pl- PROG-tie- Rec- Caus- FV
'..cause to tie each other'

The hierarchy in (5-b) yields only one possible order (from Ryan (2010, 7a, 7b) who cites Larry Hyman and Sam Mchombo p.c.).

(7) One linear order (321) from the fixed hierarchy $1_{Rec} > 2_{Caus} > 3_V$:
a. a- ku- máng- íts- an- a [321]
3Pl- PROG-tie- Caus- Rec- FV
b. *a- ku- máng- àn- its- a [312]
3Pl- PROG-tie- Rec- Caus- FV
'..cause each other to tie'

How do these patterns follow given the respective underlying hierarchies? The linear morpheme orders must Reflect the syntactic derivations below, forced by the U20 approach. Movement is driven by the EPP feature that suffixes have as part of their lexical specification.

(8) $1_{Caus} > 2_{Rec} > 3_V$ (Cause reciprocal Ving)

(6-a)

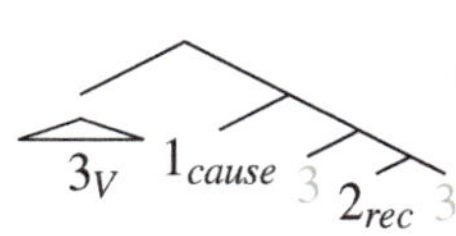

and (6-b)

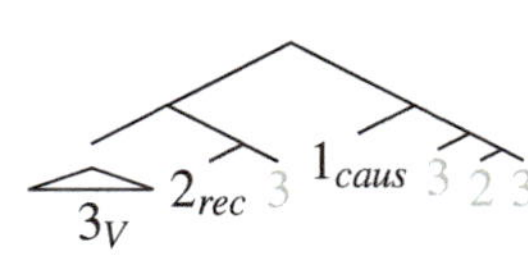

(9) $1_{Rec} > 2_{Caus} > 3_V$
(7-a)

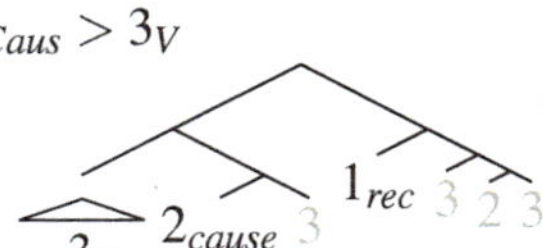

not * (7-b)

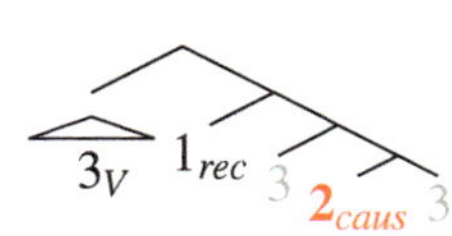

As we can observe by inspecting the derivations, the verbal constituent may pied-pipe Rec or strand it: The variability is thus in some way related to the optionality of pied-piping. The Caus suffix, however, must pied-pipe with V. Since 312 is excluded in this case, we can conclude that this is related to a prohibition on stranding Caus somehow.

What is the difference between Rec and Caus? Both are suffixes with an *EPP* feature as their lexical specification. Well-formed cases with Caus, however, always have a left sister with phonological content at the output of the syntactic derivation, i.e., at the interface with spell-out, but the reciprocal does not. If this is required for the Spec of the Caus, pied-piping of the causative must be forced in (9), yielding a single output, and ruling out stranding Caus. This suggests the following generalization needs to be accounted for: Caus requires a spec with PH content at the interface with phonology/spell-out, but Rec does not. As I propose in Koopman (2014) for different cases, this can be modeled by a further specification of the *EPP* property of a lexical entry, which Caus has (must have lexical content in spec at spell-out), but Rec does not, suggesting that the *EPP* property of Rec can be satisfied at some point in the derivation, allowing Vp to strand Rec.

Huave Morpheme Ordering: Local Dislocation or U20?

The preceding section simply gave an idea of the tasks that are involved in motivating an analysis, and pursuing the predictions of the U20 approach to morphology. A linear order of morphemes (once these are identified) must map onto a syntactic hierarchy, which should be independently motivated. The syntactic derivations that underly the linear orders must be hypothesized, and the formulation of the lexical properties that drive the syntactic derivation must be deduced, and ditto for height of movement and pied-piping parameters. The analysis must of course be internally consistent. Once an analysis is motivated, we can verify whether the linear orders indeed fall within the expected U20 patterns, or not, pursue further predictions, etc. We now turn this into practice in the next section for Huave.

A Puzzle: Huave Morpheme Order

Here, we turn to the puzzling case of morpheme ordering in Huave (San Mateo del Mar), a language isolate of Oaxaca State, Mexico, discussed by Embick and Noyer (2001; 2007). The morpheme order in Huave represents a type of mismatch between syntax and morphology, and is argued to involve *Local dislocation*, a local movement process defined in terms of adjacency, operating postsyntactically after vocabulary insertion. This local readjustment process is further claimed to care only about linear order, not about hierarchical structure. Is local dislocation motivated?

Can the U20 approach to morphology outlined above account for these orders in Huave, and can we dispense with local dislocation?

The morpheme order puzzle is illustrated below (from Embick and Noyer (2007): 320, 51–53). The example sentences vary in two ways: First, whether the subject is first person singular or plural (person and plural are discontinuous), and second, whether the tense is "present" (atemporal) or "past/completive." The verb in these examples is transitive, starting with a vowel, probably an exponent of a Voice prefix. Some affixes in Huave are always suffixal (Refl and Pl), some are "mobile," surfacing sometimes preverbally, sometimes postverbally. The puzzle concerns the alignment of affixes in the postverbal domain. Note that this is the domain where we expect to find variation under U20 because Vp moving past the affixes can interact with pied-piping.[17]

(10) Present, 1st person, sg/pl. Embick and Noyer (2007), ex. 51)

a. S- a- kohch- ay
   1- Th- cut- Refl
   ' I cut myself'

b. S- a- kohch- ay- on
   1- Th- cut- Refl- Pl
   'we (excl.) cut ourselves'

(11) Past, 1st person, sg.

a. T- e- kohch- ay- os
   PAST- Th- cut- Refl- 1
   ' I cut (past) myself'

b. *T- e- kohch- as- ay
   PAST- Th- cut- Refl- 1
   ' I cut (past) myself'

(12) Past 1st person, pl.

a. T- e- kohch- as- ay- on
   PAST- Th- cut- 1- Refl- Pl
   'We cut ourselves'

b. *T- e- kohch- ay- os- on
   PAST- Th- cut- Refl- 1- Pl
   'We cut (past) ourselves'

The order is Refl-1 in (11-a), but excluded in the context of a plural (12-b). The linear sequence 1-Refl is excluded in (11-b), but obligatory in the context of the plural (12-a). This pattern is not derivable by syntactic head movement.

[17]We (incl.) lacks −*s*− *a- kohch- ay- on* "we (incl.) cut ourselves." The default plural-n cooccurs with 1/2 person, the third person plural form is a fused form. The fact that both person and number are expressed on the plural suffix is probably important (see section (22)).

Embick and Noyer (2007) set out to capture the following generalization: A reflexive affix *-ay* appears directly before the final affix of a verb, if there is any. This is achieved by a role of local dislocation which is triggered by a morphological well-formedness condition that applies to complex verbs in Huave, and that specifically refers to the Refl affix.

(13) Refl must precede postroot-X, X a non-Root node.

Refl, it is assumed, is right peripheral to the verb inflectional complex. When no Xs occur, postroot (13) is satisfied, and (10-a) results, with Refl in final position. But when the root is followed by at least one inflectional affix, a Local Dislocation operation which left-adjoins Refl to the final affix applies to satisfy (13). This rules out (11-b) and (12-b). This yields a second position effect with respect to the edge of the verb, but only if other affixes are present.

The assumption that Refl is peripheral to the verb's inflectional complex is required to make local dislocation work. This basic position of Refl must result from the syntax, given DM; hence, it must be supported by what is known about the syntax of reflexives in general, given that the syntax of Huave reflexives has not been studied. This implies that the syntactic structure underlying (12-a) must be something like [[[V 1s] Pl] Refl], assuming head movement, with Refl c-commanding 1st of the transitive verb. This is a highly implausible syntactic structure from a typological point of view: Refl affixes are generally closer to the transitive verb than the 1st person subject. This is clearly true internal to Huave as well, as the "mobile" first person affix *−s−* must be above the Refl in transitive verbs, as shown in (10-a) and Section "Establishing a Syntactic Hierarchy and How High Vp Moves" below.[18]

Since the syntax on which this analysis has to be based makes no sense, the local dislocation analysis on which it must be based, together with the ad hoc well-formedness condition (13), must be rejected as well. It simply must be shown that a speaker can arrive at the underlying syntactic structures by undoing local dislocation. This is what the DM framework requires. The syntax of Huave affixes plays no role in this analysis at all. This means that the generalization that a reflexive affix -*ay* appears directly before the final affix of a verb, if there is any, does not translate into a linguistic analysis.

Thus, an alternative analysis for these morpheme orders pattern is necessary in any case, which takes the syntax into account. In the next sections, we test the U20 framework on these data. As I will conclude, there is no need, nor place, for local dislocation in this account.

[18]In Kim (2008) layered affix fields for Huave of San Fransisco, Refl is also closer to the verb root and then the "mobile" first person suffix *−s−*.

A Sketch of a Syntactic Analysis

Here I will develop a syntactic analysis based on Antisymmetry and phrasal movement as in the U20 approach, taking the limited data presented in the paradigm above, and see how far we can get.

Establishing a Syntactic Hierarchy and how high Vp moves

The very first step consists in determining a reasonable syntactic hierarchy, and determining height of movement of the Vp within this hierarchy. This hierarchy will give us a baseline for the derivation of the orders and properties that must be derived and interactions with pied-piping parameters. Recall that variability in suffix order, as is the case of the Huave paradigm, is expected under antisymmetry, as a consequence of variable pied-piping options. Preverbal orders are expected to show no variability, which seems to be true for Huave. This plays no role in the discussion.

Establishing a syntactic hierarchy of merge is difficult. The four items in (14), I assume, must be ordered in a unique fixed hierarchy. 1st person and Pl(ural) are discontinuous, and not bundled in a single node. Present and past interact with this hierarchy, as shown below.

(14) 1st, Pl, Refl, [Th-V]

It seems reasonable that 1st is merged above Pl, because of the person hierarchy. In languages in which person and plural are independent morphemes (Georgian, Semitic, Maasai), the exponent of person ends up consistently to the left of plural. Refl merges with the V(p), and 1st Person subject is c-commanding Refl, as we saw in Section "A Puzzle: Huave Morpheme Order". This yield the following hierarchies: Refl

(15) a. Refl> V
b. 1st>Refl
c. 1st >Pl

It is unclear, however, what the relative order of merge of Refl and Pl is. I will therefore explore both logically possible hypotheses: Either the order is *Refl > Pl*, or it is *Pl > Refl*, and let the data speak to determine the issue. Looking ahead, it turns out that both hierarchies seem correct for different varieties of Huave, with different morpheme orders.

We now have two hypotheses about the possible shape of the hierarchy that underlies the linear order. These are merges in head complement orders (but with internal Merge interspersed), in agreement with antisymmetry. A constituent containing the remnant Vp (here, Th V) will move leftward, raising the question how high they raise (and why).

(16) Hypothesis 1: $Refl > Pl$:

1st Refl Pl [Th V]
1 2 3 4

(17) Hypothesis 2: $Pl > Refl$:

1st Pl Refl [Th V]
1 2 3 4

Two further elements occur in the examples: "Present" (unmarked for tense or aspect) and "Past/completive" $-t-$. These lead to a different order w.r.t. the mobile affix -s- (-t- itself is a mobile affix, preceding transitive verbs and verbs with a voice prefix), but following intransitive verbs (big VPs), or verbs with a Voice suffix.

The linear orders reveal that the constituent containing the Vp moves to different heights. If $-s-$ always spells out the 1st person node, a reasonable assumption, we observe that $-s-$ precedes the transitive verb (in fact voice initial verbs) in the present, but follows it in the past.

(18) a. "Present/Unmarked":
$1_{1st}\ V...$
'A phrase containing the transitive verb moves above Pl/Refl, but stops below 1st person *s* in "present" tense'

b. "Past": $[t - Th\ V..]1_{1st}$ ..
'A phrase containing the transitive verb raises above 1st in "past/completive" (possibly to the C region)'

As expected under U20 derivations, the verb may or may not pied-pipe other postverbal elements. Such orders, however, are expected to comply with the U20 patterns that can be derived from a given syntactic hierarchy.

1*st* person $-s-$ is referred to in the literature as a *mobile* affix, sometimes ending up preverbal, sometimes postverbal. In the syntactic analysis sketched here, it is not the 1st affix that is mobile. It is in fact always in the same merge position, with the Vp moving to different heights, depending on the type of tense/aspect. Its placement w.r.t. the verb is not driven by a morphological property of the affix itself, in formal terms, the affix does not have an epp_V, but by properties of heads above it (in the past), or below it (in the present). This is sufficient for the discussion here.[19] Such mobile patterns are well known from the syntax. Object clitics in Romance for example follow the imperative (when the V raises to the left periphery), but precede the tensed verb (when the V stops in Agr/T). English subjects follow the finite

[19]Kim (2010) argues the placement of mobile affixes is driven by phonology. Affixes (mobile and nonmobile alike) occur at a fixed distance from the root relative to other affixes. Mobile affixes prefix to vowel initial stems, but suffix to consonant initial stems, to avoid vowel epenthesis. This is incompatible with the U20 view of morpheme order presented here, and remains to be addressed.

auxiliary when T moves to C, but precede T in declaratives, etc. The intuition that lexical items are somehow in invariant syntactic positions, with the functional elements moving around, lowering, etc., does not translate into a syntactic reality in natural languages.

Derivations: Testing Hypothesis 1: Refl > Pl

The fixed syntactic hierarchy in (19) forces specific syntactic derivations for the (limited) data presented above (annotated below). These allow us to verify that possible orders indeed fall within the licit U20 patterns, and to check if the analysis is internally consistent.

(19) 1st Refl Pl [Th V]
     1 2 3 4

(20) a. S- a- kohc- ay.
1- Th- cut- Refl
'I cut myself'

$1_1 3_V 2_{Refl}$

→Vp moves past Refl

b. S- a- kohc- ay- on.
1- Th- cut- Refl- Pl
'We cut ourselves'

$1_{1st} 4_V 2_{Refl} 3_{Pl}$

→Vp moves past Refl, strands Pl

(21) a. T- e- kohc- ay- os.
PST- Th- cut- Refl- 1
'I cut (past) myself'

PST $3_V 2_{Refl} 1_{1st}$

→Vp pied-pipes Refl

b. *T- e- kohc- as- ay
PST- Th- cut- 1- Refl
'I cut (past) myself'

*PST $3_V 1_{1st} 2_{Refl}$

→Vp must pied-pipe Refl. Refl cannot strand

(22) a. T- e- kohc- as- ay- on.
PST- Th- cut- 1- Refl- Pl
'We cut ourselves'

(PST) $4_V 1_{1st} 2_{Refl} 3_{Pl}$

→ REF and Pl must strand

b. *T- e- kohc- ay- os- on
PST- Th- cut- Refl- 1- Pl

*(PST) $4_V 2_{Refl} 1_{1st} 3_{Pl}$

→* a U20 violation!

Possible and impossible U20 patterns:
The attested morpheme orders 132, 321, 1423, and 4123 are possible U20 patterns, as expected by the theory. The ungrammaticality of 4213 order in (22-b) is expected: V and the Refl do not form a constituent to the exclusion of Plural. This order therefore cannot be derived. Nothing further needs to be said. Why (21-b) is ruled out, however, must be explained, as this order is fine, in fact obligatory in the context of the Plural.

Questions about stranding and pied-piping
Why cannot Refl strand (21-b), unless the plural is stranded as well (22-a)? (21-b) competes with (21-a), an order where pied-piping yields convergence.

Similar alternations are found in Hungarian and German (Koopman and Szabolcsi, 2000). We proposed there that pied-piping can be the unmarked option. Unmarked options, however, can be overridden by the needs of other structural elements, say requiring a small piece of structure for example (as is the case for V-second). This forces splitting the structure leading to stranding of elements which can otherwise pied-pipe. Applied to Huave, this implies that you must pied-pipe when possible, unless there is (or are) some other factor(s) that force stranding for convergence. This factor must be absent in (21-b) yielding pied-piping as the sole output. Why is this so? Reflexive can pied-pipe (21-a). Why cannot it do so in the context of a stranded plural?

It will be helpful to examine what the output of the derivation would look like. Take as point of departure the structure in (23a), where (22-a) has merged with 1st. In the Past environment, the Vp must move past 1st. There are exactly two ways in which this can happen. Spec extraction or pied-piping of the node labeled. Extraction of Vp extracts, strands the Refl, yielding the grammatical 4123 in (23b). Vp pied-piping Refl results in the ungrammatical (23c):

(23) a.
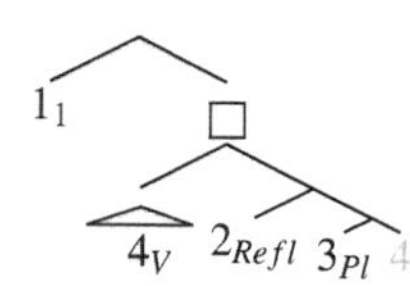

b.
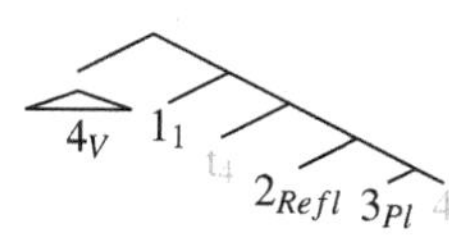

c. *
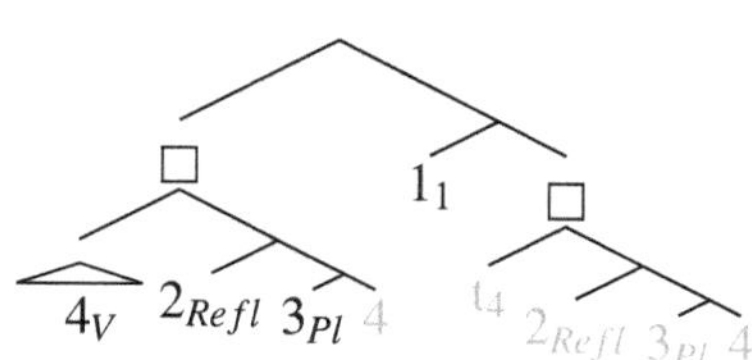

If the output of pied-piping in (23c) can be excluded on independent grounds, Refl may strand, because the unmarked option of pied-piping will not lead to convergence. Note that this derivation results in the heavily right-branching syntactic structure in (23c). Such right-branching structures in Spec position routinely (though not always) lead to ungrammaticality in the syntax of the world's languages. This problem thus relates to a well-known syntactic problem, as expected under a syntactic account. For an account that excludes this case as a problem related to depth of embedding of phonological material, see Koopman (2014): In the past environment, the Vp ends with the V being the most deeply embedded spelled-out material.

In sum, under the fixed hierarchy in Hypothesis 1, a U20 account derives the possible and impossible morpheme orders in Huave. Ungrammatical morpheme orders either cannot be generated by the grammar, or are excluded by interactions of pied-piping and stranding, partially driven by the exclusion of heavy right-branching syntactic structure in Spec positions.

An empirical prediction about variation

The U20 theory makes a strong prediction about the type of variation we expect to find between different dialects or individual speakers of Huave. Indeed, since (22-b) cannot be built from this particular hierarchy, we should not find *any* dialects or speakers who accept it, or produce it. It turns out that this order is found in the San Fransisco del Mar variety of Huave (Kim 2008).[20] This means that these orders cannot be derived from hierarchy 1. However, if the theory is correct, and if this order turns out to be possible for some speakers or dialects, it *must* be the case that this order derives from a different hierarchy.

The fact that I formulated two hypotheses about the hierarchy with no clear way of deciding between the relative order of Refl and Pl now becomes highly relevant. Perhaps both hypotheses are right, but differences in hierarchy will result in a different set of judgments under the syntactic account. The following sections show this is basically correct: The theory predicts the space of variation in morpheme orders, for hierarchies which are not universally fixed.

Local dislocation or U20

I have shown with this sketch that there is no need for local dislocation in Huave to capture these morpheme orders: A syntactic U20 approach can capture the possible and impossible morpheme orders from a fixed syntactic hierarchy, with height of movement and pied-piping parameters at play. General questions that arise can be related to well-known syntactic questions; predictions that are made can be verified and further explored.

[20]Ralf Noyer and Yuni Kim (p.c).

Derivations: Testing Hypothesis 2: Pl > Refl

We next test the fit of Hypothesis 2 on the exact same data. The two hypotheses only differ for the relative order of merge of Ref and Pl. They will yield the same outputs, except when Refl and Pl cooccur.

The data will be summarized in Table 2.3. As before, we proceed from the fixed syntactic hierarchy in (24) (Hypothesis 2). As we will see, this hypothesis cannot model these data patterns.

(24) 1st Pl Refl [Th V]
     1 2 3 4

(25) a. T- e- kohc- ay- os
     PST- Th- cut- Refl- 1
     'I cut (past) myself'
     [PST $3_V 2_{Refl} 1_{1st}$]
     →*Vp can pied-pipe Refl*

b. *T- e- kohc- as- ay
     PST- Th- cut- 1- Refl
     'I cut (past) myself'
     [*PST $3_V 1_{1st} 2_{Refl}$]
     →*Vp must pied-pipe Refl; Refl may not strand*

(26) a. T- e- kohc- as- ay- on
     PST- Th- cut- 1- Refl- Pl
     'We cut ourselves'
     (PST) [$4_V 1_{1st} 3_{Refl} 2_{Pl}$]
     →*Vp pied pipes Refl and subextracts, strands Refl and Pl*

b. *T- e- kohc- ay- os- on
     PST- Th- cut- Refl- 1
     *(PST) [$4_V 3_{Refl} 1_{1st} 2_{Pl}$]
     →*what excludes this?*

Table 2.3 A comparison of the predicted outputs under Hypothesis 1 and 2 (with pied-piping unmarked)

Ex.	*Hyp 1*:1 > *Ref* > *Pl* > *V*	*Hyp 2*: 1 > *Pl* > *Refl* > *V*
(20-a)	$1_1\ 3_V\ 2_{Refl}$	same
(20-b)	$1_{1st}\ 4_V\ 2_{Refl}\ 3_{Pl}$	$1_{1st} 4_V 3_{Refl} 2_{Pl}$
(21-a)	PAST $3_V 2_{Refl} 1_{1st}$	same
(21-b)	* PAST $3_V 1_{1st} 2_{Refl}$	same
(22-a)	(PAST) $4_V\ 1_{1st}\ 2_{Refl}\ 3_{Pl}$	(PAST) $4_V\ 1_{1st}\ 4_V\ 3_{Refl}\ 2_{Pl}$
(26-b)	*(PAST) $4_V 2_{Refl} 1_{1st} 3_{Pl}$	(PST) $4_V 3_{Refl} 1_{1st} 2_{Pl}$

Attested orders (1432, 4132) are licit U20 patterns. But so is 4312 (26-b). This order cannot be excluded either on Huave internal considerations. Here is why. In the same Past environment, Refl must pied-pipe with V, and cannot strand, as shown in (25-a) and (25-b). Since Refl also pied-pipes with V in (26-b), the problem cannot be related to V pied-piping Refl, or the output. Moreover, the *Past V 1st pl* pattern (past 312) is independently attested, showing that plural strands below 1st. Under hierarchy 2 then, there simply is no account why this string would be excluded. Since all properties converge, this string is expected to be grammatical, as illustrated in (27). This turns out to be a good thing, as we see in the next section.

(27)

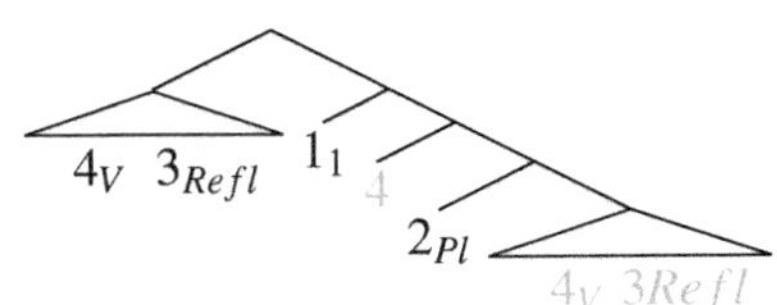

Hypothesis 2 should thus clearly and unambiguously be rejected as a possible hierarchy underlying these specific patterns. This leaves us with the quite successful Hypothesis 1.

What Patterns Are Expected for Hypothesis 2?

So far, we simply examined if hypothesis 2 could account successfully for the particular word order patterns that we described, and rejected it for the data patterns under consideration. Here, we examine the expected output orders under Hypothesis 2, keeping everything else the same, and compare this with the expected outcomes under hypothesis 1. The results are summarized in Table 2.3. This table yields predictions about what variation we can find in Huave dialects.

As for the first three rows, the linear strings *1st V Refl, 1st V refl Pl, and Pst V Refl 1st* are fine under either hypothesis. The order *past V 1st Refl* of (21-b) is excluded in the same way for both hierarchies: Pied-piping is unmarked. Since stranding Refl is not independently forced, stranding Refl is excluded. Stranding is forced for *Past V 1st Pl* (22-a) in the same fashion: Pied-piping would result in *Past V Refl Pl 1*. In both cases, this violates right branch depth of embedding. In short, we expect no variation in Huave for these orders depending on the two hierarchies.

But the two hierarchies do lead to different predictions for rows 5 and 6. The order *pst V Refl 1s Pl* of (26-b) is ruled out under hypothesis 1, but perfect under hypothesis 2. The order *V 1st Refl Pl* (26-a) is perfect under hypothesis 1, but its expected grammaticality depends on whether subextraction from a complex specifier, a potential island violation, is allowed or not. We do not get much help from the syntax, as this question has never been completely resolved.[21] As argued in Koopman and Szabolcsi (2000), subextraction from a complex specifier must be excluded in the derivation for verbal complexes in Hungarian. Cinque (2005), p.c. noted that this order is "possibly spurious" for nominal U20 patterns, but believes now that it should be allowed (it occurs frequently enough in his extended U20 database). Subextraction must be ruled out for several cases of morpheme orders in Wolof, as shown in Koopman (2015). But Abels (2011), however, shows this order is documented within Germanic.

If subextraction from a complex specifier is excluded, 4132 should be excluded in principle as well as an island violation. In short, the predictions for grammaticality under hypothesis 2 depend on whether subextraction is allowed or not.

Expected Patterns of Variation Within Huave

Table 2.4 now summarizes the only predicted variation in morpheme orders for Huave dialects or speakers for the set of data we have considered, depending on whether subextraction is allowed or not.

What is known about variations of such strings in different varieties of Huave? There are four dialects of Huave: San Mateo (which is the dialect with the data reported so far), Santa Mar′ıa (a dialect Rolf Noyer worked on extensively), San Dionisio, and San Francisco del Mar (Kim 2008; 2010). The data reported here, modeled by hypothesis 1, are solidly established for San Mateo and Santa Mar′ıa (Ralph Noyer, p.c). But in San Fransisco del Mar, (22-b) is fine (Yuni Kim, p.c and Kim (2010)), in accordance with the hierarchy in hypothesis 2:

(28) t- a- xut- ey- as- an (or: t-a-xut-e-s-an)
PAST- Th- hide- Refl- 1- Pl
'we (excl.) hid ourselves'

The theory furthermore predicts that (22-a) should be accepted if subextraction is possible, but should be excluded in the San Francisco dialect if subextraction from a complex specifier is ruled out. Yuni Kim (p.c) volunteered that she had not verified the negative data, but thought she never heard it. The verifications of the full empirical predictions for Hypothesis 2a versus 2b will thus have to wait further work.

Ralf Noyer (p.c) also points out that (Stairs and Hollenbach 1969) mention in a footnote that the alternative order in (22-a) which he gives as ungrammatical is possible, as noticed by Gregory Stump. Noyer's consultants, however, do *not*

[21]See Koopman (2015) for a suggestion under what circumstances subextraction in the syntax could be expected to be possible: What is at issue is whether this configuration is always an island, or sometimes.

Table 2.4 Predicted patterns of variation in Huave morpheme orders

	Hyp 1 1 > *Ref* > *Pl* > V	Hyp 2a 1 > *Pl* > *Refl* > V	Hyp 2b no subextr. 1 > *Pl* > *Refl* > V
(22-a)Pst-V-1st-Refl-V	✓	✓	
(22-b)Pst-V-Refl-1st		✓	✓

accept this alternative order: The facts represented by Hypothesis 1 are clear. The published literature does not mention this order as a possible order either. Given the argument presented here, however, we can make sense of these apparently problematic data. This alternative order could very well have come from a speaker with an internal grammar that reflects the hierarchy under Hypothesis 2. We may never know. But, given the theory that I have sketched here, this is the type of variation that is expected, and thus no cause for concern. On the contrary, the theory can be used and should be used to pursue possible variation.

An important point is that the linear order in (28) is *not* derivable from the hierarchy in Hypothesis 1. The theory therefore leaves no choice: If such orders are attested, they must reflect a *different* hierarchy. As this hierarchy cannot contradict universal hierarchies, the variation in Merge must be located in an area where such variation is allowed. In fact, it is encouraging that where we found indeterminacy in the order of merge, this indeterminacy actually may provide insights in how closely related varieties may differ exactly. In other words, the theory makes specific predictions about patterns of variation in different varieties of Huave speakers.

Conclusion

We conclude that there is no motivation to adopt Local dislocation for Huave, even within DM, and every reason to extend the syntactic account to the morphology of Huave more generally, and put the theory to test on other potentially problematic cases. As I showed, a syntactic account can in fact be constructed, based on a direct interface of syntax and phonology, which accounts for the typology of word order patterns in syntax *and* morphology, as expected under a single computational engine for syntax and morphology. There is every reason to extend the syntactic account to Huave morphology more generally in the future, and put the theory to test on other potentially problematic cases that have been argued to motivate postsyntactic reordering.

To evaluate different frameworks, as stated at the beginning of this chapter, it matters how well the frameworks account for the empirical data, not just for individual languages but for human languages in general, whether they generate predictions that can be verified, and how appropriate they are for the interfaces with phonology and semantics.

The account developed here fares well with respect to these criteria. It can capture the various aspects that underly the empirical data. Further analytical problems that arise can be related to well-known syntactic puzzles or phenomena. The framework generates predictions that can be verified, and it is appropriate for the interface with phonology—the linear order is read off the syntactic derivation—as well as semantics in so far as the hierarchical structures underlying the linear orders encode scope. The interface is important. Any DM type account of morpheme ordering must be able to show how morpheme order relates to the syntax in a particular language, and show that this is a reasonable syntax.

In many ways, this chapter here suggests that Baker's Mirror Principle has to be true under the syntactic account:

(29) **Mirror Principle** Baker (1985, p. 4)
'Morphological derivations must directly reflect syntactic derivations (and vice versa)'

It simply took a different understanding of syntax than was possible at the time, building on general progress of the field, with an ever increasing focus on comparative syntax.

While there are well-known surface violations of the Mirror order principle, i.e., orders that cannot be derived by head movement, we expect these violations to fall within the possible syntactic patterns under the syntactic U20 approach in the framework presented here. This is an important question for the future research agenda.

References

Abels, K. 2011. Hierarchy-order relations in the germanic verb cluster and in the noun phrase. *Groninger Arbeiten zur Germanistischen Linguistik* 53 (2): 1–28.

Abels, K., and A. Neeleman. 2009. Universal 20 without the LCA. In *Merging Features: Computation, Interpretation, and Acquisition*, ed. J. Brucart, A. Gavarro, and J. Solá, 60–79. Oxford: Oxford University Press.

Baker, M. 1985. The mirror principle and morphosyntactic explanation. *Linguistic Inquiry* 16 (3): 373–416.

Barbiers, S. 2005. Theoretical restrictions on geographical and individual word order variation in Dutch three-verb clusters. In *Syntax and variation: Reconciling the biological and the social*, 233–264. Amsterdam/Philadelphia: John Benjamins.

Biberauer, T., A. Holmberg, and I. Roberts. 2014. A syntactic universal and its consequences. *Linguistic Inquiry* 45 (2): 169–225.

Bobaljik, J. 2015. *Distributed morphology, to appear in a handbook.*

Bobaljik, J.D. 2012. *Universals in comparative morphology: Suppletion, superlatives, and the structure of words*, vol. 50. MIT Press.

Buell, L.C. 2005. Issues in Zulu verbal morphosyntax. ProQuest.

Caha, P. 2009. The nanosyntax of case. PhD dissertation. Tromsoe.

Chomsky, N. 1992. A minimalist program for linguistic theory, vol. 1. *MIT Working Papers in Linguistics*. Cambridge, Massachusetts: MIT.

Cinque, G. 2010. *The syntax of adjectives: A comparative study*. MIT Press.
Cinque, G. 2009. The fundamental left-right asymmetry of natural languages. In *Universals of language today*, 165–184. Berlin: Springer.
Cinque, G. 2005. Deriving greenberg's universal 20 and its exceptions. *Linguistic inquiry* 36 (3): 315–332.
Cinque, G., et al. 1994. On the evidence for partial n-movement in the romance DP. In *Path towards universal grammar*, ed. G. Cinque, J. Koster, J.-Y. Pollock, L. Rizzi, and R. Zanuttini, 85–110. Washington, DC: Georgetown University Press.
Embick, D., R. Noyer. 2007. Distributed morphology and the syntax/morphology interface. *The Oxford handbook of linguistic interfaces* 289–324.
Embick, D., and R. Noyer. 2001. Movement operations after syntax. *Linguistic Inquiry* 32 (4): 555–595.
Greenberg, J.H. 1963. Some universals of grammar with particular reference to the order of meaningful elements. In *Universals of language*, ed. J. Greenberg. Cambridge, Massachusetts: MIT Press.
Halle, M., and A. Marantz. 1993. Distributed morphology and the pieces of inflection. In *The view from building 20*, ed. K. Hale, and S.J. Keyser, 111–176. Cambridge, Massachusetts: MIT Press.
Harley, H. 2012. Semantics in distributed morphology. *Semantics: International Handbook of Meaning* 3.
Hoekstra, T. 1999. Parallels between nominal and verbal projections. In *Specifiers*, ed. D. Adger, B. Plunkett, G. Tsoulas, and S. Pintzuk, 163–187. Oxford: Oxford University Press.
Hyman, L.M. 2003. Suffix ordering in Bantu: A morphocentric approach. In *Yearbook of Morphology 2002*, 245–281. Berlin: Springer.
Joshi, A. 1985. How much context-sensitivity is necessary for characterizing structural descriptions. In *Natural language processing: Theoretical, computational and psychological perspectives*, ed. D. Dowty, L. Karttunen, and A. Zwicky, 206–250. NY: Cambridge University Press.
Julien, M. 2002. *Syntactic heads and word formation*. Oxford University Press.
Kayne, R. 2010. Toward a syntactic reinterpretation of harris and halle (2005). *Die Berliner Abendbla¨tter Heinrich von Kleists: ihre Quellen und ihre Redaktion* 2 (4).
Kayne, R.S. 2005. Movement and silence, vol 36. Oxford University Press on Demand.
Kayne, R.S. 2000. On the left edge in UG: A reply to Mccloskey. *Syntax* 3 (1): 44–51.
Kayne, R.S. 1994. *The antisymmetry of syntax*. Cambridge, Massachusetts: MIT Press.
Kim, Y. 2010. Phonological and morphological conditions on affix order in huave. *Morphology* 20 (1): 133–163.
Kim, Y. 2008. Topics in the phonology and morphology of San Francisco del Mar Huave. ProQuest.
Koopman, H. 2015. Generalized u20 and morpheme order, under review.
Koopman, H. 2014. Recursion restrictions: Where grammars count. In *Recursion: Complexity in Cognition*, 17–38. Berlin: Springer.
Koopman, H. 2005. Korean (and Japanese) morphology from a syntactic perspective. *Linguistic Inquiry* 36 (4): 601–633.
Koopman, H.J., and A. Szabolcsi. 2000. *Verbal complexes*. Cambridge, Massachusetts: MIT Press.
Muriungi, P.K. 2009. Phrasal movement inside bantu verbs: Deriving affix scope and order in ki-itharaka. PhD thesis, Universitetet i Tromsø.
Muysken, P. 1981. Quechua word structure. *Binding and filtering* 279–326.
Myler, N. 2013. Exceptions to the mirror principle and morphophonological "action at a distance": The role of "word"-internal phrasal movement and spell out. New York: ms., New York University.
Pollock, J.Y. 1989. Verb movement, universal grammar, and the structure of ip. *Linguistic inquiry* 365–424.
Ryan, K.M. 2010. Variable affix order: Grammar and learning. *Language* 86 (4): 758–791.

Sportiche, D., H. Koopman, and E. Stabler. 2013. *An introduction to syntactic analysis and theory*. New York: Wiley.

Stabler, E. 2011. Computational perspectives on minimalism. In *Oxford Handbook of Linguistic Minimalism*, 617–641. Oxford University Press.

Stairs, E.F., B.E. Hollenbach. 1969. Huave verb morphology. *International Journal of American Linguistics* 38–53.

Starke, M. 2010. Nanosyntax: A short primer to a new approach to language. *Nordlyd* 36 (1): 1–6.

Torrence, H. 2003. Verb movement in wolof. *Papers in African linguistics* 3: 85–115.

Wurmbrand, S. 2006. Verb clusters, verb raising, and restructuring. *The Blackwell companion to syntax* 229–343.

Chapter 3
Tense and the Realization of the Feminine Plural in Hindi-Urdu

Rajesh Bhatt and Stefan Keine

Introduction

This chapter examines the realization of the plural feature in the context of the feminine feature in Hindi-Urdu. We argue that the plural feature is only realized in the presence of a feminine feature if this plural feature is in the context of finite tense. Our analysis gives a detailed treatment of agreement morphology in Hindi-Urdu and provides an independent way of characterizing finiteness in the language.

In agreement environments, Hindi-Urdu displays pervasive neutralization of the plural feature in the context of the feminine feature. This can be exemplified by the oft-cited paradigm for the agreeing genitive marker *ka:*, which displays the three-way distinction in *ka:/ke/ki:* and not a four-way distinction in *ka:/ke/ki:/kĩ:*. We document this pattern of neutralization and contrast it with closely related languages such as Punjabi, Marathi, Kashmiri, and Sindhi where we show that there is no such neutralization. We show that plural is in fact realized by nasalization in the context of the feminine feature in certain environments. We argue that these environments all involve the agreeing participle in the context of tense. Further, we show that to determine whether the plural is realized or not, we cannot just make reference to the surface forms. Whether the plural is realized or not depends upon the morphosyntactic properties of the silent auxiliary verb involved in these contexts. The proposal deepens our understanding of Hindi-Urdu agreement morphology, the structural location of participles, and the representation of Tense in Hindi-Urdu.

R. Bhatt (✉)
Department of Linguistics, University of Massachusetts Amherst, Amherst, USA
e-mail: bhatt@linguist.umass.edu

S. Keine
Department of Linguistics, University of Southern California, Los Angeles, USA
e-mail: keine@usc.edu

G. Sengupta et al. (eds.), *Perspectives on the Architecture and Acquisition of Syntax*, DOI 10.1007/978-981-10-4295-9_3

Plural Neutralization in the Feminine

Hindi-Urdu displays agreement in both gender and number. However, number is neutralized in the context of the feature feminine. This seems quite systematic and can be seen with adjectives, the past/passive participle, the habitual participle, the progressive auxiliary, the infinitive, and the agreeing genitive postposition.

Adjectives agree in number and gender with the subject if they are predicative and with the noun phrase they modify if they are attributive. The agreement is visible only with adjectives that end in *-a:*.

(1) certain adjectives that end in *a:*, e.g., *lamba:* 'tall' (both attributive and predicative contexts)

	SG	PL
MASC	lamba:	lambe
FEM	lambi:	lambi:

The adjectivalizer *va:la:* inflects in a similar fashion: *va:la:/va:le/va:li:/va:li:* as do modifiers of adjectives such as *itna:/utna:/jitna:/kitna:* "this/that/how$_{rel}$/how$_{q}$ much."

The passive/past participles, the habitual participle, and the progressive auxiliary agree with their subject/object depending upon the case borne by these arguments.

(2) passive/past participles, e.g., *ka:ṭ-a:* 'cut-Pfv'

	SG	PL
MASC	ka:ṭ-a:	ka:ṭ-e
FEM	ka:ṭ-i:	ka:ṭ-i:

(3) habitual participle, e.g., *ka:ṭ-ta:* 'cut-Hab'

	SG	PL
MASC	ka:ṭ-ta	ka:ṭ-te
FEM	ka:ṭ-ti:	ka:ṭ-ti:

(4) the progressive auxiliary *raha:*

	SG	PL
MASC	raha:	rahe
FEM	rahi:	rahi:

Infinitival verbs agree but only in contexts of long-distance agreement where they agree with a long-distance agreeing object.

(5) infinitive, e.g., *ka:ṭ-na:* 'cut-Inf'

	SG	PL
MASC	ka:ṭ-na:	ka:ṭ-ne:
FEM	ka:t-ni:	ka:ṭ-ni:

Finally, we turn to the genitive postposition which agrees in number and gender with the possessum.

(6) the genitive postposition, e.g., *Tina ka:* 'Tina GEN'

	SG	PL
MASC	Tina ka:	Tina ke
FEM	Tina ki:	Tina ki:

The similative postposition *jaisa:* 'like' and the suffixal genitive in *-ra:* that appears with personal pronouns pattern with the genitive postposition and agree with the noun that follows it.

We can abstract a common agreement pattern across all these contexts: *-a:/-e/-i:*. Note that this pattern of agreement makes a three-way distinction and not a four-way distinction. Number is neutralized in feminine contexts in Hindi-Urdu. The neutralization of number in feminine contexts is not a general characteristic of Indo-Aryan languages. Punjabi, Marathi, Sindhi, and Kashmiri do not neutralize number in feminine contexts. Here are examples of some of these contexts for Punjabi where we see number being expressed in feminine contexts.

(7) certain adjectives that end in *a:*, e.g., *caŋga:* 'good' (both attributive and predicative contexts) (Punjabi, Bhatia (1993): 83, ex. 258)

	SG	PL
MASC	caŋga:	caŋge
FEM	caŋgi:	caŋgiã:

The Punjabi adjectivalizer *va:la:* inflects in a parallel fashion: *va:la:/va:le/va:li:/va:liã:*.

(8) past participles, e.g., *uṭṭhia*: 'rise-Pfv' (Punjabi, from Tolstaya (1981), Chap. 3, p. 45)

	SG	PL
MASC	uṭṭhia:	uṭṭhe:
FEM	uṭṭhi:	uṭṭhiã:

Habitual participles in Punjabi inflect similarly: From the verb *likhṇa:* 'to write,' we get *likhda:/likhde/likhdi:/likhdiã:* and so do infinitives (Gurmeet Kaur p.c.).is no plural neutralization in the feminine,

(9) the genitive postposition, e.g., *da*: (Punjabi, Bhatia (1993): 182)

	SG	PL
MASC	da:	de
FEM	di:	diã:

The Punjabi progressive auxiliary *ría:* behaves similarly: *ría:/ráe/rái:/ráiã:*

We see here that Hindi-Urdu and Punjabi agreement in the environments differs systematically with respect to neutralization of number in feminine contexts: Hindi-Urdu neutralizes number systematically in the presence of the feminine feature, while Punjabi does not. We find a similar systematicity in Kashmiri (Wali and Koul 1997), Marathi, and Sindhi (Trumpp 1872: 327–328).

(10) adjectival agreement without number neutralization in contexts of feminine agreement:

	MSG	MPL	FSG	FPL
PUNJABI	-a:	-e	-i:	-iã:
MARATHI	-a:	-e	-i:	-ya:
SINDHI	-ō	-ā	-ī	-iũ:
KASHMIRI	-mut	-mɨt'	-mɨts	-mɨtsɨ

(Marathi also has neuter gender; the forms for those are *-ə/-i:*. The paradigm shown for Kashmiri is for the perfect participle. Unlike the other languages, the adjectival agreement paradigm is not purely concatenative.) Of the languages surveyed, only Gujarati patterns with Hindi-Urdu in neutralizing number in the feminine.

It also has neuter as a gender, and there is no number neutralization with the neuter.

(11) certain adjectives that end in *-o,* e.g., *saro* 'good' (Doctor 2004: 26)

	SG	PL
MASC	saro	sara
FEM	sari	sari
NEUT	sarũ	sarã

The adjectival agreement paradigm for Gujarati—*-o/-a/-i/-ũ/-ã*—is also the agreement paradigm used by all the agreeing participles (the present participle, the past participle, the future participle, the remote past participle, the future agentive participle, and the future imperative participle which is identical to the gerundial infinitive) (Doctor 2004: 39–40, 45–47), modifiers of adjectives that end in *-o* (Doctor 2004: 67), and agreeing postpositions (the genitive *-no, jevũ, sərkhũ* 'like') (Doctor 2004: 32, 71).

Looking across these languages, we note two generalizations. The first is that the same pattern of inflection, which we can call the participial pattern, holds across a range of syntactic environments—underived adjectives, infinitives, agreeing postpositions, modifiers of adjectives, and participles. The second is that in the languages where there is no plural neutralization in the feminine, the plural feature is realized by a distinct segment—*-ã:* in Punjabi, *-a:* in Marathi, *-ũ:* in Sindhi, and -ɨ in Kashmiri—in addition to a segment that realizes the feminine feature. In this, it contrasts with the expression of plural in the context of the masculine feature. All four languages use a single morpheme that expresses both the masculine feature and the plural feature.

Having set up this crosslinguistic background, it is worth noting that the neutralization of number in feminine contexts is a fact about agreement contexts. There is no such systematic neutralization of number in feminine contexts with nouns, where the number and gender features can be thought of as intrinsic.

(12) *laṛka:* 'boy' versus *laṛki:* 'girl'

	SG	PL
MASC	laṛka:	laṛke
FEM	laṛki:	laṛkiyã:

That this is a restriction related to agreement can be seen by looking at the *va:la:* construction. This construction can be used to construct properties. So 'X va:la:' denotes a property associated with X when it modifies an NP. 'X va:la:' can also stand on its own as an argument and in that case it denotes the one associated with X.

(13) a. *nakhre va:la: laṛka:*
tantrums VALA.MSg boy
'the boy with tantrums'

b. *nakhre va:la:*
tantrums VALA.MSg
'the (masculine) one with tantrums'

But if we look at the full inflection of *va:la:* when it modifies an NP versus when it stands on its own, we see that the modifier *va:la:* neutralizes number in the feminine while the freestanding one does not.

(14) modifier *va:la:*

	SG	PL
MASC	nakhre va:la: laṛka:	nakhre va:le laṛke
FEM	nakhre va:li: laṛki:	nakhre va:li: laṛkiyã:

(15) freestanding *va:la:*

	SG	PL
MASC	nakhre va:la:	nakhre va:le
FEM	nakhre va:li:	nakhre va:liyã:

The fact that the freestanding form does not display number neutralization tells us something important: Number neutralization is not simply a general syncretism of the feminine singular and the feminine plural in Hindi-Urdu. The freestanding contexts show us that the language is perfectly capable of making the distinction. Our characterization of number neutralization needs to be sensitive to the structural configuration in which the participle finds itself.

Environments Without Number Neutralization in the Feminine

Plural is not always neutralized in the presence of the feminine feature. We survey here environments where plural is in fact realized in the presence of the feminine feature. These environments will involve some of the elements that we used to demonstrate number neutralization in the first place: the past participle, the habitual participle, and the progressive auxiliary.

The Freestanding Past Participle

A notable environment where there is no number neutralization is that of the freestanding perfective participle that marks past tense. Plural in the presence of the feminine is obligatorily realized via nasalization.

(16) freestanding past participle, e.g., *ka:ṭ-a:* 'cut-Pfv'

	SG	PL
MASC	ka:ṭ-a:	ka:ṭ-e
FEM	ka:ṭ-i:	ka:ṭ-ĩ:

The freestanding past participle is to be distinguished from the past participle and the passive participle. The realization of the feminine plural aside, these have the same form. The distinction between the freestanding past participle and the (non-freestanding) past/passive participle is a syntactic one: The freestanding participle is the highest verbal element in a minimal finite clause, while the others are further embedded. The embedding can involve being the complement of an auxiliary verb or being embedded as an NP modifying reduced relative.

We see this contrast in (17). In (17a), the participle is the highest verbal element and we see that feminine plural marking with nasalization is obligatory. In contrast, in (17b), the participle combines with a past auxiliary to form the past perfect. In this structure, the participle is not the highest verbal element in its clause and we see that the participle appears without nasalization.[1]

(17) a. *Ram=ne ṭehniyã: ka:ṭ-ĩ:/*ka:ṭ-i:*
Ram=ERG branches.FPL cut-PFV.FPL/cut-PFV.FSG
'Ram cut the branches'

b. *Ram=ne ṭehniyã: ka:ṭ-i: thĩ:/*thi:*
Ram=ERG branches.FPL cut-PFV.FSG be.PST.FPL/be.PST.FSG
'Ram had cut the branches'

Expression of FPl via nasalization is impossible when this participle is used as a passive participle and when it is used to form a participial relative.

(18) a. *ṭehniyã: kal ka:ṭ-i:/*ka:ṭ-ĩ: gayĩ:/gayi:*
branches.FPL yesterday cut-PFV.FSG/cut-PFV.FPL go.PST.FPL/go.PST.FSG
'The branches were cut yesterday'

b. *[[kal kaṭ-i:/*kaṭ-ĩ:] ṭehniyã:]*
yesterday cut$_{unacc}$-PFV.FSG/cut$_{unacc}$-PFV.FPL branches.FPL
'the branches (that were) cut yesterday'

[1] We are being cautious here and not claiming that nasalization is impossible here. In our judgement, feminine plural marking on the participle is dispreferred, but it seems to be well-attested online. Non-nasalization is also equally well-attested. So for now our claims are limited to the environments where FPl must be expressed via nasalization. We will return to environments where there is optionality/speaker variation with respect to the expression of FPl.

The Habitual Participle and the Progressive Auxiliary

Unlike the past participle, the habitual participle and the progressive auxiliary cannot be freestanding in the sense defined above. To form a well-formed sentence, an auxiliary is needed. (19) with the habitual participle in *-ta:* and (20) with the progressive auxiliary *raha:*, both involve a present auxiliary, but a past auxiliary or a future auxiliary would do just as well.

(19) *ve larkiyã: seb kha:-ti: *(hɛ̃)*
those girls apple eat-HAB.F be.PRS.PL
'Those girls eat apples'

(20) *ve larkiyã: seb kha: rahi: *(hɛ̃)*
those girls apple eat PROG.F be.PRS.PL
'Those girls are eating apples'

As discussed earlier, we find number neutralization in these environments.[2] But if we examine environments where the habitual participle and the progressive auxiliary become freestanding, then the pattern changes and plural must be realized in the context of the feminine feature, as nasalization. We turn to two such environments next.

Negation Triggered Auxiliary Deletion

Bhatia (1979) noted that in the presence of negation, participles/auxiliaries that otherwise require a tensed auxiliary can be freestanding.

(21) Progressive: Aux obligatory
a. *Ram seb kha: raha: *(hɛ)*
Ram apple eat PROG.M.SG be.PRS.SG
'Ram is eating apples'

Progressive + negation: Aux optional
b. *Ram seb nahĩ: kha: raha:*
Ram apple NEG eat PROG.M.SG
'Ram is not eating apples'

(22) Habitual: Aux obligatory
a. *Ram seb kha:-ta: *(hɛ)*
Ram apple eat-HAB.M.SG be.PRS.SG
'Ram eats apples'

Habitual + negation: Aux optional
b. *Ram seb nahĩ: kha:-ta:*
Ram apple NEG eat-HAB.M.SG
'Ram does not eat apples'

[2]As with the case of the past participle discussed in the previous section, we will largely focus on environments where there is no number neutralization, i.e., expression of the plural feature is obligatory. Judging from online usage, there are speakers who allow for nasalization of non-freestanding habitual participles/progressive auxiliaries. Based on our own introspective judgements, we assume that such nasalization is optional. We cannot rule out the possibility that there are speakers for whom nasalization is obligatory in these environments. If such speakers exist, we can analyze their grammars as being like that of the languages discussed in Section "An Initial Generalization and an Initial Analysis" which do not display number neutralization.

For reasons that we do not understand, the negated freestanding participle/auxiliary can only be interpreted as a present tense sentence as indicated in the translations of the freestanding structures in (21) and (22). The restriction does not directly follow from properties of *nahĩ:* 'neg,' which is compatible with both past and present auxiliaries.[3]

(23) a. *Ram seb nahĩ: kha: raha: hɛ/tha:*
Ram apple NEG eat PROG.M.SG be.PRS.SG/be.PST.SG
'Ram is/was not eating an apple'

b. *Ram seb nahĩ: kha:-ta: hɛ/tha:*
Ram apple NEG eat-HAB.M.SG be.PRS.SG/be.PST.SG
'Ram does/did not eat apples'

In other words, *nahĩ:* allows the present auxiliary, but not the past auxiliary, to go missing. What happens to the habitual participle and the progressive auxiliary when the presence of *nahĩ:* allows them to be freestanding? We find that as with the freestanding past participle, plural must be marked as nasalization in the presence of the feminine feature.

(24) Freestanding progressive:
a. *ve laṛkiyã: seb nahĩ: kha: rahĩ:/*rahi:*
those girls apple NEG eat PROG.F.PL/PROG.F
'Those girls are not eating apples'

Freestanding habitual:
b. *ve laṛkiyã: seb nahĩ: kha:-tĩ:/*kha:-ti:*
those girls apple NEG eat-HAB.F.PL/eat-HAB.F
'Those girls don't eat apples'

The Past Habitual and the Counterfactual

Another environment where the habitual participle can be freestanding involves the counterfactual. In fact, in these environments an overt auxiliary is impossible.

(25) counterfactuals

a. *agar Ram mehnat kar-ta: (*hɛ/*tha:), to zaru:r pa:s ho ja:-ta: (*hɛ/*tha:)*
if Ram hardwork do-HAB.M.SG be.PRS.SG/be.PST.SG then definitely pass be go-HAB.M.SG be.PRS.SG/be.PST.SG
'If Ram had worked hard, he would've definitely passed'

b. *ka:sh Ram mehnat karta: (*hɛ/*tha:)*
wish Ram hardwork do-HAB.M.SG be.PRS.SG/be.PST.SG
'I wish Ram worked hard'

And as one might expect now, in these environments, we find that there is no number neutralization in the feminine. Plural must be marked as nasalization in the presence of the feminine feature.

[3]That said, *nahĩ:* is crucial for allowing the present tense auxiliary to go unexpressed. The negation marker *na:* does not allow the present tense auxiliary to be absent.

(26) counterfactuals

a. *agar ve laṛkiyā̃: mehnat kar-tī̃:/*kar-ti:, to zaru:r pa:s ho*
if those girls hardwork do-HAB.F.PL/do-HAB.F then definitely pass be
*ja:-tī̃:/*ja:-ti:*
go-HAB.F.PL/go-HAB.F
'If those girls had worked hard, they would've definitely passed'

b. *ka:sh ve larkịyā̃ mehnat kartī̃:/*kar-ti:,*
wish those girls hardwork do-HAB.F.PL/do-HAB.F
'I wish those girls worked hard'

A related case is that of the narrative past habitual. In sequences of sentences describing past habitual actions, the participle can be freestanding. In these cases, unsurprisingly the freestanding participle only has past reference. What is surprising is that auxiliary cannot go missing when describing a sequence of present habitual actions.

(27) *un dinõ Ram 6 baje uṭh-ta:. sna:n kar-ta:. aur phir 7 baje sku:l ja:-ta:.*
those days Ram 6 o'clock rise-HAB.M.SG bath do.HAB.M.SG and then 7 o'clock school go-HAB.M.SG
'Those days Ram would wake up at 6am. He'd take a bath and then go to school at 7 a.m'

We have now seen three ways in which a past habitual can become freestanding—via negation, which yields a present tense meaning, via the narrative past habitual, and via the counterfactual. So in principle, the same string can have three different interpretations: negative present habitual, negative past habitual, and negative counterfactual. This is shown below. In the following example, the subject has feminine plural features, and we see that there is no number neutralization; plural must be realized.

(28) Negative present habitual

a. *ve subah sna:n nahī̃: kart-ī̃:/*kar-ti:*
3.PL morning bath Neg do-HAB.F.PL/do-HAB.F
'She (honorific) doesn't bathe in the morning'

Narrative Past habitual

b. *un dinõ Auntie-ji: 6 baje uṭh-tī̃:/*uṭh-ti:. ve subah sna:n nahī̃:*
those days Auntie-Hon 6 o'clock rise-HAB.F.PL/rise-HAB.F 3.PL morning bath Neg
*kar-tī̃:/kar-ti:. si:dhe sku:l ja:-tī̃:/*ja:-ti:.*
do.HAB.F.PL/do.HAB.F directly school go-HAB.F.PL/go-HAB.F
'Those days Auntie would wakeup at 6am. She wouldn't bathe in the morning but would go directly to school'

Counterfactual

c. *ka:sh ve subah sna:n nahī̃: kar-tī̃:/*kar-ti:*
wish 3.PL morning bath Neg do -HAB.F.PL/do-HAB.F
'I wish she (honorific) bathed in the morning'

We see here that the same string can correspond to three different meanings. Therefore, we take this to tell us that these freestanding structures involve extra inaudible structure which is responsible for the meaning differences we find.

An Initial Generalization and an Initial Analysis

The generalization that has emerged so far seems quite straightforward: There is number neutralization in the context of the feminine feature in Hindi-Urdu. This number neutralization disappears if the relevant context functions as a freestanding participle or if it functions as a nominal expression.

Here is a way to model these facts. We assume that number and gender head their own nodes with number higher than gender. This would yield a structure like the following for a participial structure.

(29) external structure of a participle

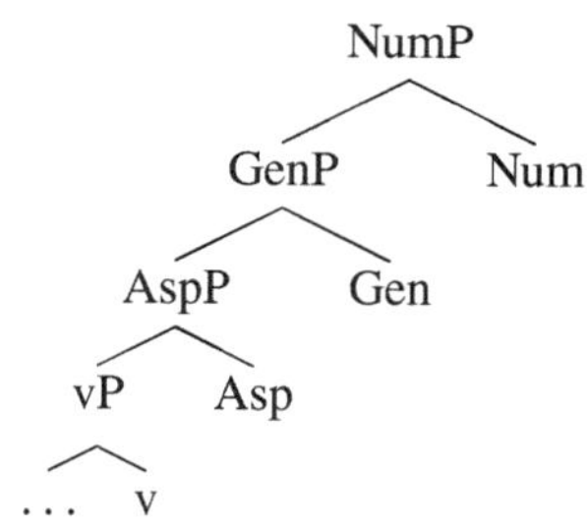

We further assume that head movement combines the verbal root with v and then with Asp, Gen, and Num. Within the context of a postsyntactic realizational theory of morphology such as Distributed Morphology, let us consider the following realizational rules for a language without number neutralization in the feminine.[4] Here, we show the case for Punjabi.

(30) *Punjabi realizational rules*:

a. /-e/ ↔ [M.PL]
b. /-a:/ ↔ [M]
c. /-i:/ ↔ [F]
d. /-ã:/ ↔ [PL]

[4]Note that these rules make no reference to the [SG] feature. This requires further comment. One possibility is that there simply is no such feature in the syntax; under this conception, only plural DPs have a number specification. While this conception would work well for the data at hand, we will need to make reference to the [SG] feature while handling the paradigm for the present auxiliary, and hence, we will work with an architecture where the morphology does not have to spell out all syntactic features. It must spell out anything that it can but if there is no realizational rule for a feature, that feature can just go unrealized without any concomitant deviance.

Head movement in the syntax creates the following complex head, [[[[V v] Asp] Gen] Num]. Following the classical model of Distributed Morphology developed in Halle and Marantz (1993) and Halle and Marantz (1994), postsyntactic morphology realizes abstract syntactic heads. It does so by inserting one exponent into each syntactic head, a process called *vocabulary insertion*. Vocabulary insertion is subject to the Subset Principle. If more than one exponent satisfies this principle, the most specific exponent is chosen (by Panini's Principle, i.e., the Elsewhere Principle). Portmanteau morphemes, i.e., morphemes that simultaneously realize more than one syntactic head, are triggered by *fusion* rules, which combine two syntactic heads into a single one. Applied to (30), the existence of the exponent *-e*, which simultaneously expresses [masculine] and [plural], motivates the fusion rule in (31):

(31) *Masculine plural fusion rule*:

. . .] M] PL] → . . .] [M PL]]

Fusion applies in this context—masculine plural—in all of the Indo-Aryan languages that we discuss here. The resulting structure is then realized by the rules in (30).

(32) *Punjabi participles*

a. participle with [M.PL] features:
input to realizational component after fusion (31): [[[[V v] Asp] [M PL]]

- there is a special form for [M.PL], and hence it must be used, giving us [V-v-Asp-**e**].

b. participle with [F.PL] features:
input to realizational component (no fusion): [[[[[V v] Asp] F] PL]

- [F] and [PL] are realized separately and in the order given by the structure, giving us [V-v-Asp-**i-ã:**].

The structure assumed has number located higher than gender. This together with the realizational rule in (30d) derives the generalization that in the languages without number neutralization, plural in the presence of feminine is always marked by a distinct exponent and that this exponent appears after the exponent of the feminine feature.

Under this account, Hindi-Urdu differs minimally from Punjabi and other languages where there is no number neutralization with respect to (30d).

(33) *Hindi-Urdu realizational rules*:

a. /-e/ ↔ [M.PL]
b. / ˜ / ↔ [PL /___[T]]
c. /-ã:/ ↔ [PL /___[n]]
d. /-i:/ ↔ [F]
e. /-a:/ ↔ [M]

Crucially, in Punjabi, the [PL] on its own is always realized by *-ã:*. In Hindi-Urdu, the realization of this feature is context-sensitive. In the context of T, it is realized as a nasalization and in the context of an *n* head, it is realized as *-ã:*. In the absence of such heads, it simply lacks a realization. Number neutralization is in this treatment encoded implicitly—the plural feature by itself has no realization in Hindi-Urdu, unless it is in the context of T or n. We assume a structural characterization of the notion of context—the context of T is the head of the complement of T. The case of participles is shown below. The head of the NumP associated with the AspP is not in the immediate context of T, while the head of the NumP associated with the AuxP is. Consequently a PL feature on the lower Num head (the Num head of the AspP) will not be realized while a PL feature on the higher Num head (the Num head of the AuxP) will be.

(34) participle plus auxiliary:

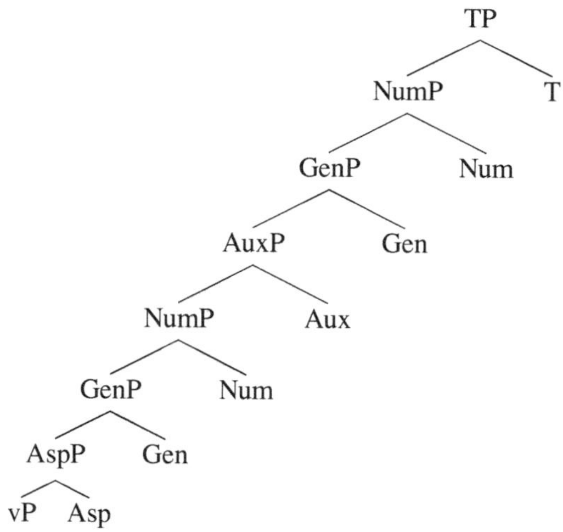

The other environments where we find number neutralization—infinitives, postpositions, untensed auxiliaries, adjectives, and modifiers of adjectives—are also not sisters of TP and hence a PL feature there is not in the immediate context of T. We are also able to explain why number neutralization disappears when a participle becomes freestanding. It is plausible that in these cases, the freestanding participle is in fact in the immediate context of T as shown in the following structure.

(35) freestanding participle:

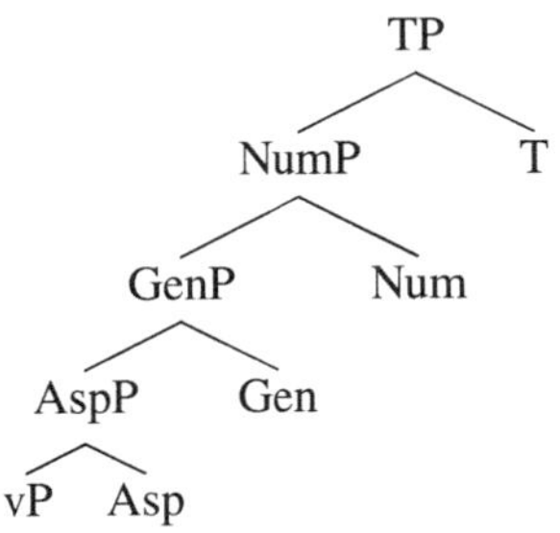

Finally (33e) handles the case of nominals where [PL] is realized by *-ã:*.

The Role of Person and a Revised Generalization

The analysis proposed in the previous section works well but it runs into a confound when we look beyond agreement with the 3rd person. In all the examples considered so far, the agreement trigger has had third person features. We have not looked at cases where the agreement trigger has first or second person features. This might seem to be an innocent omission as in general participial/adjectival agreement tends to not involve person features (cf. Baker 2011). So the expectation would be that the person feature of the agreement trigger would not influence participial/adjectival agreement. However, it turns out that person does influence the agreement on freestanding participles. We find that freestanding participles with plural feminine 1st person subjects pattern with plural feminine 3rd person subjects in lacking number neutralization.

(36) *ham/ve laṛkiyã: mehnat nahĩ: kar-tĩ:/*kar-ti:*
we/they girls hardwork Neg do-HAB.F.PL/do-HAB.F
'We girls/those girls don't work hard'

(37) *ham/ve laṛkiyã: mehnat nahĩ:kar rahĩ:/*rahi:*
we/they girls hardwork Neg do Prog.HAB.F.PL/Prog.HAB.F
'We girls/those girls aren't working hard'

But plural feminine 2nd person subjects display number neutralization.

(38) *tum laṛkiyã: mehnat nahĩ: kar-ti:/*kar-tĩ:*
you girls hardwork Neg do-HAB.F/do-HAB.F.PL
'You girls don't work hard'

(39) *tum laṛkiyã: mehnat nahĩ: kar rahi:/*rahĩ:*
you girls hardwork Neg do Prog.HAB.F/Prog.HAB.F.PL
'You girls aren't working hard'

Now recall that freestanding habitual participles can actually appear in a number of syntactico-semantic contexts. Exemplified above is the case where negation allows for a freestanding habitual participle with present reference. Next we consider cases where the freestanding habitual participle is allowed by counterfactuals and the narrative past habitual.

(40) Counterfactual

a. *ka:sh tum laṛkiyã: mehnat kar-̃tı:/*kar-ti:*
'wish' you girls hardwork do-HAB.F.PL/do-HAB.F
'I wish you girls worked hard'

Narrative Past Habitual

b. *un dinõ tum laṛkiyã: khu:b mehnat kar-̃tı:/*kar-ti:* . . .
those days you girls lot hardwork do-HAB.F.PL/do-HAB.F
'In those days, you girls worked very hard. . .'

Here we find that plural must be expressed. The contrast between (38)/(39) on the one hand, where freestanding participles display number neutralization and (40), where they do not initially seems quite puzzling as at least on the surface it looks as if one and the same object is behaving differently with respect to number neutralization. This contrast is also the reason why we cannot sustain the analysis proposed in the previous section. The analysis derives the generalization it is based on, namely that there is no number neutralization with freestanding participles. But as (38)/(39) show us, this generalization is wrong. So what is the correct generalization? Here is the distribution of number neutralization across the environments that we have examine so far.

(41) Number neutralization across environments
(all agreements triggers have feminine and plural features)

	1/3 PERSON	2 PERSON
All Non-Freestanding Participles	Yes	Yes
Freestanding Present Habituals	No	**Yes**
Freestanding Narrative Past Habituals	No	No
Freestanding Counterfactuals	No	No

We believe that the correct generalization surfaces once we consider the covert ways in which the three superficially identical freestanding habitual participles differ, discussed in Section "The Freestanding Past Participle". The first kind, where the freestanding participle is licensed by negation, is always interpreted with present tense reference (see (21) and (22)). The narrative past habitual has, as the name suggests, past reference (see (27)). The case of the counterfactual (see (25) and (26)) is less clear but following the crosslinguistic generalizations discussed in Iatridou (2000), it is plausible that there is a past component in the makeup of the counterfactual. Therefore let us assume that the first kind of freestanding participle involves a covert present tense auxiliary while the other two involve a covert past tense auxiliary.

Next let us examine the paradigms of the present tense and the past tense auxiliaries. The present tense auxiliary only agrees in person and number while the past tense auxiliary only agrees in number and gender.

(42) the present tense auxiliary *hɛ*
(involved by hypothesis in the makeup of the freestanding participles licensed by negation)

	SG	PL
1	hũ	**hɛ̃**
2	hɛ	**ho**
3	hɛ	**hɛ̃**

(43) the past tense auxiliary *tha:*
(involved by hypothesis in the makeup of the freestanding habitual licensed by counterfactuals and the narrative past habitual)

	SG	PL
M	tha:	the
F	thi:	**thĩ:**

Focusing on the bold faced cells in these tables, we can extract the forms of the auxiliaries that would correspond to various potential number neutralization configurations. To test number neutralization, we will keep the gender as feminine and the number as plural. This means we will only manipulate person and the covert makeup of the freestanding participle in question.

(44) the form of the auxiliary that could appear with negated habituals versus narrative habitual pasts

	NEGATED HABITUAL	NARRATIVE PAST
1F.PL	hɛ̃	thĩ:
2F.PL	**ho**	thĩ:
3F.PL	hɛ̃	thĩ:

Note that all the cells in the above table have nasalization except the boldfaced cell that corresponds to the 2F.PL subject of a negated habitual/progressive. So the final generalization can be stated as follows:

(45) *Realization of the plural*:
If the tensed auxiliary that would appear with a particular freestanding participle has nasalization (see (44)), then the freestanding participle will too.

The new generalization makes reference to "the tensed auxiliary that would appear with a particular freestanding participle." How is this to be implemented? Let us explore the possibility that freestanding participles have a covert tensed auxiliary associated with them. Postpositions, participial reduced relatives, adjectives, and modifiers of adjectives are clearly not associated with a tensed auxiliary. Participles and the progressive auxiliary that appear with an overt tensed auxiliary are transparently associated with a tensed auxiliary, but the generalization only applies to covert auxiliaries.

This is an unusual generalization as it makes reference to a very particular fact about the form of a covert element, namely whether it has nasalization or not, to determine the shape of the freestanding participle. How may we represent this generalization? A simple generalization along the lines of the analysis in the previous section will not suffice. In that analysis, a plural associated with the participle received a realization in the context of T. But in this case, it is not quite the properties of the participle and the T head that determine whether we get number neutralization or not. The determining factor seems to be the actual form of the relevant covert auxiliaries.

A Morphological Analysis

The generalization concerning the realization of the plural feature laid out in (45) can be derived if we take the morphological makeup of the auxiliaries seriously. The idea is that the plural forms with nasalization are morphologically more complex than the forms without nasalization. In these plural forms, the plural feature is realized by a distinct exponent as opposed to the other forms where a single exponent realizes multiple features.

Let us use the past tense auxiliary, the paradigm for which is repeated below, to illustrate this proposal concerning morphological complexity. The past auxiliary only inflects for number and gender.

(46) the past tense auxiliary *tha:*

	SG	PL
M	tha:	the
F	thi:	**thĩ:**

The interesting contrast is between the masculine plural and the feminine plural. The feminine plural involves one designated exponent for feminine (*-i:*) and one for plural (namely, nasalization). The masculine plural, on the other hand, employs a single exponent (*-e*) to express number and gender. The special behavior of masculine singular follows immediately from the fusion rule in (31). The feminine plural is thus morphologically complex in a way that the masculine plural is not and we take this complexity to be structurally represented. The structures created by successive head movement, which form the input to vocabulary insertion, are given in (47). (47b) is the result of fusion (31).

(47) a. masculine singular: [$_{T}$ [$_{Num}$ [$_{Gen}$ Aux M] SG] T]
 b. masculine plural: [$_{T}$ [$_{Aux}$ Aux [M PL]] T]
 c. feminine singular: [$_{T}$ [$_{Num}$ [$_{Gen}$ Aux F] SG] T]
 d. feminine plural: [$_{T}$ [$_{Num}$ [$_{Gen}$ Aux F] PL] T]

Next let us consider the participle where ordinarily we get number neutralization of the plural in the context of the feminine. We will assume that despite number neutralization, a participle with feminine plural features has a complex representation that consists of [F] and [PL]. That is, agreement in all phi-features is syntactically represented. It is just a fact about Hindi-Urdu that [PL] on its own has a zero realization.

We can now take a look at what happens with a freestanding participle with a covert past tense auxiliary. The interesting case here concerns feminine plural features and involves the following configuration:

(48) a. *feminine plural freestanding participle:*
 . . . [$_{Num}$ [$_{Gen}$ Part(iciple) F]PL] ~~[$_{T}$ [$_{Num}$ [$_{Gen}$ Aux F]PL] T]~~
 b. *masculine singular freestanding participle:*
 . . . [$_{Part}$ Part [M PL]] ~~[$_{T}$ [$_{Aux}$ Aux [M PL]] T]~~
 '~~(strikethroug~~h indicates that the auxiliary is syntactically present but is not realized overtly.)'

To complete the proposal, we propose the following realizational rules.

(49) *Hindi-Urdu realizational rules*:

 a. /-e/ ↔ [M,PL]
 b. / ˜ / ↔ **PL** / ___ ~~[$_{T}$ [$_{Num}$ [. . .] **PL**] **T**]~~
 c. / ˜ / ↔ **[PL / [[___] T]]**
 d. /-i:/ ↔ [F]
 e. /-a:/ ↔ [M]

These realizational rules differ from the realizational rules from (33) primarily in the context that conditions the overt realization of the [PL] feature. Earlier we had this feature being realized anytime it was in the context of T. Now only T's with a [PL] specification count. (49b) states that a plural feature is realized by nasalization if it is local to a plural feature that is immediately dominated by a node of type T and which is not itself realized. This rule triggers nasalization on participles if there is a covert auxiliary with feminine plural features (48a). Crucially, if the covert auxiliary contains masculine plural features, these features undergo the fusion rule

(31) and as a result will not fulfill the context requirement of (49b), as shown in (48b). The second nasalization rule in (49c) realizes a plural feature that is in a complex head with T, i.e., a plural feature on an auxiliary.

To illustrate, consider first a case of feminine plural with an overt auxiliary. The schematic structure (after head incorporation has taken place) is:

(50) participle plus past auxiliary: the FPL case

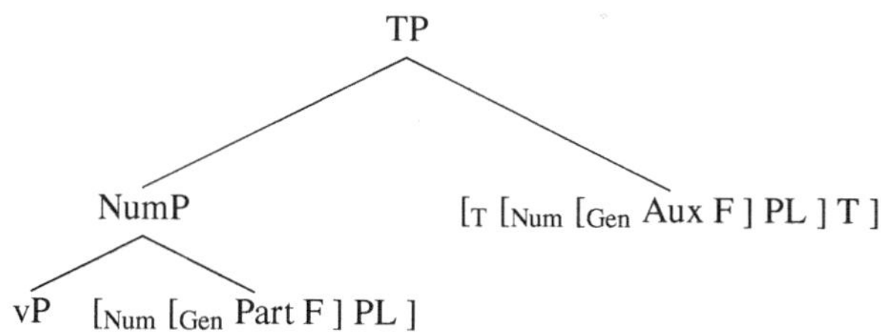

The [PL] feature under T is realized via nasalization by the rule in (49c). The [PL] associated with the participle is in the context of a plural T but this is an overt T and hence the participial [PL] is not realized.

Next, consider a feminine plural case with a covert auxiliary:

(51) freestanding participle with silent past auxiliary: the FPL case

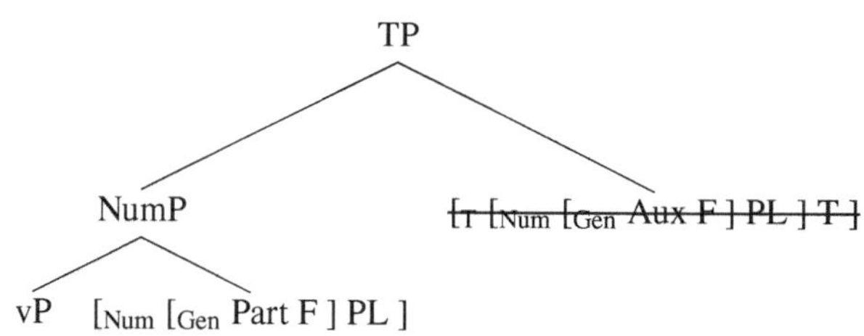

Here the rule (49b) can apply and results in nasalization on the participle.

For completeness, let's also consider the cases of a participle and auxiliary, overt or covert, with [M, PL] features. As we have seen, fusion of [M] and [PL] applies in this case:

(52) freestanding participle with overt/silent past auxiliary: the MPL case

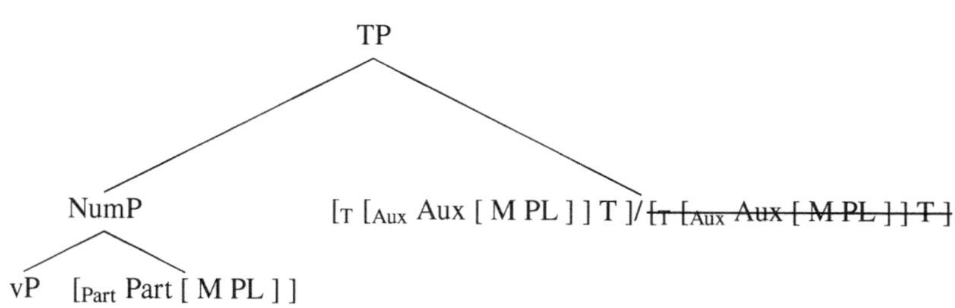

The features of the participle are realized completely independently of the features of T. Whether T is realized overtly or not, all the features of the participle are spelled out by the morpheme *-e* in (49e). Because a single feature cannot be realized twice, no issue of realizing a freestanding [PL] feature bundle arises.

The empirical impact of the revised proposal becomes clearer once we look at the present tense auxiliary, which inflects for person and number but not for gender. The paradigm for it is repeated below.

(53) the present tense auxiliary *hɛ*

	SG	PL
1	hũ	**hɛ̃**
2	hɛ	**ho**
3	hɛ	**hɛ̃**

Note that the [2PL] involves the portmanteau morpheme *ho*, which simultaneously expresses 2nd person and plural number. Just like in the case of masculine plural, this portmanteau morpheme motivates the existence of the fusion rule in (54), which fuses a 2nd person feature on T and a plural feature into a single head.[5]

(54) *2nd person plural fusion rule*:

. . .] PL] 2] → . . .] [2 PL]]

The interesting cases for us involve the plural column. Fusion applies in the context of [2] and [PL] but not in the context of [1/3] and [PL]. Abstracting away from gender agreement, which is not expressed in the paradigm in (53), this gives us the following featural representations:

(55) *Representation of plural forms of the present tense auxiliary*:

a. 1st Plural: [$_{T}$ [$_{Num}$ Aux PL] 1]
b. 2nd Plural: [$_{T}$ Aux [PL 2]]
c. 3rd Plural: [$_{T}$ [$_{Num}$ Aux PL] 3]

In the 2nd plural, the person and number feature are fused and therefore both expressed by a portmanteau morpheme. This contrasts with the 1st and 3rd plural, where plurality is expressed by a designated element, i.e., nasalization.

We now take a look at a freestanding participle with a covert present tense auxiliary with a number of feature combinations. The fusion rule (31) applies in masculine plural configurations, and the fusion rule (54) applies in 2nd person plural cases. As a result, in the case of feminine 2nd plurals (56b), fusion rule (54) applies to the covert auxiliary. In masculine 1/3 plural cases (56c), fusion rule

[5]We would also need to address the [1SG] case. Following the logic of our proposal, fusion also applies in the context of [1] and [SG].

(31) applies to the participle. Finally, in masculine 2nd plural cases (56d), both fusion rules apply.

(56) *Covert auxiliary is a present tense auxiliary:*

a. *feminine1/3 plural freestanding participle:*
 … [$_{\text{Num}}$ [$_{\text{Gen}}$ Part F] PL] ~~[$_{\text{T}}$ [$_{\text{Num}}$ Aux PL] 1/3]~~

b. *feminine 2 plural freestanding participle:*
 … [$_{\text{Num}}$ [$_{\text{Gen}}$ Part F] PL] ~~[$_{\text{T}}$ Aux [PL 2]]~~

c. *masculine 1/3 plural freestanding participle:*
 … [$_{\text{Part}}$ [M PL]] ~~[$_{\text{T}}$ [$_{\text{Num}}$ Aux PL] 1/3]~~

d. *masculine 2 plural freestanding participle:*
 … [$_{\text{Part}}$ [M PL]] ~~[$_{\text{T}}$ Aux [PL 2]]~~

We now turn to the question of how the abstract syntactic structures in (56), which are created by head movement and fusion, are morphological realized. The cases where the agreement controller has masculine plural features (56c, d) are the easiest to handle. In these cases, fusion yields a [M, PL] feature bundle. By Panini's Principle (the Elsewhere Principle), the most specific rule—namely (49a)—always wins out over the less specific (49b). As a result, only the realization of freestanding [PL] features is context-sensitive; the realization of [PL] features that have fused with another feature is not dependent on the context. Thus, no nasalization appears on the participle in the case of [M, PL].

When the agreement controller has feminine plural features, the [PL] feature on the participle and the [F] feature on the participle do not fuse. (49a) is therefore not applicable. Now, the realization of the [PL] feature depends upon the syntactic context. If this [PL] feature finds itself in the context of a [PL] feature on a covert T, the contextual restriction of (49b) will be met and this [PL] feature will be realized via nasalization. Otherwise, it will not be realized. The contextual restriction is met in (56a), with a 1/3PL present auxiliary. In these auxiliaries, the [PL] feature on the auxiliary does not fuse with the [1/3] person feature and so there is a freestanding [PL] feature on T to condition the realization of the freestanding [PL] feature on the participle as nasalization. But this is not the case in (56b), where we have a 2PL present auxiliary in which the [PL] feature fuses with the [2] person feature. Here is the final set of realizational rules, augmented to handle person. The rest of the system stays the same.

(57) *Hindi-Urdu realizational rules* (final version)

a. /-e/ ↔ [M,PL]
b. /˜/ ↔ PL /____ ~~[$_{\text{T}}$ [$_{\text{Num}}$ [. . .] PL] T]~~
c. /˜/ ↔ [PL / [[____] T]]
d. /-i:/ ↔ [F]
e. /-a:/ ↔ [M]
f. /-o/ ↔ [2,PL]
g. /-ũ:/ ↔ [1,SG]
h. /-ɛ/ ↔ [PERSON]

In this analysis, the morphological distinctions that we have appealed to—namely whether [PL] on an auxiliary receives a distinct exponent or whether it is realized as part of a portmanteau—play a crucial role. Whether or not rule (57b) applies is determined by whether fusion of person and number by (54) takes place. This derives the curious generalizations in (41) and (45). Number is neutralized in the second person on freestanding present habitual participles because these involve a covert present tense auxiliary, whose overt forms in (42) reveal it to undergo fusion of [2] and [PL], hence bleeding the nasalization rule in (57b). By contrast, the freestanding narrative past habitual participle and the freestanding counterfactual participle use the covert past tense auxiliary (43), which does not fuse [2] and [PL]. Rule (57b) can hence apply and insert nasalization onto the participle. As a result, the number distinction is morphologically preserved only in the latter case. In this way, we derive the fact that nasalization disappears on the participle if the covert auxiliary is present tense and if the agreement is 2nd person plural—the combination that does not induce fusion.

Note that that, as before, we have two distinct rules that introduce nasalization ((57b) and (57c), respectively). A [PL] feature bundle under T is always realized as nasalization. And a [PL] feature in the immediate context of a silent T[PL] is also realized with nasalization. The restriction to a silent T[PL] is significant because otherwise we consistently get double nasalization, i.e., nasalization on the auxiliary and nasalization on the participle. While this is attested in online usage, it seems degraded to our judgement. An example is provided in (58). While standardly there is no nasalization on the participle, for some speakers the participle can carry nasalization alongside the auxiliary:

(58) *Ram=ne ṭehniyā̃: ka:ṭ-i:/%-ĩ: thĩ:*
Ram=ERG branches.FPL cut-PFV.FSG/%-PFV.FPL be.PST.FPL
'Ram had cut the branches'

We assume that while double nasalization is an option for some speakers, it is optional even for them. The system so far does not produce nasalization on the participle in (58). Modeling optional double nasalization would require the following optional realizational rule, which is similar to (57b), but drops the covertness requirement imposed on the auxiliary.[6]

[6]Sakshi Bhatia has suggested to us that double nasalization might have an entirely different phonological source based on the phenomenon of prenasalization—a spread of nasalization from a nasalized auxiliary to a participle. Prenasalization would explain why some speakers accept sentences like the following.

i. *%uncle-ji: naha: rahẽ hɛ̃*
uncle-Hon bathe Prog.MPL.PL be.PRS.3PL
'Uncle is bathing'

Here under our analysis, the progressive only has [M, PL] features which get fully spelled out *-e*. There is no [PL] feature left to realize. Consequently, the double nasalization rule cannot be

(59) *Optional rule for deriving double nasalization*:

/ ˜ / ↔ PL / ___ [T [Num [. . .] PL] T]

Like (57b), the rule in (59) is conditioned only if no fusion of the plural feature as taken place.

A More Syntactic Analysis

The morphological analysis developed in the previous section is able to account for the data at hand, but the analysis relies on access to how features are grouped together by the exponents that realize them in order to condition the realization of other features. For example, a [PL] feature on a participle is either overtly realized or not depending upon how the matrix present tense auxiliary groups together its person and number features. If, as in the case of the second person plural, the features are grouped together, participial [PL] goes unrealized. If no fusion takes place and the features are grouped separately as in 1st plural cases, then participial [PL] is realized. It is reasonable to assume that these fusion rules apply during Spell-Out. But this raises a problem—if, as is standardly assumed, Spell-Out proceeds cyclically up the tree (Bobaljik 2000), then at the point at which the participle is being spelled out, the tensed auxiliary has not been spelled out. Then, it is not obvious where the difference between [[1] [PL]] and [[2 PL]] would come from. Therefore, in this section, we consider an alternative treatment which does not need to make reference to such information.

---

used to generate (i). Once we admit prenasalization as a source for double nasalization, it becomes an open empirical question whether the grammar also has (59). We leave the choice between these rules for future work which should also carefully delineate the availability of double nasalization. We find (i) and all other cases of double nasalization with the exception of perfects quite degraded. However, informal surveys of online usage suggest that there is much variation here.

It should be noted that while a prenasalization account can be used to explain double nasalization, it is not obvious that we can appeal to prenasalization for handling freestanding participles. In particular cases where the possibility of nasalization depends upon the properties of the silent auxiliary would require a rather abstract notion of prenasalization. Such an account would also need to explain why otherwise optional and variable prenasalization in double nasalization contexts becomes obligatory with freestanding participles. We also see a clear empirical problem. While (i) is marginally acceptable for some, its freestanding counterpart in (ii) is completely unacceptable.

ii. **uncle-ji: nahĩ: naha: rahẽ*

uncle-Hon Neg bathe Prog.MPL.PL

'Uncle is not bathing'

A prenasalization account that derives obligatory nasalization on a freestanding participle from the nasalization on a silent auxiliary should do the same in (ii), contrary to fact.

This alternative treatment follows the morphological treatment with the exception that the realization of [PL] is not conditioned on the internal grouping of features; instead, we condition the realization of [PL] on syntactic features of the auxiliary. We replace the morphological rule in (60a) by the rule in (60b)—it should be noted that the [PL] in the conditioning context in (60a) refers to a morphological feature bundle, while the [–2,PL] in the conditioning context in (60b) refers to a structure that contains a PL feature but does not have a 2nd person feature.

(60) a. *Morphological Rule:*
/˜/ ↔ **PL** / ___ ~~[$_{T}$ [$_{Num}$ [. . .] **PL**] **T**]~~
b. *Syntactic Rule:*
/˜/ ↔ **PL** / ___ ~~[$_{T}$ [$_{Num}$ [. . .] **PL**] **–2**]~~

What the new rule in (60b) states is that [PL] is realized by nasalization in the immediate context of a silent T with a plural feature whose person feature is not 2nd person. Among the present tense auxiliaries with plural features, 1st person and 3rd person auxiliaries qualify, while 2nd person auxiliaries do not. Past tense auxiliaries lack a person specification and so all plural past tense auxiliaries qualify. The resulting system makes the same predictions as the morphological system—the second person plural present tense auxiliary was the one environment that did not condition the realization of participial [PL]. However, it is not subject to the criticism we leveled at the morphological system. The system can be embedded in a standard cyclic Spell-Out system.

However, we believe that as set up, this system is in fact less explanatory than the morphological system. By making direct reference to how the features are encoded, the morphological system is able to explain why the second person plural present tense auxiliary is special. In the new system, the fact that this auxiliary is special is merely encoded. It does not follow from anything. In principle, nothing would prevent us from having a system with exactly the current exponents but where the special form was, e.g., the 1st person plural present tense auxiliary instead. It seems like by merely encoding the special form we are missing a generalization. Unfortunately at this point, we are unable to do better than these two attempts. Both attempts work. The first one is explanatory, but there are questions about its implementation. The second one is easy to implement, but it is not explanatory. We hope that future research will bring forth a system that is both explanatory and implementable within an existing Spell-Out system.

Remaining Issues

Freestanding Past Participles

The first case of a freestanding participle that we looked at involved freestanding past participles. What is special about these in the context of Hindi-Urdu is that unlike the habitual participle and the progressive auxiliary, the past participle can stand on its own without any extra support, in a manner of speaking. The freestanding past participle is how the simple past tense is conveyed in Hindi-Urdu. In Section "The Freestanding Past Participle", we discussed how freestanding past participles need to be distinguished from the superficially similar past/passive participle. One clear way in which these differ is in the realization of the plural feature in the context of feminine. In the freestanding past participle, the plural feature is always realized as nasalization (even in 2PL configurations). This is shown in (61), repeated from (17) above. Plural is not expressed on the passive participle or on the past/passive participle used as a reduced relative, as shown in (62), repeated from (18).

(61) *Ram=ne ṭehniyã: ka:ṭ-ĩ:/*ka:ṭ-i:*
Ram=ERGbranches.FPL cut-PFV.FPL/cut-PFV.FSG
'Ram cut the branches'

(62) a. *ṭehniyã: kal ka:ṭ-i:/*ka:ṭ-ĩ: gayĩ:/gayi:*
branches.FPL yesterday cut-PFV.FSG/cut-PFV.FPL go.PST.FPL/go.PST.FSG
'The branches were cut yesterday'
b. *[[kal kaṭ-i:/*kaṭ-ĩ:] ṭehniyã:]*
yesterday cut_{unacc}-PFV.FSG/cut_{unacc}-PFV.FPL branches.FPL
'the branches (that were) cut yesterday'

The situation of the past participle when used with an auxiliary is in between—realization of the plural feature in the context of feminine seems to be optional, falling under the rubric of 'double nasalization,' illustrated in (58). In our proposal, [PL] can be realized as nasalization in one of two ways: It can be directly under T, or it can be in the local context of a silent T[PL] (or T[-2PL], depending upon which of the two analyses one adopts). For the habitual participle and the progressive auxiliary, we concluded that they were in the context of a tensed auxiliary, which is overt some times and silent in the freestanding cases. What is the situation for the freestanding past participle (61)?

Let us explore the option that the freestanding past participle involves a silent auxiliary. What would this auxiliary be? We could let it be the past auxiliary or the present auxiliary. The problem that arises then is that the past participle together with the past auxiliary and the past participle with the present auxiliary both have semantics that are distinct from the semantics of the simple past conveyed by the freestanding past participle. The semantics of the past participle together with the past auxiliary could be very roughly characterized as akin to the past perfect, and the semantics of the past participle together with the present auxiliary could be very roughly characterized as akin to the present perfect. The remaining option then is the idea that the freestanding past participle moves to T. Nasalization would then be immediately follow, due to the rule in (57c), which inserts nasalization if there is an unrealized plural feature in T. (61) then follows. Of course, this analysis will need to notate somewhere that past participle can move to T, while the habitual participle and the progressive auxiliary cannot. The past tense semantics will follow from the aspectual semantics of the perfective aspect on the past participle.

The Case of tum

We conclude this chapter with a puzzle about the feature specification of the second person pronoun *tum*. Like English 'you,' even though *tum* has singular reference, it triggers plural agreement. This is in contrast to *tu:*, which triggers singular agreement. *tum* is used for addresses that are social equals of the speaker, while *tu:* for people are who are either intimate with or socially lower than the speaker. Unlicensed use of *tu:* can be perceived as rude.

(63) *tum na:c-te/na:c-e ho/the*
you dance-HAB.MPL/dance-PFV.MPL be.PRS.2PL/be.PST.MPL
'You$_{equal}$ (male) dance/used to dance'/'You$_{equal}$ (male) have/had danced'

(64) *tu: na:c-ta:/na:c-a: hɛ/tha:*
you.SG dance-HAB.MPL/dance-PFV.MSG be.PRS.2SG/be.PST.MSG
'You$_{familiar/inferior}$ (male) dance/used to dance'/'You$_{familiar/inferior}$ (male) have/had danced'

Based on these, it seems reasonable to treat *tu:* as having singular number and *tum* as having plural number for the purposes of agreement. The gender is contributed by the gender of the referent. So if *tum* is used for a female addressee, we would expect it to have [2FPL] features. This seems correct initially as the following cases show.

(65) *tum na:c-ti:/na:c-i: ho*
you dance-HAB.F/dance-PFV.F be-PRS.2PL
'You$_{equal}$ (female) dance'/'You$_{equal}$ (female) have danced'

(66) *mɛ̃ ca:h-ta: hũ: [ki tum vahã: na:c-ti: hui: ja:-o]*
I want-HAB.MSG be.PRS.1PL that you there dance-HAB.F be.PFV.F go-SBJV.2PL
'I want that you go there dancing'

The participle agrees with the feminine feature and the auxiliary in person and number, supporting the contention that this *tum* has [2FPL] features. However, the picture looks rather different in the following cases.

(67) *tum na:c-ti:/na:c-i: thi:/*thĩ:*
you dance-HAB.F/dance-PFV.F be.PST.F/be.PST.FPL
'You$_{equal}$ (female) used to dance'/'You$_{equal}$ (female) had danced'

(68) *tum nahĩ: na:c-ti:/*na:c-tĩ:*
you Neg dance-HAB.F/dance-HAB.FPL
'You$_{equal}$ (female) don't dance'

Given that we believe that *tum* has [2FPL] features, these examples are puzzling. In (67), we would expect the past auxiliary to display plural agreement; instead, we find singular agreement. And in (68), we have a freestanding participle, and hence, we would expect the PL feature to be realized via nasalization. But nasalization is not possible here. Curiously, plural agreement becomes obligatory if we add a plural NP to *tum* and thereby make it semantically plural.

(69) *tum laṛkiyã: na:c-ti:/na:c-i: thĩ:/*thi:*
you girls dance-HAB.F/dance-PFV.F be.PST.FPL/be.PST.F
'You girls used to dance'/'You girls had danced'

We do not have an explanation for this puzzling state of affairs. There does seem to be the following peculiar generalization:

(70) a. *tum* with singular reference has [PL] features for agreement purposes if those PL features are realized as part of a feature bundle with other features such as [MPL] and [2PL] but not if those [PL] features would be realized by themselves, i.e., by nasalization. In such a case, *tum* lacks [PL] features.
b. *tum* with plural reference has [PL] features across the board.

Perhaps the [PL] feature bundle obligatorily has plural semantics, which would be incompatible with *tum* having singular reference. But this would mean that the semantics of particular feature could vary depending upon how the feature is realized. A further problem with this line of thought is that the features of *tum* would have to be dependent on the elements it is agreeing with; when agreeing with elements where the agreement would result in a [MPL] or [2PL] feature bundle, *tum* must have [PL] features, but when agreement would result in a [PL] feature bundle, *tum* is allowed to not have [PL] features.[7] We leave a solution to the mysterious case of *tum* for future research.

[7]It might be instructive to look at singular *tum* with a feminine addressee together with a verb in the future. The Hindi-Urdu future is morphologically complex consisting of a subjunctive part that agrees in number and person and a participial part that agrees in number and gender. So we might expect that when a future agrees with a feminine singular reference *tum*, the subjunctive part will agree with [2F] and the participial part with either [FPL] or [F] depending upon the feature representation of *tum*.

i. *tum kab a:-o-gi:/*a:-o-gĩ:?*
you when come-SBJV.2PL-Part.F/come-SBJV.2PL-Part.FPL
'When will you come?'

References

Baker, M. 2011. When agreement is for number and gender but not person. *Natural Language & Linguistic Theory* 29: 875–915.

Bhatia, T.K. 1993. *Punjabi: A cognitive-descriptive grammar*. Routledge, London: Descriptive Grammars.

Bhatia, T.K. 1979. Negation in South Asian languages. In *South Asian languages analysis*, vol. 1, ed. B. Kachru, H. H. Hock, and Y. Kachru, 1–12. Department of Linguistics, University of Illinois, Urbana-Champaign.

Bobaljik, J. 2000. The Ins and Outs of Contextual Allomorphy. In *University of Maryland Working Papers in Linguistics 10*, ed. K. Grohmann, and C. Struijke, 35–71. College Park, University of Maryland.

Doctor, R. 2004. *A grammar of Gujarati*. Munich: LINCOM Europa.

Halle, M., and A. Marantz. 1994. Some key features of Distributed Morphology. In *Papers on phonology and morphology, MIT Working Papers in Linguistics*, vol. 21, ed. A. Carnie, H. Harley, and T. Bures, 275–288. Cambridge, MA: MITWPL.

Halle, M., and A. Marantz. 1993. Distributed Morphology and the pieces of inflection. In *The view from Building 20: Essays in linguistics in honor of Sylvain Bromberger*, ed. K. Hale, and S.J. Keyser, 111–176. Cambridge, MA: MIT Press.

Iatridou, S. 2000. The grammatical ingredients of counterfactuality. *Linguistic Inquiry* 31 (2): 231–270.

Tolstaya, N.I. 1981. *The Panjabi language: A descriptive grammar*. Translated by G.L. Campbell. London/Boston: Routledge & Kegan Paul/Henley.

Trumpp, E. 1872. *Grammar of the Sindhi Language compared with the Sankrit-Prakrit and the cognate Indian vernaculars*, Osnabrück: Biblio Verlag. Reprinted in 1970.

Wali, K., and O.N. Koul. 1997. *Kashmiri: A cognitive-descriptive grammar*. Routledge, London: Descriptive Grammars.

We find that only singular agreement is possible here leading to a paradoxical situation where one and the same *tum* needs to be [2PL] for the subjunctive part but singular for the participial part. But in fact, the participial component of the future seems to not realize the plural in the context of the feminine across the board. Consider the following case of a semantically plural *tum*. Even in this case, the participial component does not display nasalization.

ii. *tum laṛkiyā̃: kab a:-o-gi:/*a:-o-gī̃:?*
you girls when come-SBJV.2PL-Part.F/come-SBJV.2PL-Part.FPL
'Whenwill you girls come?'

Hence, there is no paradox with *tum* here. But the fact that the participial part displays number neutralization is puzzling if we assume that the whole future verb is under T. Given the system we have proposed, that would lead to realization of plural in a feminine context. A way to make sense of the facts is that while the subjunctive component of the future is under T, the participial component is outside the scope of T. Consequently, a [PL] feature bundle does not receive any realization.

It is possible to find examples online where there is nasalization on the participial component of the future but such cases sound very degraded to our ear. Moreover, these cases with nasalization on the participial component (e.g., *kar-ẽ-gī̃:* "do-SBJV.2PL-PART.FPL") are outnumbered greatly by the cases without nasalization on the participial component (e.g., *kar-ẽ-gi:* "do-SBJV.2PL-PART.FPL"). We will therefore not analyze cases such as *kar-ẽ-gī̃:*.

Chapter 4
English *One* and *Ones* as Complex Determiners

Richard S. Kayne

Introduction

Perlmutter (1970) took prenominal *one* to be the same element in both of the following:

(1) John has written only one paper this year

(2) Mary has just written one hell of a paper

Despite the fact that the numeral interpretation perceived in (1) seems to be absent in (2). Other examples of a similarly non-numeral pre-N *one* are found in:

(3) There's one John Smithfield here to see you

(4) One day, he'll realize that we were right

In support of Perlmutter's unified approach to these two types of *one* is the fact that all are equally incompatible with plural nouns:

(5) *He's written only one papers this year

(6) *She's just written one hell of papers

(7) *There's one John Smithfields here to see you

(8) *One days, he'll realize that we were right

In this chapter, I will attempt to extend a unified approach to *one* to encompass, in addition, the *one* of:

(9) I have a red car and you have a blue one

R.S. Kayne (✉)
New York University, New York, USA
e-mail: richard.kayne@nyu.edu

G. Sengupta et al. (eds.), *Perspectives on the Architecture and Acquisition of Syntax*, DOI 10.1007/978-981-10-4295-9_4

Despite the fact that this *one* is compatible with a plural:

(10) I have red cars and you have blue ones

That this attempt has initial plausibility comes from a point made by Llombart-Huesca (2002: 60) to the effect that the *one* of (9) and (10) shares with the *one* of (1)–(4) an incompatibility with mass nouns. Parallel to (1)–(4), we do not have the following:

(11) *He lost only one blood in the accident

(12) *You've just had one hell of fun

(13) *There's one Domino Sugar all over the table

(14) *One money, (and) you'll succeed

Nor, parallel to (9) or (10) do we have:

(15) *I like red wine and you like white one

(16) *She's had good luck but he's had bad one

The fact that plural *ones* is possible in (10) will turn out, as I will try to show, not to be incompatible with taking the *one* of (9), as well as the *one* of (10), to be essentially the same as the *one* of (1)–(4).

One Is not a Noun

The *one* of (1)–(4) looks like a determiner of some sort. But the *one* of (9) and (10), especially insofar as it is postadjectival, looks at first glance like a noun, and in that sense looks quite unlike determiner *one*. If the *one* of (9) and (10) were really a noun, though, it would have to be recognized as an extremely odd one, since, unlike ordinary nouns, it cannot be a bare plural[1]:

(17) *I have cars and you have ones, too

---

[1]Cf. Stirling and Huddleston (2002: 1515), Payne et al. (2013: 798, 812).

Payne et al. (2013: 812) suggest that bare **ones* is "preempted by …*some*". This does not seem descriptively correct (quite apart from the absence of a clear notion of preemption). Consider, for example:

(i) Bicycles have wheels and unicycles have wheels/*ones, too.

Here, *ones* is bad, as usual, but *some* is inappropriate:

(ii) ?…and unicycles have some, too

with (ii) rather having the status of:

(iii) ?…and unicycles have some wheels, too.

Similarly, there is to a large extent no completely bare *a one*[2]:

(18) *I have a car and you have a one, too

which would be surprising if *one* were a noun. In addition, as noted by Llombart-Huesca (2002: 61), *one* cannot be immediately preceded by a numeral in sentences like[3]:

(19) *You have three cars but I only have two ones

in which respect *one* is again behaving in an un-noun-like fashion. The conclusion must be, in agreement with Llombart-Huesca (2002: 62),[4] that the *one* of (9) and (10) is not a noun.

One Is a Determiner

If *one* is never a noun, then a unified approach to all instances of *one* will lead to the conclusion that *one* is in all cases a determiner, just as it is in (1)–(4), in which case the phrase *a blue one* in (9) must contain two determiners. Furthermore, in:

(20) We have only one blue one

one blue one must contain two determiners that are identical in form.
This conclusion, to the effect that English allows two (sometimes identical) indefinite determiners in what looks like one DP, is less surprising than it might appear, given the existence in some English (e.g., mine) of[5]:

(21) It'll take us a half a day to finish that job

in which *a half a day*, with two identical determiners, is perfectly natural. Similarly, Wood (2002) had noted, for some English (in this case, not mine)[6]:

(22) a such a wonderful book

[2]In standard English as opposed to the dialects discussed in McDonald and Beal (1987: 48) and Beal et al. (2012: 57). Stirling and Huddleston (2002: 1513n) give *You're a one!* as idiomatic. (It would be of interest if these exceptions had no counterpart with plural *ones*.) The general impossibility of bare **a one* was noted by Perlmutter (1970: 236).

[3]As noted by Perlmutter (1970: 236) and Lakoff (1970: 630). Halliday and Hasan (1976: 97) say that one hears *two ones* especially in children's speech; this needs to be looked into. As does the fact that a Google search yields a number of examples with completely bare *ones*, which may point to the existence of an as yet unstudied variety of English.

[4]Llombart-Huesca's arguments were not taken into account by Payne et al. (2013).

[5]Cf. also the multiple definite articles of Greek, as discussed by Alexiadou and Wilder (1998) among others.

[6]Schibsbye (1970: 285) had noted *a half a dozen eggs*. Probably also belonging here are *a helluva good show* and *a gem of a film*. On other Germanic languages, see, for example, Barbiers (2005) and Wood (2013) and references cited there.

One and *a/an*

Of course, there is a discrepancy between (21) and (22), which contain two instances of the indefinite article *a/an*, and (20), which contains two instances of *one*. But this discrepancy is arguably a relatively minor one, in particular if interpreted against the background of Perlmutter (1970), Barbiers (2005; 2007) both of whom argue in favor of a close relation between prenominal *one* and the indefinite article. Perlmutter (1970: p. 234) more specifically took English to have, as a source for the indefinite article, "a rule which obligatorily converts unstressed proclitic *one* to *an*."[7]

Perlmutter's formulation/rule was not immediately able, as he himself noted, to account for generic-like *a/an*, given the absence of a comparable (stressed) generic prenominal *one* that would be its source[8]:

(23) A spider has eight legs and many eyes

(24) One spider has eight legs and many eyes

The generic-like reading of (23) does not seem to carry over to (24).
The rule that Perlmutter suggested was meant to treat pairs like:

(25) That was a hell of a paper

(26) That was one hell of a paper

As involving, respectively, an unstressed and a (somewhat) stressed variant of the same element *a/one*, with the same interpretation. As just noted, the kind of pairing that holds for (25) and (26) does not hold for (23) and (24). In part similarly, the intended pairing breaks down for:

(27) too long a book,

which has no counterpart with *one*:

(28) *too long one book

A third such problem for Perlmutter's conversion rule lies in:

---

[7]Left open by this emphasis on phonology is the fact that English sometimes allows a stressed indefinite article, as in:

(i) I can't give you the book, but I can give you a book,

in which *a* rhymes with *say*. This stressed *a* does not license NP-ellipsis:

(ii) *…but I can give you a.

suggesting that Borer's (2005: 111n) primarily phonological account of the impossibility of (ii) with unstressed *a* is not general enough.

[8]He suggests generic *a* might perhaps derive from *any one*, but note:

(i) Any/*A spider whatsoever would be able to eat that insect.
(ii) Hardly any/*a spider would eat that insect.
(iii) Not just any/*a spider could have done that.

(29) a few books

(30) *one few books

where, again, the indefinite article has no *one* counterpart to serve as a plausible source.

A fourth problem for the pairing of *a* and *one* can be shown in:

(31) They're selling one-drawer desks in the back of the store

(32) *They're selling a-drawer desks in the back of the store

in which, this time, prenominal *one* is possible, but cannot be replaced by *a/an*. Despite these several discrepancies between *one* and *a/an*, I will, in partial agreement with both Perlmutter and Barbiers, take there to be a significant relation between *a/an* and *one*, to be spelled out in the next section.

One Is a Complex Determiner Containing a Classifier

Let me execute the idea that *a/an* is a reduced form of *one* in a different way from Perlmutter (and Barbiers). Let me start from generic-like (23) and (24) and in particular from (23) versus (24) being reminiscent of a fact from Chinese. According to Cheng and Sybesma (1999: 533–534; 2012: 640), a singular classifier in Chinese cannot occur within a generic DP (whether or not *yi* ("a/an/one") is present).[9]

This leads me to think that *one* cannot occur in (24) with a generic-like reading for the same reason that singular classifiers are excluded from Chinese generic DPs, which in turn leads to the following proposal:

(33) An English DP with *one* contains a singular classifier

(Conversely, an English DP with *a/an* can (perhaps must) lack a classifier.) That *one* is associated with a singular classifier, while *a/an* is not, is close to Perlmutter's idea that *a/an* is a "reduced form" of *one,* though by expressing the notion of "reduction" in terms of the more specific notion of the presence versus absence of a classifier, we can formulate an account of (23) versus (24) that Perlmutter's less specific proposal was unable to do. More precisely put, the phrase *one spider* in (24) must, by (33), contain a singular classifier. But, judging from Chinese, singular classifiers are plausibly incompatible with generic readings. Therefore, (24) cannot be a generic type of sentence in the way that (23) can be.

In Cardinaletti and Starke's (1999) terms, we might want to go further and relate the fact that *one* is associated with extra-syntactic material (the singular classifier) to the fact that *one* is (arguably) morphophonologically "bigger" than *a/an*. We can do this as follows. *One* is to be understood as bimorphemic and in particular as

[9] Cf. Simpson et al. (2011: 188) on Vietnamese; also Simpson and Biswas (2015: 7) on Bangla.

"w- + an" where *w-* (as I will write it) is the classifier and *an* the indefinite article.[10] The difference in vowel quality between *one* and *an* might be due to independent properties of English phonology, perhaps involving (in part) stress. The necessary pronunciation of the *n* of *one* even before a consonant, as opposed to the necessary dropping of the *n* of *an* before a consonant, might again just be phonology. Or it might also be related to syntax, especially if the order "classifier–indefinite article" (*"w- + an*; cf. (Ghosh 2001, Chap. 3), on some Tibeto-Burman having "CLF Num N" order) is produced by leftward movement from a structure in which the indefinite article precedes the classifier.[11]

From this perspective, the additional contrasts (beyond the generic one) mentioned earlier between *one* and *a/an* look as follows. The contrast in:

(34) We have a/*one few days left

can be attributed to a clash between the classifier *w-*, that is, part of *one,* and the silent noun NUMBER (capitalization will indicate silence) that accompanies *few,*[12] in a way that is parallel to:

(35) We have (only) a/*one small number of days left

as well as to:

(36) Mary has written a/*one number of papers this year

In all of (34)–(36), *number*/NUMBER is not allowed to co-occur with the classifier contained in *one.* In the variants of (34)–(36) with *a*, there is no comparable classifier, just the indefinite article, and so no clash. (The clash in question may in turn be related to the classifier-like status of *number*/NUMBER itself in these sentences—cf. Liao 2015).

As for:

(37) too long (of) a/*one book

it looks like the classifier that is part of *one* blocks the preposing of the degree phrase (I return to (37) below).

Finally, the restriction shown in:

(38) They're selling one-drawer/*a-drawer desks in the back of the store

may be linked to:

(39) They're real Brooklyn-lovers

(40) They're real (*the) Bronx-lovers

---

[10]An alternative that I will not pursue might be to take *one* to be monomorphemic and to cooccur with a silent classifier.

[11]Cf. Leu (2015: 116) on German *ein* being moved across.

[12]Cf. Kayne (2002a; 2005a).

via a prohibition against bare articles appearing within compound-like structures, with the classifier contained in *one* protecting it, in a way that remains to be spelled out, from this prohibition.[13]

English *Ones*, Spanish *Unos,* and French *Uns*

If *one* is a complex determiner (containing two subparts, namely a classifier and an indefinite article),[14] then *ones* in examples like:

(41) They have blue ones

must be an even more complex determiner with (at least) three subparts, namely a classifier, an indefinite article, and plural *-s*. An immediate objection might be that *ones* cannot be followed by an overt noun, as shown in:

(42) *They have blue ones cars

unlike more familiar determiners.

This objection to the determiner status of *ones* is weaker than it looks, for two kinds of reasons. The first has to do with the fact that Spanish allows sentences like:

(43) Yo tengo unos libros. ("I have some/a few books")

in which the noun *libros* is preceded by a determiner *unos* that resembles English *ones*.[15] Both *unos* and *ones* contain a plural *-s*. In addition, *uno* (or *un* or *una*) is the Spanish counterpart of English numeral *one* and often of the English indefinite article *a/an*, which we saw earlier to be closely related to *one*. Without saying that *unos* and *ones* are identical in composition (whether *unos* (sometimes) contains a classifier is unclear), the similarity between *unos* and *ones*, combined with the fact that *unos* is followed by an overt noun in (43), shows that the language faculty does not systematically frown on determiners of the *ones* type.

Of course we would also like to understand why *unos* and *ones* differ in certain ways, e.g., in (42) versus (43) with respect to whether they can be followed by an overt N. A possibility that comes to mind is that (42) is excluded in English for the same reason (whatever it is) that an adjective cannot be followed by plural *-s* if it is also followed by an overt N:

---

[13]Why *one* acts differently here from demonstratives remains to be understood. Relevant to the formulation of the prohibition in question is:

(i) two (beautiful) (*the) seventh inning home runs
versus

(ii) ?two (beautiful) top of the seventh inning home runs.

[14]On the complexity of (most) determiners, see Leu (2015).

[15]As noted by Jespersen (1961, Sect. 10.12).

(44) They have other(*s) cars

If so, then we have at the same time an account of the contrast between (41) and (42), which now reduces to the contrast between (44) and (45).

(45) They have other*(s)

If we set aside demonstratives,[16] plural *-s* in English has the property that it cannot be followed by an overt noun (within the relevant DP[17]), as shown in both (42) and (44). In some cases, as in both (41) and (45), deleting the overt N makes plural *-s* possible.

Spanish plural *-s* can, on the other hand, readily be followed by an overt noun, as in:

(46) buenos libros ("good books"),
(47) muchos libros ("many books")

as opposed to English:

(48) good(*s) books,
(49) many/*manies books

so the well-formedness of (43) is not surprising.

A second difference between *unos* and *ones* lies in the fact that *unos* cannot be immediately preceded by an adjective in the way that *ones* can be in (41):

(50) *Yo tengo buenos unos (libros). ("I have good some/a few (books)")

This is not specific to plural *unos*; it also holds for singular *un(o), una*, even in those cases where English allows *a/an* to be preceded by an adjective (and a degree word):

(51) You have too big a house
(52) *Tú tienes demasiado gran(de) una casa

This property of the Spanish indefinite article appears to hold quite generally across Romance languages. Whatever turns out to underlie it, it seems likely that it will not affect the relevance of *unos* to *ones*, i.e., the fact that the existence of *unos* lends plausibility to the determiner status of *ones*.

French *uns* differs from Spanish *unos* in that French *uns* cannot be immediately followed by an overt noun (and in that way resembles English *ones*). French has:

(53) Les uns sont partis, les autres sont restés. ("the ones are left, the others are stayed")

but not:

(54) *Les uns enfants sont partis, les autres (enfants) sont restés

[16]If the final consonant of *these* and *those* is the plural *-s*, then demonstratives fall outside the text statement (cf. Kayne 2010a). Alternatively, Bernstein (2015) has argued that the final consonant in *these* and *those* is a genitive *-s*.

[17]In *students that age*, there is probably a silent preposition intervening between *students* and *that age*.

Adding (nonappositional) *enfants* ("children") to *les uns* in (53) is not possible. *Uns* is also possible in French in:

(55) Quelques-uns sont tombés. ("some ones are fallen")

Again, adding a noun like *livres* ("books") is not possible:

(56) *Quelques-uns livres sont tombés

What French adds to the discussion can be shown in:

(57) Jean a mis quelques livres sur la table. ("J has put some books on the table")

(58) *Jean a mis quelques-uns sur la table

Quelques-uns is possible as a preverbal subject in (55), but not as a postverbal object in (58) and in this respect differs sharply from "*quelques* + overt noun," as shown in (57), suggesting that *uns* is not a noun, just as *ones* is not (and *unos* is not), if the discussion so far is on the right track.

What *uns* is is a (complex) determiner (*un* + *s*), with *un* an indefinite article/numeral and *-s* a plural morpheme. This is indirectly supported by the fact that (55) versus (58) is a contrast found quite generally with indefinite determiners in French (and Italian), for example:

(59) Trois sont tombés. ("three are fallen")
(60) *Jean a mis trois sur la table. ("J has put three on the table")

with both (58) and (60) requiring the addition of clitic *en* ("of them/thereof")[18]:

(61) Jean en a mis quelques-uns sur la table
(62) Jean en a mis trois sur la table

The parallelism between *trois* and *quelques-uns* shown in (55)–(62) supports taking *quelques-uns* to be a (highly) complex determiner, of which determiner *uns* is a subpart. In no way, apart from the very presence of *-s*, does *uns* in French act like a (plural) noun. Indirectly, then, French *uns* increases the likelihood that it is correct to take English *ones* not to be a noun, but rather a determiner.

Defusing the Objection. Part II

The possible objection to the determiner status of *ones* based on the impossibility of (42) repeated here:

(63) *They have blue ones cars

[18]On *en* corresponding most closely to English *thereof*, see Kayne (2004). On the subject–object asymmetry at issue in the text, see Pollock (1998).

in addition to being weakened by the considerations of the previous section concerning Spanish *unos* and French *uns*, is further weakened by the observation that the contrast between (63) and (64):

(64) They have blue ones

is not specific to English *ones*. What I have in mind involves French interrogative *quel* (plural *quels,* for masculine gender), a close counterpart of English *which,* as in:

(65) Which linguists have you invited?
(66) Quels linguistes as-tu invités?

If the lexical noun modified by *which* or *quels* is silent, we have:

(67) Which have you invited?
(68) Lesquels as-tu invités?

English seems straightforward, but in French, in (68), instead of *quels,* we get *lesquels,* which is the definite article *les* followed by *quels.* The link to *ones* rests on the contrast between (68) and:

(69) *Lesquels linguistes as-tu invités?

French interrogative *lesquels* is like *ones* in disallowing an immediately following overt N (within the same DP); that is, (69) is parallel to (63) (and (68) to (64)). To the extent that *(les)quels* is, as seems clear, a complex determiner and not a noun (any more than English *which* is), we have indirect evidence that *ones*, too, is a complex determiner and not a noun.

Derivations

The question arises as to how best to understand this common behavior of *ones* and *lesquels*. Let me begin with (69) versus (68), which seem to differ only in that (69) has a lexical noun *(linguistes*) while (68) has a silent noun. That difference does not by itself account for the difference in acceptability between (69) and (68). Consider, then, the proposal in Kayne (2006) to the effect that a silent noun does not end up in the same position as its pronounced counterpart. In that spirit, let us take *lesquels* in (68) to be, not "les quels NOUN," but rather[19]:

(70) [les NOUN] quels

Assume further that (70) must be derived from:

(71) quels [les NOUN]

[19]This differs in part from Kayne (2008a, Sect. 7).

by leftward movement of "*les* NOUN," so that a fuller variant of (70) (and (68)) is:

(72) [les NOUN] quels <[les NOUN]>

In other words, the definite article *les* can come to precede interrogative *quels* in (68) only via movement (internal merge). Assume more specifically that this movement operation reflects the noun in question needing to reach a position in which it will not be pronounced.[20] If so, then, if the noun is not silent, the movement operation in question will not take place. In which case, *les* will not come to precede interrogative *quels*.[21] That will exclude (69), as desired.[22]

Along the lines just sketched, consider the following approach to (63) versus (64), repeated here:

(73) *They have blue ones cars
(74) They have blue ones

Ones is a complex determiner. The adjective *blue* here modifies *cars* or, in (74), its silent counterpart CARS. In (73), *blue* is not adjacent to *cars*, contrary to expectations. Put another way, (73) shows an "Adj Det N" order, rather than the expected (for English) "Det Adj N" order. This is, I think, part of the reason for (73)'s unacceptability.

The challenge is then to simultaneously understand the contrasting acceptability of (74). In the spirit of Hendrick's (1990) analysis of *too big a car*, and in line with (72), let me take (74) to have a derivation reflected in:

(75) [blue CARS] ones <[blue CARS]>,

in which "[blue CARS]" moves past "ones," starting from the expected "Det Adj N" configuration.[23] As in the case of (72), the movement in question will be linked to the (ultimate) silence of the noun, so that it could not apply to "ones [blue cars]" to yield:

(76) *They have blue cars ones

any more than it could apply to yield (73). As for the impossibility of:

(77) *ones blue cars

---

[20]There might also be a link here to Kayne's (2002b) idea that antecedents need to be reached via movement.

[21]Why *lesquels* acts differently in nonrestrictive relatives remains to be understood. Cf. Grevisse and Goosse (2011: §619).

[22]A remaining question is why French does not then allow:

(i) *Quels les linguistes as-tu invités?

[23]Cf. Greenberg (1966), Cinque (2005) though neither attempted to integrate articles. A separate question is whether their "Dem Num Adj N" reflects external merge alone, or whether internal merge is also involved. See also Shlonsky (2004).

Barbiers (2005: 172) has the idea that DP moves, triggered by focus, to spec of *one* in Northern Brabantish, in a partially similar way.

it may be that in English (vs. Spanish *unos*) there is a problem with the two instances of plural *-s*. As for:

(78) *one (blue) cars

it may "simply" be a question of agreement.[24] In any event, there is now a key similarity between (74) and the equally acceptable:

(79) They have too blue a car

Insofar as both have an adjective preceding a determiner.

Concerning the contrast between (73) and (79), a solution is suggested by Turkish *bir* ("a"/"one"). According to Kornfilt (1997: 106), *bir* can either precede or follow an adjective, i.e., one can have in Turkish either "*bir* Adj N" or "Adj *bir* N"; however, when *bir* precedes the adjective, it corresponds to English numeral *one;* when *bir* follows the adjective, it corresponds to the English indefinite article.

This leads to the following possibility. English *one* (classifier + indefinite article) must end up in a higher position within DP than the position of the indefinite article alone.

The indefinite article can be preceded by an adjective, as in (79), or be followed by one, as in the usual case:

(80) They have a blue car

The position of *one*, though, is sufficiently high that it may not be preceded by an adjective, as shown in (73). There is one exception, of course, namely (74). Thinking of Cinque (2005), the generalization is:

(81) An adjective can come to precede *one* only if moved along with a noun

In English, this noun must be silent, so (74) contrasts with (76).

For Hendrick (1990), *blue* in (79) comes to precede *a* as the result of a wh-like movement operation in which *blue* is pied-piped by *too* (or another degree word). In the absence of an appropriate degree word, the adjective is not allowed to precede *a*:

(82) *They have blue a car

Thinking of (21) and (22) above, though, it might be that an adjective can precede an indefinite article in English even in the absence of a degree word, as long as the indefinite article is silent, in which case (80) would be[25]:

(83) …a blue A car

---

[24]With a possible link to:

(i) A group of three/?two students is waiting in your office.
(ii) *A group of one student is waiting in your office.
and/or to:
(iii) all three of Mary's three children.
(iv) *every single one of Mary's (one) child.

[25]Cf. Tat (2011) for a similar proposal on Turkic languages.

with A the silent article. If so, then (79) might be:

(84) ...A too blue a car

and similarly for the colloquial:

(85) They have too big of a car
which might be:
(86) ...A too big of a car

as suggested by the large number of Google hits for phrases like *a too big of a car* (not possible for me).

A Further Restriction on *Ones*

The derivation of (74) briefly sketched in the preceding section takes the adjective in *blue ones* to originate, as a modifier of *cars*/CARS, below the determiner *ones*. Not all adjectives are compatible with *ones* the way that *blue* is in (74), however. For example, *few* is an adjective, to judge by the series *few, fewer,* and *fewest*. Yet we have (for my English):

(87) Few linguists went to that talk and few (*ones) to this talk

Similarly:

(88) Mary has written few papers this year, but John has written even fewer *ones)
(89) This year, of all the graduate students, it's John who's written the fewest papers/*ones

Since *few, fewer,* and *fewest* happily occur with all sorts of (plural) nouns, this is another indication that *ones* is not a noun, but rather a (complex) determiner.

In all likelihood, thinking of Kayne's (2002a; 2005a) proposal to the effect that *few* is necessarily a modifier of *number*/NUMBER, the facts of (87)–(89) reduce to those of[26]:

(90) Only a small number of linguists went to that talk and only a small number (*of ones) to this talk
(91) Mary has written only a small number of papers this year, but John has written an even smaller number (*of ones)
(92) This year, of all the graduate students, it's John who's written the smallest number of papers/*ones

[26]*Many* acts like *few* here, as opposed to *numerous*: (i) We've bought?numerous/*many ones. The reason is that *numerous* is not a modifier of NUMBER in the way that *few* and *many* are. For more details, see Kayne (2002a).

In (90)–(92), *number of* cannot be followed by unmodified *ones*. In (87)–(89), the same holds for NUMBER OF, as in:

(93) *...and few NUMBER OF ones to this talk

with silent NUMBER and probably silent OF.

The restrictions shown in (87)–(92) fall sharply away if an adjective or adjectival phrase is added, for example:

(94) John has written many papers, but few good ones

(95) Only a small number of good ones were written this year

This fact about *few* (and *fewer* and *fewest*, and also *a few*) is almost certainly the same fact that we see with numerals[27]:

(96) John has written three *(good) ones this year

The Licensing Role of Adjectives

The way in which the adjective in (94)–(96) "saves" those sentences is arguably not specific to English *ones*. French has:

(97) Vous avez acheté de *(bons) vins. ("you have bought of (good) wines")

French allows a plural DP to have the form "*de* Adj N,"[28] but does not (apart from polarity contexts) allow DPs of the form "*de* N." If we think of this fact as indicating that in (97) the adjective is licensing the preposition *de*,[29] there is a clear point of similarity to the licensing of *ones* in (94)–(96).

Of importance is the fact that in French a postnominal adjective or relative does not suffice for such licensing:

(98) *Vous avez acheté de vins excellents. ("you have bought of wines excellent")

(99) *Vous avez acheté de vins qui sont bons. ("...of wines which are good")

The link with *ones* is strengthened by the fact that (94)–(96) become to my ear unacceptable if the pre-*ones* adjective is replaced by a (reduced) relative:

(100) *John has written many papers, but few ones that are any good

---

[27]Payne et al. (2013: 814) give, without appreciating the nonunicity of English, two examples of definite *the five ones*... which are for me only marginally acceptable, probably in a way related to the discussion in Section "The" below.

[28]Cf. Pollock (1998, note 24).

[29]In French, this *de* can also be licensed by a following determiner, as in:

(i) Vous avez acheté des (bons) vins. ("you have bought of-the (good) wines") in which case an adjective is no longer necessary.

(101) *John has written many papers, but few ones worth reading
(102) *?Only a small number of ones that are good have been written this year
(103) *?Only a small number of ones as good as ours have been written this year
(104) *John has written three ones that you'll like this year
(105) *John has written only three ones worth reading this year

A licensing property comparable to that shown in (97), again involving prenominal (but not postnominal) adjectives or reduced relatives has been discussed by Leu (2015: 16) for colloquial Slovenian, based on work by Marušič and Žaucer (2006). Colloquial Slovenian has an unstressed nondemonstrative definite article that requires such adjectival licensing, as shown in:

(106) ta *(nov) pes ("the new dog")

Leu (2015: 13) also discusses similar facts found in some Scandinavian languages (and in Swiss German).

Although these Slovenian and Scandinavian facts are not identical to the French ones, they share a common property. In each case, what is licensed by the adjective is arguably some kind of determiner. In Slovenian and in the relevant Scandinavian languages, it is a definite article; in French, it is a preposition that may be part of an indefinite determiner.[30] In none of these cases is it a noun that is being licensed. Consequently, the resemblance to the licensing of English *ones* by a pre-*ones* adjective shown in (87)–(105) indirectly reinforces the determiner status of *ones*.[31]

It is not easy to see what exactly distinguishes those determiners that require licensing by an adjective and those that do not.[32] In English, numerals and *few* need no adjective, even when the associated noun is silent:

(107) Mary has written four papers this year, but John has written only three
(108) Many papers are started, few are finished

Similarly for *some*, with a deleted/silent plural noun:

(109) Some will be finished

and for plural demonstratives:

(110) These will be finished

---

[30]For recent discussion of this kind of French *de*, see Ihsane (2008).

[31]An example of licensing by a pre-*ones* reduced relative in English is: (i) There are a few old letters on the chair and a few recently arrived ones on the table.

On adjectives and reduced relatives more generally, see Cinque (2010). The text cases are to be distinguished from cases in which the licensing modifier need not be prenominal; see Longobardi (1994, note 12) on determinerless nouns in preverbal subject position.

[32]The indefinite article requires licensing by an adjective in:
(i) You must have spent a *(good, beautiful) three weeks in Italy.
(ii) You should invite a*(n other) four people.

Singular demonstratives are partly different:

(111) This will be finished

While (111) is acceptable, the silent noun it contains would seem to be THING and cannot be dependent on an antecedent in the way that the silent noun of (110) can be.

Of interest here is one other determiner in English that looks as if it requires, in a certain kind of context, adjectival licensing of the sort under discussion. Consider:

(112) People are often in need of help
(113) Very poor people always need help

The noun *people* in (113) can be deleted/silent, but in that case a definite article is required:

(114) The very poor always need help
(115) *Very poor always need help

Having silent PEOPLE together with a definite article is not possible in (112), however:

(116) *The are often in need of help

In effect, the *the* of (114) needs licensing by an adjective (phrase). As in (98)–(105), a relative clause is not sufficient:

(117) *The who have little money are often in need of help

Nor is a reduced relative of the sort that is otherwise postnominal:

(118) *The lacking money are often in need of help

The adjectival licensing requirement of this *the*, then, is similar to that of *ones*. In both cases, a certain determiner requires an adjective in the context of a silent noun. This parallelism further reinforces the determiner status of *ones*.

Of all the adjective-requiring determiners discussed, though, *ones* is the only case in which the licensing adjective precedes the determiner in question. Thinking of the discussion around (75) above, in which it was proposed that the adjective preceding *ones* originates below *ones*, it may be that the licensing of *ones* by the adjective takes place prior to that movement,[33] in which case all the determiners in question will turn out to be licensed by a following adjective.

This statement will also cover (for my English)[34]:

(119) We bought a blue one yesterday

[33]And similarly for: (i) too long (of) a book

In the cases he discusses, Leu (2015: 92) has the determiner and adjective forming a constituent. Extended to *ones*, this would mean that (at the point of licensing) *ones* + adjective is a constituent.

[34]Cf. note 2.

(120) *We bought a one yesterday, too

Since the indefinite article does not normally require an adjective, it seems likely that the contrast between (119) and (120) rests on singular *one* also needing an adjectival licenser here. As in the other determiner cases discussed, a relative clause is not sufficient, in my English:

(121) *We bought a one yesterday that was really beautiful

Nor is a reduced relative of the postnominal sort[35]:

(122) *We bought a one worth reading

In some English (not exactly mine), though, it is possible to have:

(123) We bought not a one

In this English, either *not* itself must be the licenser, or else there must be a silent SINGLE making (123) quasi-equivalent to[36]:

(124) We bought not a single one

which is fully acceptable to me. (Again, the fact that *one* in (119)–(122) requires an adjective reinforces the determiner status of *one*.)

Nonrestrictive Adjectives

Some notion of contrast or focus seems to be relevant to the licensing role that adjectives play with *one* (cf. Halliday and Hasan (1976: 95, 97) and Llombart-Huesca (2002: 73):

(125) People who read interesting books generally profit considerably from the reading of those interesting books/*ones
(126) People who read an interesting book generally profit considerably from the reading of that interesting book/*one

---

[35]As opposed to:

(i) We bought a recently published one

with a reduced relative that is prenominal.

[36]For another case of a silent adjective with no antecedent, see Kayne (2005a, Sect. 7) on GOOD. Possibly the English that accepts *not a one* has it as:

(i) ...not SINGLE a one

with SINGLE preceding, rather than following, the indefinite article, with this position for SINGLE licensed by the presence of *not* (via movement of the phrase "not SINGLE" from postnominal position directly to pre-*a* position)—cf. Troseth (2009) on *not very good of a book*.

It may be that a nonrestrictive adjective cannot be itself license *one(s)*, much as Llombart-Huesca suggests that noun ellipsis is not possible with a nonrestrictive adjective in Spanish. If so, a possible account might rest on the discussion around (75) above, in which it was proposed that the adjective preceding *ones* originates below *ones*, in which case it might be that nonrestrictive adjectives cannot originate below *one(s)*, from which it would follow that they cannot license *one(s)*.

Numeral *One*

Numeral *one* needs no adjective, even in the presence of a silent noun:

(127) John has written three papers. Two are on phonology and one is on syntax
(128) There are three books on the table. Only one is worth reading

In this respect, numeral *one* behaves like other numerals, as illustrated in (107) above. This may at first seem unsurprising, but Barbiers (2007) has shown that *one* is quite different from other numerals in some ways, in particular in not lending itself (in a great many languages) to regular ordinal formation:

(129) The first/*oneth chapter is the most interesting

Barbiers's point about the special behavior of *one* can be further strengthened by noting that in many Romance languages *one* is the only numeral that shows agreement in gender. In addition, we can note that in French complex numerals that are multiples of 100 (or 1000), *one* is the only numeral that cannot appear, as shown, for example, in:

(130) deux cents ("two hundred"), trois cents ("three hundred")...
(131) cent
(132) *un cent ("one hundred")[37]

French also displays an asymmetry between *one* and other numerals in that in the additive compound numerals 21, 31, 41, 51, 61, 71, an overt coordinating element *et* ("and") is necessary, for example:

(133) vingt-et-un livres ("twenty-and-one books")

whereas with 22, 23, ... 32, 33... no coordinating element appears, for example[38]:

(134) vingt-deux livres ("twenty-two books")

---

[37]With 1000, French has:

(i) (*un) mille linguistes ("a thousand linguists")

Possible, with a complex numeral containing *one* as a subpart, is:

(ii) trente-et-un mille linguistes ("thirty and one thousand linguists").

[38]Though there may be a silent one present, to judge by the obligatory pronunciation of the final consonant of *vingt* in 22, 23...

If numeral *one* is unlike other numerals in various ways, then the fact that in (127)–(128) numeral *one* acts, with respect to the need or non-need for adjectival licensing, like other numerals and not like the *one* of (120), or like *ones*, needs to be accounted for. The proposal that comes to mind is that the exceptionality of numeral *one* relative to adjectival licensing is only apparent and that numeral *one* is in fact necessarily accompanied by an adjective. More specifically, thinking of the discussion of (123), let me take sentences with numeral *one* such as:

(135) John has two brothers and one sister

to have the analysis:

(136) …and one SINGLE sister

with a silent adjective corresponding to *single*.[39] In some cases, *one* is natural with a following overt *single*:

(137) You haven't written one single paper this year

It should be noted that the title of this section is somewhat misleading. If this chapter is on the right track, *one* is consistently to be understood as "classifier + indefinite article." There is no single morpheme that would correspond exactly to "numeral 1." More than that, *one* itself is the same ("classifier + indefinite article" combination) in all its instances. Some instances of *one* are numeral-like in that they contrast readily with other numerals, as in (135). Other instances of *one* are not, e.g., in *two blue ones*.

Thus, the term "numeral *one*" must be taken to pick out those instances of *one* that occur in a syntactic context whose overall interpretation lends itself to contrast with other numerals. If (136) is correct, then that context will include an adjective like *single*/SINGLE. In some cases, overt *only* is very natural:

(138) John has two brothers but only one sister

Silent ONLY might be present in other cases. If *only* is adjectival, it itself might be able to serve as licenser for *one*, perhaps in some cases instead of SINGLE. Whatever the correct details, it seems extremely likely that the language faculty treats "numeral 1" as complex, not simplex (i.e., not as a primitive).

Ordinals

The idea that numeral *one* is to be understood as in (136) is in partial agreement with Barbiers's (2005; 2007) claim that *one* is very different from *two* and numerals higher than *two*. He took numeral *one* to be a stressed, focussed version of the

---

[39]There is a point of similarity here with Borer's (2005: 196) proposal that Hebrew '*exád* ("one") is an adjective interpreted as "single".

indefinite article.[40] The present proposal does not rely directly on the notion of "focus," using instead the presence of SINGLE.

As mentioned in the previous section, Barbiers emphasized the relative systematicity of the crosslinguistic absence of a regularly formed ordinal based on *one*:

(139) Mary was the first/*oneth linguist to have proposed that

From the present perspective, this must reflect the inability of ordinal *-th* to combine either with the complex determiner *one* or with SINGLE or *single*:

(140) *the (a/one) single-th linguist

Presumably, the numerals from *two* on up (apart from complex numerals having 1 as a subpart) do not (necessarily) involve SINGLE. (Why ordinal *-th* differs from the *-ce* of *once*, which can combine with *one*,[41] needs to be elucidated.)

One(s) and Demonstratives

There is a clear contrast (in my English—cf. note 2) between (120), repeated here:

(141) *We bought a one yesterday, too

and:

(142) We bought that one yesterday, too

This may indicate that demonstrative *that* (or *this*) is capable by itself of licensing *one* independently of the presence of a canonical adjective, perhaps because demonstratives have something significant in common with adjectives.[42] Things are more complex, however, since in some English (e.g., mine), there is a contrast between the singular case of (142) and its plural counterpart:

(143) *We bought those ones yesterday, too

For those speakers who accept (143), there seems to be no extra complexity. But for speakers like me, who reject (143), the question is why the plural case should be different from the singular. (Again, we can note that taking *ones* to be a noun would incorrectly lead to the expectation that (143) should be acceptable to all.) Not surprisingly, by now, adding an adjective to (143) makes it acceptable to all (as far as I know):

(144) We bought those blue ones yesterday

---

[40] As mentioned in an earlier footnote, this view of *one* faces a challenge dealing with stressed *a*, as in:

(i) We don't need some chocolates, we need a chocolate

with *a* pronounced to rhyme with *say*.

[41] On *once*, see Kayne (2014).

[42] Cf. Leu (2007; 2015, Chap. 2).

Llombart-Huesca (2002: 77), by taking the appearance of *one(s)* to be a last-resort strategy (her *one*-support) that comes into play only when NP-ellipsis is not available, could perhaps relate my rejection of (143) to my accepting:

(145) We bought those yesterday, too

The problem, however, is that even if the language faculty sometimes has recourse to last-resort strategies (which isn't clear), that sort of approach to (143) would have difficulty accounting for the fact that many speakers accept both (143) and (145). (I don't know with certainty if there are speakers who accept (143) and reject (145).)

Complementarity between *one(s)* and NP-ellipsis fails to hold in various other cases, too.[43] In the context of a shirt store, I accept both of the following:

(146) The blues/blue ones are selling well this week

In the context of a daycare center for children, I accept both of these:

(147) The three-year olds/three-year old ones are easier to manage than the others

And without any special context, both of the following:

(148) The others/other ones are even less expensive

and similarly for:

(149) There are others/other ones on the table

as well as (with no *-s* in the NP-ellipsis variant):

(150) John gave several talks. Only the first (one) was understandable

(151) Each (one) was good in a different way

(152) The tallest (one) of the three is really very tall

(153) The taller (one) of the two is really very tall

Failure of complementarity also holds with *that* (and *this*), though with a difference in interpretation:

(154) Give me that

(155) Give me that one

These two singular demonstrative examples are both possible, but not quite on a par. This can be shown clearly in examples where the antecedent is human:

(156) That linguist prefers phonology, while this *(one) prefers syntax

With *that one* or *this one*, the antecedent can readily be a human noun like *linguist*, or not. With *that* or *this* alone, the understood antecedent cannot be human. In fact, it arguably cannot be any ordinary noun, a relevant example being:

[43]As noted by Halliday and Hasan (1976: 97).

(157) That decision was made by committee, while this *(one) was made by John alone

With *this one*, (157) is extremely close in interpretation to:

(158) That decision was made by committee, while this decision was made by John alone

With *this* alone, (157) is possible, but not with the same interpretation.[44] A way to understand this difference is to take (154) to be as in:

(159) ...that THING

and (155) to be as in:

(160) ...that one NOUN

in which the silent NOUN necessarily has an antecedent (and similarly for (156)).

THING in (154)/(159), on the other hand, does not need or take an antecedent in anything like the same sense. Rather the interpretation is close to the also possible:

(161) Give me that thing

The ability of THING to appear in this way in (154)/(159) is probably related to its special behavior in[45]:

(162) something else

(163) *some book else

If so, the absence of a true plural for (154), which is very clear is some cases:

(164) I've been wondering that/*those myself

(165) How can you possibly think that/*those?

will link to:

(166) *somethings else

supporting the presence of THING in (154).

As Edwin Williams (p.c.) has pointed out to me, *thing* is also special in that it cannot readily be the antecedent of *one(s)* (more precisely, from the perspective of (160), of the silent NOUN that accompanies *one(s)*). Examples of this are[46]:

---

[44]As noted by Halliday and Hasan (1976, 96).

[45]Cf. Leu (2005).

[46]The first example has a DP apparently case-licensed by *wonder*, in contrast to Pesetsky (1991: 6) Note the contrast with adjectives, for example:

(i) *We're sure it's time to leave and they're sure the same thing.

It may be that the property of *thing* at issue is (to some extent) limited to abstract, as opposed to object, *thing*, a distinction that some languages make explicit; cf. Zepeda (1983: 53, 55) on double counterparts of *nothing* and *what*.

(167) They've been wondering if it's time to leave and we've been wondering the same thing. In fact, you've been wondering the same thing/*one, too, haven't you?

(168) How come you did such a smart thing last night, but such a stupid thing/?? one this morning?

(169) John said something and Bill said something/*someone else

In the variants of (167)–(169) with *one*, there must be "...one NOUN," much as in (160). The question is why this silent NOUN cannot readily take *thing* in (167)–(169) as antecedent. The answer might perhaps be that *thing* is in these examples classifier-like[47] and that having a classifier-like NOUN associated with *one* would clash with the fact that *one* itself contains a classifier, as suggested earlier.

Singular Versus Plural

Let us return now to (143), i.e., to the fact that English speakers differ from one another on *(*) those ones*. We have seen earlier that *ones* is readily licensed by an immediately preceding adjective, as in[48]:

(170) They bought three *(blue) ones yesterday

Whereas if *ones* is immediately preceded by a determiner (broadly construed), we generally have unacceptability, as in[49]:

(171) *They bought few/a small number of/three/several/some ones yesterday

For speakers like me who reject **those ones*, demonstrative *those* (as well as *these*) is acting like the other determiners of (171). Speakers who accept *those ones* and *these ones* may be taking *those/these* to be adjectival; alternatively they are taking the silent THERE/HERE that accompanies *those/these* to be adjectival.[50]

The contrast, for one set of speakers, between singular *this one, that one* and plural **these ones, *those ones* leads to the question whether the adjectival licensing relevant to plural *ones* is at all relevant to (certain instances of) singular *one*. In fact, (171) has a parallel with some singular determiners:

---

[47]Though "thing" seems to be compatible with various classifiers in Cantonese, see Matthews and Yip (1994: 106).

[48]On "immediately," note:
(i) They spent a beautiful three weeks/*ones in France last year.

[49]Conceivably there is a point of contact here with:
(i) Someone(*s) else called.

[50]Cf. especially Leu (2015: 32) on Norwegian.

(172) John was attending some class (or other) yesterday and Mary was attending some class/*some one (or other) yesterday, too

(173) Mary made one mistake and John made one mistake/*one one, too

As with plural *ones*, adding an adjective changes the acceptability status:

(174) Mary made one bad mistake and John made one bad one, too

With singular *some,* there is clearly improvement, even if the result is not entirely natural:

(175) (?) John was attending some weird class yesterday and Mary was attending some weird one (yesterday), too

In addition, I find that *every* is to some degree like singular *some*, in some cases:

(176) As for spiders, every?(single) one has eight legs

whereas with *each* we have:

(177) Each spider/one will be found to have eight legs

Why singular *one* is compatible with a preceding determiner to a greater extent than plural *ones* is left an open question.

Possessors

That "adjectival," as far as the licensing of *ones* is concerned, might go beyond ordinary adjectives to include THERE/HERE, as suggested in the discussion of (171), is indirectly supported by some curious facts concerning possessors, which in my English are not by themselves licensers of *ones*:

(178) *Mary's papers are usually stronger than John's ones

Yet I find the following more acceptable:

(179) ?Men's shoes are usually less expensive than women's ones

As if *women's* here could count as adjectival in a way that *John's* could not.[51]

The nonlicensing property of possessors shown in (178) carries over for me to singular *one*:

---

[51]Another kind of example with something adjectival, but not strictly speaking an adjective is:

(i) John makes lots of remarks, including lots of over-the-top ones.

Note also:

(ii) *I've read neither John's papers nor Mary's ones

versus

(iii) ?I've read neither yesterday's newspapers nor today's ones

(180) *Mary's paper is stronger than John's one

As expected by now, adding an adjective makes them acceptable:

(181) We appreciate John's recent one(s)

both with *ones* and with *one*, reflecting the fact that the licensing conditions for *ones* and *one* are to a degree similar.

Human *One*

There is a clear contrast in my English between (172) and:

(182) Let's invite someone

Here, *one* can be immediately preceded by *some* (and similarly for *every, any* and *no*), in direct contrast with (172). One might "just" say that this *one* is different, which it of course is. But a primary claim of this chapter is that all instances of *one* are in fact the same in their internal makeup (the more specific claim is that all are classifier + indefinite article) and that it is the syntactic contexts in which *one* occurs that differ.

Since *someone, everyone, noone,* and *anyone* are basically restricted to humans, it is natural to link the *one* in them to the *one* of:

(183) When one is hungry, food becomes essential

which is also restricted to humans. This link is strengthened by the fact that neither (182) and (183) allows *ones* to replace *one*[52]:

(184) *Let's invite someones

(185) *When ones are hungry, food becomes essential

A sentence like (183) is in turn close to:

(186) When a person is hungry, food becomes essential

Thinking of the proposal in Kayne (2005a, appendix) to the effect that *John* is "John PERSON," as well as of the discussion of (114) above, it becomes natural to think of (182) and (183) as containing[53]:

(187) some one PERSON; one PERSON

with *one* a determiner, as it now always is.

[52]There may or may not be a link to:

(i) The plates were piled one on top of the other.

(ii) *The plates were piled ones on top of the other(s).

[53]The extent to which this kind of analysis should be extended to French *on*, or to Italian *si*, or to German *man* is left open here; for relevant discussion, see Cinque (1988), Malamud (2013).

A discrepancy between (182) and (183) concerns *else*:

(188) Let's invite someone else

(189) *When one else is hungry, …

This contrast between (188) and (189) suggests that *else* in (188) depends on the presence of the determiner *some*.[54] Thinking of the similarity between *someone else* and *some other person*:

(190) Let's invite some other person

and more generally between *else* and *other*, it may be that *one* in (188) is licensed by quasi-adjectival *else*, rather than by *some*. (As for (182), or even (183), it might be that PERSON itself plays a licensing role for *one*, rather than *some* doing so (in (182)); alternatively a silent adjective might be present.)

The impossibility of (184) of course recalls:

(191) Let's invite somebody/*somebodies

which may reflect a common prohibition against plural. If so, and if the *one* of *someone* has, as I have been suggesting in this section, the same complex determiner status as other instances of *one*, we seem to be faced with a curious choice. Either *body* here must be analyzed parallel to *one*, i.e., as a complex determiner, or else *somebody* and *someone* are not as perfectly parallel to each other as they at first look.

The latter possibility appears to be supported by the following difference, brought to my attention by Edwin Williams (p.c.):

(192) He's a real somebody/??someone

(193) He's a real nobody/??noone

With plurals, the distinction is for me even sharper:

(194) They're real somebodies/*someones

(195) They're real nobodies/*noones

With *somebody, nobody,* there is a natural interpretation as "a really important/unimportant person" that is less readily available with *someone, noone*, and similarly (but more strongly) in the plural. What this suggests is that rather than matching the *one* of *someone*, the *body* of *somebody* better matches PERSON itself, i.e., it may be that while *someone* is[55]:

---

[54]An arguably similar sensitivity to the presence of a determiner is shown in (nonstandard):

(i) Let's go somewheres (else).
(ii) *Wheres (else) should we go?

For relevant discussion, see Kayne (2007a, Sect. 3).

[55]Cf. the nonequivalence of *somewhere* and *someplace* discussed in Kayne (2007a) Also:

(i) He's living in the middle of nowhere/*noplace.

(196) some one PERSON

somebody is:

(197) some (ONE) body

with *body* receiving a (partially) idiomatic interpretation akin to that of *person*.
The unacceptability of **someones*, **noones* in (194), (195) recalls that of:

(198) *John ate some apples and Bill ate some ones, too

(199) *John has no friends and Bill has no ones, either,

thereby indirectly supporting the common determiner status of the *one* of *someone, noone,* and the *one* of *some red one, no good one*.[56]

The

The generalization that other determiners are not licensers for plural *ones* has one sharp exception that holds for all speakers (as far as I know)[57]:

(200) Bring us the ones that you consider worth reading

This kind of sentence is perfectly acceptable without any overt prenominal adjective, contrary to various cases discussed earlier, for example:

(201) *Bring us three ones that you consider worth reading

On the other hand, with neither an adjective nor a relative clause, (200) becomes unacceptable[58]:

(202) *Bring us the ones

Why a relative clause seems to be able to act as a licenser for *ones* in (200) but not in (201) is not clear. Relevant is the status of:

(203) ?Bring us ones that you consider worth reading

with no determiner preceding *ones*. In my English, (203) is deviant to some degree, as shown also (for me) in:

---

[56]This way of looking at things makes sense of *nobodies* vs. **noones*, while leaving open the contrast between *They're nobodies* and

(i) *They have nobodies else.

[57]Note that the "head" of the relative here contains not just *ones* but also at least one silent NOUN.

[58]As opposed to some special cases like:

(i) John and Mary have both signed up, but so far they're the only ones.

These may involve a deleted relative—cf. Stirling and Huddleston (2002: 1513n), and for a sustained proposal, (Collins 2014).

(204) Don't bring us heavy ones

(205) ?Don't bring us ones that are heavy

Yet (203) and (205) are acceptable to many, with such speakers presumably allowing the relative to act as licenser, given:

(206) *Bring us ones

For my English, the contrast between (200) and (203) suggests that *the* is playing a key role, too.[59] That the definite article can contribute to the well-formedness of DPs with *ones* is indirectly supported by the comparable role played by demonstrate *those/these* in:

(207) We'd like to buy *(??those) three ones, please

While **three ones* by itself is bad, adding a demonstrative improves things to some extent,[60] perhaps especially for those who accept *those ones/these ones*.

Just Singular *One*

A remaining question is why the following is possible without any adjective or modifier of any sort:

(208) We bought one, too

In agreement with Payne et al. (2013, 798), I take this instance of *one* to be closer to the *one* of:

(209) We bought one book

than to the *one* of:

(210) We bought an expensive one

In essence, the question is when exactly singular *one* needs an adjective. As an initial approximation, we may have:

(211) Only when preceded (within the relevant DP) by another determiner does singular *one* need to be preceded by an adjective

---

[59]Possibly via a silent prenominal THERE that might be relevant to the contrast between English and Dutch concerning "the…one…" noted by Barbiers (2005: 163). Jespersen (1961, Sect. 10.12) notes that some Jutland dialects allow a counterpart of definite *that abominable one*, as opposed to standard Danish.

[60]As opposed to adding *some* in:

(i) Mary has published some twenty papers/*ones in the last five years.

The *-s* of *Ones*

Saying that *ones* is plural normally goes with the (usually implicit) assumption that *one* and plural *-s* form a constituent. But that assumption is not straightforward.[61] Nor is it in the case of *others*, as in:

(212) Give me the others

which I take to have an analysis as in:

(213) ...the other NOUN s

where *-s* is associated with the silent noun rather than directly with *other*.[62] An imaginable alternative would have *other* itself sometimes being a noun in addition to usually being an adjective. There are, however, reasons for thinking that at least this kind of category multiplication/neutrality is not made available by the language faculty.

If, in addition to being an adjective, *other* could also sometimes be a noun, one would wrongly expect the following to be straightforwardly possible:

(214) ?Give me that other

(215) *You've eaten every (single) other

Furthermore, there is a striking fact having to do with the interaction between *other* and other adjectives. One has:

(216) The other American invasions took place years ago

(217) The other American ones took place years ago

If *other* could also be a noun, one would wrongly also expect to have[63]:

---

[61]Cf Koopman and Szabolcsi (2000), Julien (2002).

[62]Cf Kayne (2003).

[63]The impossibility of this kind of example was noted by Stirling and Huddleston (2002: 1524), who did not, however, draw the conclusion that *other* is always an adjective. Their reason was that *the others* is possible, combined with the belief that adjectives never take plural *-s* in English.

British and American English seem to differ in that only British English has, with a simple numeral:

(i) Mary has three millions in the bank,

in which the *-s* is likely associated with silent POUND. In (my) American English, this *-s* does not appear:

(ii) Mary has three million in the bank.

though DOLLAR(S) is presumably present. Her and Tsai (2015: 592) note the existence of doublets like:

(iii) There are three grand pianos/grands in the storeroom,

which they interpret as showing that *grand* in (iii) is a noun. Alternatively, it is an adjective occurring with either *piano* or PIANO. The monetary *grands* (possible for some speakers) that they discuss in their Sect. One is not a noun is compatible with monetary *grand* being an adjective,

(218) *The American others took place years ago

Whereas if *other* is consistently an adjective, (218) reduces to:

(219) *The American other invasions took place years ago

The appearance of plural *-s* following a silent noun is allowed in a variety of adjectival cases, not just with *others*:

(220) They have two four-year olds

(221) If I had a choice among those crayons, I'd take all the reds

(222) In that linguistics department, the first-years are under a lot of pressure

In other cases, this is not possible, for reasons yet to be determined:

(223) *Speaking of invasions, the Americans took place years ago

(224) Those three books are more interesting than these four(*s)

It seems almost certain that the *-s* of *ones* has the same property as the *-s* of *others* (and the *-s* of *four-year olds, reds* and *first-years*), namely this *-s* is associated with a silent noun, rather than simply with *one* itself. For example, the following[64]:

(225) I prefer red cars, but you prefer blue ones

is to be analyzed, parallel to (213), as containing as a subpart[65]:

(226) … blue one CAR-s

in the same way. The question whether the specific analysis of monetary *grand* proposed in Kayne (2012) is on the right track is beyond the scope of this chapter.

[64]With the indefinite article in place of *one*, we get the impossible:

(i) *…but you prefer blue a's

Presumably, this is the same fact as:

(ii) *John has a car and you have a, too.

in turn akin to:

(iii) John likes the *(car), too.

[65]*One* here is associated with plural "CAR s," contrary to:

(i) We have one car(*s).

Thinking of Heim (1987), van Riemsdijk (2005), and Leu (2008), this might suggest:

(ii) … blue one KIND CAR -s.

in which *one* goes with silent KIND (or some other additional NOUN) and *-s* with silent CAR. Pursuing this possibility would be beyond the scope of this chapter.

Restrictions on What Follows *One(s)*

Baker (1978: 415) considered sentences like the following[66]:

(227) *In this university, the students of physics are generally stronger than the ones of chemistry

For Baker, this kind of example merits a full *. To my ear, this sentence is deviant, but not dramatically so. Baker took this kind of restriction to constitute an argument in favor of an innate component to the language faculty. Payne et al. (2014) try to show that Baker's argument does not go through, by observing, via a corpus study, various (relatively) acceptable examples of the same general sort as (227). I myself would tend to accept:

(228) ?The assassination of the prime minister had taken place two years before the one of the president

Baker had taken (227) to indicate that *one(s)* could not be followed by what would correspond to a complement of the antecedent, i.e., that *one(s)* could not replace N, as opposed to N-bar. For those speakers who fully accept examples like (228), this cannot be right as a general characterization of *one(s)*.

From the perspective of this chapter, *one(s)* does not "replace" a lexical noun at all; rather, in, say, (228), *one* is followed by a silent counterpart of *assassination*. Moreover, since I have argued elsewhere that nouns do not take complements,[67] restrictions like the one shown in (227), for those who reject it,[68] must be formulated otherwise.

Baker's argument for an innate component to the language faculty is strengthened by the finding of more sharply unacceptable examples than (227) itself, such as in the following:

(229) A large number of syntacticians were talking with a large number/*one of phonologists

(230) Mary has a whole lot of money; John has a whole lot/*one of money, too

(231) The kinds of horses we need are easier to find than the kinds/*ones of cows we need

(232) Mary likes those kind of horses and John likes those kind/*one of horses, too

---

[66]Cf. Stirling and Huddleston (2002: 1515) for judgments like Baker's.

[67]Cf. Kayne (2008b).

[68]Payne et al. (2014) gave me the impression, perhaps wrongly, that they believe that there is one "English." For a sharply opposing view, see Kayne (1996; 2013). On the richness of syntactic variation within what we call English, see Algeo (2006), Kortmann et al. (2005), Zanuttini and Horn (2014), and many other such works.

(233) What do you think of those absurd goings-on and of these even more absurd goings-on/*ones-on?

(234) A quiet taking out of the trash will be less onerous than a loud taking/*one out of the garbage

In these cases of sharp unacceptability (as in many others discussed in this chapter), a lot must depend on built-in principles, as Baker (1978) had it, apart from the details of his proposal.

From the present perspective, what is more specifically at issue in (229)–(234) must have to do with the silent NOUN following *one(s)*. If Kayne (2006) is on the right track, that translates into the question of what the silent noun can leave behind when it moves. Which in turn probably becomes the question of what can (non-contrastively) scramble out before such (remnant) movement takes place. For example, in the unacceptable variant of (234), with **...a loud one out of the garbage*, we might have:

(235) ...one TAKING out...

and it may well be that a particle like *out* is not amenable to such scrambling.[69]

Similarly, in the unacceptable variant of (229), with **...a large one of phonologists*, we would have:

(236) ...one NUMBER of phonologists

and it may be that *of phonologists* is not amenable to the required noncontrastive scrambling.

Other Determiners That Look Like Pronouns

In taking the position that *one* and *ones* are in all instances complex determiners, I have been taking a position akin to the one taken by Postal (1966) for personal pronouns such as *he* and *she*, which he analyzes as being types of definite articles. (Postal took *ones* itself to be a [+*Pro*] noun.) Assuming Postal's determiner analysis to be correct for at least third-person pronouns, the position I have arrived at here claims that both third-person pronouns (*he, she, it, they*) and *one(s)* are determiners, the difference being that third-person pronouns are (as in Postal 1966) definite determiners (associated with a silent or deleted noun), whereas *one* and *ones* are for me indefinite determiners (associated with a silent or deleted noun).

The (complex) determiner status that third-person pronouns and *one(s)* have in common may be reflected in what looks like a shared restriction concerning

[69]With a point of similarity to:

(i) *their explanation away of the problem

which must also involve noncontrastive scrambling, if Kayne (2008b) is on the right track.

compound-like phrases. Having a third-person pronoun within a compound is not possible[70]:

(237) *Nixon's supporters didn't realize how many him-haters there were

The restriction illustrated in (237) is probably best understood as a restriction involving the silent noun associated with the third-person pronoun. Compounds do not admit silent nouns within them (which may in turn be interpreted as a prohibition against movement of the noun (or NP) from within a compound up to the position of its antecedent, thinking of the discussion of (229)–(236).

Consider now *one*. Numeral *one* is allowed to appear in a compound:

(238) One-drawer file cabinets are not very useful

There may well be a silent SINGLE associated with *one* in such examples, as in (136) above, but that SINGLE has no antecedent (and the noun *drawer* is overt), so movement need not be involved. On the other hand, the *one* of *a red one* does involve an antecedent, and so arguably the silent noun following *one* in *a red one* has moved. This is what I think underlies the restriction on this subtype of *one* that resembles (237):

(239) One-drawer file cabinets are less useful than two-drawer/*two-one file cabinets

(240) First-time house buyers are less experienced than second-time house/ *second-time one buyers

(241) John is a black-bear-lover and Mary is a brown-bear/*brown-one lover

In the versions with *one* of each of these examples, *one* is associated with a silent noun that has arguably had to move to reach its antecedent, if Kayne (2002b) is on the right track. Such movement out of a compound is prohibited.

It is of interest that compounds do not prohibit subparts of them from being involved in a certain kind of antecedent relation if there is no silent element at issue:

(242) John is a black-bear lover and Mary is an animal lover, too

(243) John is a black-bear lover, whereas Mary is an animal hater

Here, destressed *animal* takes *black bear* as a kind of antecedent, or subject of predication.[71]

---

[70]Cf. Postal (1969), Harris (2006).

[71]In the following:

(i) John is a self-promoting scoundrel,

the antecedent of *self* must not be *John*, but rather the silent subject of *promote*. The relation between that subject and *scoundrel* needs looking into.

In:

(ii) We're having a three-wine dinner tonight,

there may well be a silent KIND, as in Kayne (2003, note 26), but that KIND has no compound-external antecedent, just as SINGLE does not in the text discussion.

Postal (1966) also mentions dialects that allow:

(244) you'uns; we'uns

Standard English has neither this nor:

(245) *you ones; *we ones

As Postal notes, standard English does allow:

(246) you honest ones; we smart ones

in a way that is by now familiar, instantiating the adjectival licensing that we have seen in a variety of cases, as well as the nonlicensing by a certain kind of determiner, in (245). (Possibly, the availability in some dialects of (244) is related to the nonpronunciation of the initial/w/of *ones*, which might reflect the absence of a classifier.)

Conclusion

One and *ones* are complex determiners whose relation to their antecedent, when they have one, is mediated by a silent noun. They are never themselves nouns taking an antecedent directly.

The question arises as to why the language faculty would turn its back on an analysis of *one* and *ones* as anaphoric nouns in certain cases. A possible answer might be in part the one given in Kayne (2002b) for personal pronouns, namely that the antecedent-pronoun relation is necessarily mediated by movement of a "double" of the pronoun. This might hold, now, not only for *he, she…*, but also for *one(s)*, even though the character of the double would be different in the two cases. With personal pronouns, the double is a DP, with *one(s)* a NP.

A broader question now arises. Why would the language faculty use movement (internal merge) to express antecedent–"pronoun" relations in general? The most interesting answer I can think of is given in[72]:

[72]Cf. Kayne (2010b). As formulated, the text statement, which has implications for the derivation of relative clauses and *tough*-movement, also prohibits instances of Agree that do not also involve internal merge—cf. Koopman (2003; 2005), Kayne and Pollock (2012; 2014).

On NPI-licensing as involving movement, see Chomsky (1973: 242) (for the particular case of *not…many*) and especially Collins and Postal (2014). On topicalization and (a certain kind of) left-dislocation, note the reconstruction effects that hold (for me) in:

(i) His youngest daughter every man is especially fond of.
(ii) As for his youngest daughter, every man is bound to think she's a genius.

Similarly:

(iii) His youngest daughter is easy for a man to admire.

(247) All non-local syntactic relations necessarily involve internal merge (movement)

That is, there is no possibility, in a derivational syntax, of "coindexing" or directly relating two phrases in any way distinct from internal merge (or external merge, in a highly local fashion).

Acknowledgements Earlier versions of this chapter were presented at the University of Cambridge, England, in June 2009; at the Workshop on Bare Nouns, Paris VII, in November 2009; at the Giornata di Dialettologia, University of Padua, in June 2010; at the Chinese University of Hong Kong, at the National Chiao Tung University, Taiwan, and at the University of Rome 3 in April 2013. I am grateful to all those audiences for useful comments and questions.

References

Algeo, J. 2006. *British or American English?*. A Handbook of Word and Grammar Patterns: Cambridge University Press.

Alexiadou, A., and C. Wilder. 1998. Adjectival modification and multiple determiners. In *Possessors, predicates and movement in the determiner phrase*, ed. A. Alexiadou, and C. Wilder, 305–332. Amsterdam: John Benjamins.

Baker, C.L. 1978. *Introduction to generative-transformational syntax*. Prentice-Hall, Englewood Cliffs, New Jersey.

Barbiers, S. 2007. Indefinite numerals one and many and the cause of ordinal suppletion. *Lingua* 117: 859–880.

Barbiers, S. 2005. Variation in the morphosyntax of *one*. *Journal of Comparative Germanic Linguistics* 8: 159–183.

Beal, J.C., L. Burbano-Elizondo, and C. Llamas. 2012. *Urban north-eastern English: Tyneside to Teesside*. Edinburgh University Press.

Bernstein, J. 2015. The expression of case across English demonstrative forms, talk presented at New York University.

Borer, H. 2005. *In name only*. Oxford: Oxford University Press.

Cardinaletti, A., and M. Starke. 1999. The typology of structural deficiency: a case study of the three classes of pronouns. In *Clitics in the languages of Europe*, ed. H. van Riemsdijk, 145–233. Berlin: Mouton de Gruyter.

Cheng, L.L.-S., and R. Sybesma. 1999. Bare and not-so-bare nouns and the structure of NP. *Linguistic Inquiry* 30: 509–542.

Cheng, L.L.-S., and R. Sybesma. 2012. Classifiers and DP. *Linguistic Inquiry* 43: 634–650.

Cinque, G. 2010. *The syntax of adjectives. A comparative study*. Cambridge, Mass: The MIT Press.

Cinque, G. 2005. Deriving Greenberg's universal 20 and its exceptions. *Linguistic Inquiry* 36: 315–332.

Cinque, G. 1988. On *Si* constructions and the theory of *Arb*. *Linguistic Inquiry* 19: 521–581.

Collins, C. 2014. Relative clause deletion. New York: New York University.

Ghosh, R. 2001. *Some aspects of determiner phrase in Bangla and Asamiya*. Doctoral dissertation, Tezpur University, Assam.

Greenberg, J.H. 1966. Some universals of grammar with particular reference to the order of meaningful elements. In *Universals of language*, 2nd ed, ed. J.H. Greenberg, 73–113. Cambridge, Mass.: The MIT Press.

Grevisse, M. & Goosse, A. 2011. *Le Bon Usage. 75 Ans*, De Boeck Duculot, Brussels.

Halliday, M.A.K., and R. Hasan. 1976. *Cohesion in English*. London: Longman.

Harris, A.C. 2006. Revisiting anaphoric islands. *Language* 82: 114–130.

Heim, I. 1987. Where does the definiteness restriction apply? Evidence from the definiteness of variables. In *The representation of (in)definiteness*, ed. E.J. Reuland, and A.G.B. ter Meulen, 21–42. Cambridge, Mass.: The MIT Press.

Hendrick, R. 1990. Operator binding in NP. In A. Halperin (ed.) *Proceedings of the Ninth West Coast Conference on Formal Linguistics*. Chicago: University of Chicago Press.

Her, O.-S., and H.-C. Tsai. 2015. On silent elements: a case study of *grand* and its silent entourage. *Natural Language & Linguistic Theory* 33: 575–605.

Ihsane, T. 2008. *The layered DP. Form and meaning of French indefinites*. Amsterdam: John Benjamins.

Jespersen, O. 1961. *A modern English grammar on historical principles. Part II. Syntax. First Volume*. London and Ejnar Munksgaard, Copenhagen: George Allen & Unwin.

Julien, M. 2002. *Syntactic heads and word formation*. New York: Oxford University Press.

Kayne, R.S. 2014. *Once* and *twice*. In *Inquiries into linguistic theory and language acquisition. Papers offered to Adriana Belletti*, ed. C. Contemori and L. Dal Pozzo. CISCL Press: Siena (also in *Studies in Chinese Linguistics* (2015) 36, 1–20).

Kayne, R.S. 2013. Comparative syntax. *Lingua* 130: 132–151.

Kayne, R.S. 2012. A note on *grand* and its silent entourage. *Studies in Chinese Linguistics* 33: 71–85.

Kayne, R.S. 2010a. Why isn't *this* a complementizer? In *Comparisons and contrasts* (also in *Functional structure from top to toe: A Festschrift for Tarald Taraldsen*, ed. P. Svenonius. New York: Oxford University Press.

Kayne, R.S. 2010b. The DP-internal origin of datives, talk given at the 4th European Dialect Syntax Workshop in Donostia/San Sebastián.

Kayne, R.S. 2010c. *Comparisons and contrasts*. New York: Oxford University Press.

Kayne, R.S. 2008a. Some preliminary comparative remarks on French and Italian definite articles. In *Foundational issues in linguistic theory. Essays in Honor of Jean-Roger Vergnaud*, ed. R. Freidin, C.P. Otero and M.L. Zubizarreta, 291–321. Cambridge, Mass.: MIT Press (reprinted in (2010c) *Comparisons and Contrasts*).

Kayne, R.S. 2008b. Antisymmetry and the lexicon. *Linguistic Variation Yearbook* 8: 1–31 (also in *The Biolinguistic enterprise: New perspectives on the evolution and nature of the human language faculty*, ed. A.M. di Sciullo and C. Boeckx, 329–353. London: Oxford University Press (2011)) (reprinted in *Comparisons and Contrasts*).

Kayne, R.S. 2007a. A short note on *where* verses *place*. In *Miscellanea di Studi Linguistici offerti a Laura Vanelli da amici e allievi padovani*, ed. R. Maschi, N. Penello and P. Rizzolatti, 245–257. Forum, Udine (reprinted in *Comparisons and Contrasts*).

Kayne, R.S. 2006. On parameters and on principles of pronunciation. In *Organizing grammar. Linguistic studies in Honor of Henk van Riemsdijk*, ed. H. Broekhuis, N. Corver, R. Huybregts, U. Kleinhenz and J. Koster, 289–299. Berlin: Mouton de Gruyter (reprinted in (2010c) *Comparisons and Contrasts*).

Kayne, R.S. 2005a. On the syntax of quantity in English. In *Movement and silence* (also in *Linguistic theory and South-Asian languages. Essays in Honour of K.A. Jayaseelan*, ed. J. Bayer, T. Bhattacharya and M. T. Hany Babu, John Benjamins, Amsterdam.

Kayne, R.S. 2005b. *Movement and silence*. New York: Oxford University Press.

Kayne, R.S. 2004. *Here* and *there*. In *Syntax, lexis & lexicon-grammar*, ed. C. Leclère, E. Laporte, M. Piot, and M. Silberztein, 253–273. *Papers in Honour of Maurice Gross*, John Benjamins, Amsterdam (reprinted in (2005b) *Movement and Silence*).

Kayne, R.S. 2003. Silent years, silent hours. In *Grammar in focus. Festschrift for Christer Platzack*, ed. L.-O. Delsing et al., vol 2, 209–226. Lund: Wallin and Dalholm (reprinted in Kayne (2005)).

Kayne, R.S. 2002a. On some prepositions that look DP-internal: English *of* and French *de*. *Catalan Journal of Linguistics* 1: 71–115 (reprinted in *Movement and Silence*).

Kayne, R.S. 2002b. Pronouns and their antecedents. In *Derivation and explanation in the minimalist program*, ed. S. Epstein and D. Seely, 133–166. Malden, Mass.: Blackwell (reprinted in (2005b) *Movement and Silence*).
Kayne, R.S. 1996. Microparametric syntax. Some introductory remarks. In *Microparametric syntax and dialect variation*, ed. J.R. Black and V. Motapanyaneix–xviii. Benjamins, Amsterdam (reprinted in *Parameters and Universals*).
Koopman, H., and A. Szabolcsi. 2000. *Verbal complexes*. Cambridge, Mass: The MIT Press.
Kornfilt, J. 1997. *Turkish*. London: Routledge.
Kortmann, B., T. Herrmann, L. Pietsch, and S. Wagner (eds.). 2005. *A comparative grammar of British English dialects. Agreement, gender, relative clauses*. Berlin: Mouton de Gruyter.
Lakoff, G. 1970. Global rules. *Language* 46: 627–639.
Leu, T. 2015. *The architecture of determiners*. New York: Oxford University Press.
Leu, T. 2008. *What for internally*. *Syntax* 11: 1–25.
Leu, T. 2007. These HERE demonstratives. In *Proceedings of the 30th Annual Penn Linguistics Colloquium, Penn Working Papers in Linguistics*, ed. T. Scheffler, J. Tauberer, A. Eilam and L. Mayol, vol 13(1), 141–154.
Leu, T. 2005. Something invisible in English. *UPenn Working Papers in Linguistics* 11(1): 143–155 (*Proceedings of PLC 28*).
Liao, W.-W.R. 2015. Once upon an Invisible TIME: On frequentative phrases in Chinese. *Studies in Chinese Linguistics* 36: 21–33.
Llombart-Huesca, A. 2002. Anaphoric *one* and NP-ellipsis. *Studia Linguistica* 56: 59–89.
Longobardi, G. 1994. Reference and proper names. *Linguistic Inquiry* 25: 609–665.
Malamud, S.A. 2013. (In)definiteness-driven typology of arbitrary items. *Lingua* 126: 1–31.
Marušič, F., and R. Žaucer. 2006. The 'definite article' TA in colloquial Slovenian. *Formal Approaches to Slavic Linguistics* 14: 189–204.
Matthews, S., and V. Yip. 1994. *Cantonese: A comprehensive grammar*. London: Routledge.
McDonald, C., and J.C. Beal. 1987. Modal verbs in Tyneside English. *Journal of the Atlantic Provinces Linguistic Association* 9: 43–55.
Payne, J., G.K. Pullum, B.C. Scholz, and E. Berlage. 2013. Anaphoric *one* and its implications. *Language* 89: 794–829.
Perlmutter, D.M. 1970. On the Article in English. In *Progress in linguistics*, ed. M. Bierwisch, and K.E. Heidolph, 233–248. The Hague: Mouton.
Pesetsky, D. 1991. Zero syntax, vol 2. Infinitives. MIT: Mass.
Pollock, J.-Y. 1998. On the syntax of subnominal clitics: Cliticization and ellipsis. *Syntax* 1: 300–330.
Postal, P.M. 1966. On so-called 'pronouns' in English. In *Report of the seventeenth annual roundtable meeting on linguistics and language studies*, ed. F.P. Dineen, 177–206. Washington, D.C.: Georgetown University Press (reprinted in *Modern studies in English* (1969), ed. D.A. Reibel and S.A. Schane. Englewood Cliffs, New Jersey: Prentice-Hall).
Postal, P. 1969. Anaphoric Islands. *Chicago Linguistic Society* 5: 205–239.
Riemsdijk, H. Van. 2005. Silent nouns and the spurious indefinite article in Dutch, in M. Vulchanova and T. Åfarli, *Grammar & Beyond: Essays in honour of Lars Hellan*, 163–178, Novus Press, Oslo.
Schibsbye, K. 1970. *A modern English grammar*, 2nd ed. London: Oxford University Press.
Shlonsky, U. 2004. The form of Semitic noun phrases. *Lingua* 114: 1465–1526.
Simpson, A., and Biswas, P. 2015. *Bare nominals, classifiers and the representation of definiteness in Bangla, handout of talk presented at FASAL-5*, Yale University.
Simpson, A., H.L. Soh, and H. Nomoto. 2011. Bare classifiers and definiteness. A cross-linguistic investigation. *Studies in Language* 35: 168–193.
Stirling, L., and R. Huddleston. 2002. Deixis and Anaphora. In *The Cambridge grammar of the English language*, ed. R. Huddleston, and G.K. Pullum, 1449–1564. United Kingdom: Cambridge University Press, Cambridge.

Tat, D. 2011. APs as reduced relatives: The case of *Bir* in some varieties of Turkic. In *Proceedings of WAFL7. MIT Working Papers in Linguistics*, 62.

Troseth, E. 2009. Degree inversion and negative intensifier inversion in the English DP. *The Linguistic Review* 26: 37–65.

Wood, J.L. 2002. Much about *Such*. *Studia Linguistica* 56: 91–115.

Wood, J.L. 2013. Indefinite determiner doubling. Abstract of talk presented at the Germanic Linguistics Annual Conference, 19, SUNY Buffalo.

Zanuttini, R., and L.R. Horn. 2014. *Micro-syntactic variation in North American English*. New York: Oxford University Press.

Zepeda, O. 1983. *A Papago grammar*. Tucson: University of Arizona Press.

Chapter 5
Parallel Work Spaces in Syntax and the Inexistence of Internal Merge

K.A. Jayaseelan

Introduction

As is well-known, current minimalist theory does not make a distinction between Move and Merge. Move is only remerge and nothing more.

It seems to be commonly agreed that the first-time merge of a phrase—e.g., the merge of the external argument in Spec, vP—is from a different Work Space where the phrase is built up; for this reason, this operation is called External Merge. The picture we have is that of different Work Spaces that exist in parallel in the mind. One of these is of course dedicated to the main derivation. Regarding the other Work Spaces, there appears to be an assumption—which has never been articulated or examined, to my knowledge—that they are (in a peculiar way) ephemeral: Once the phrase built up in a certain Work Space has been plugged into the main derivation, that Work Space disappears. For this reason, when we want to remerge a phrase, we are forced to source it from its merged position in the main derivation; this is why remerge is called Internal Merge. Even when we want to remerge a phrase with a syntactic object that exists completely independently in another Work Space—as in proposals about sideward movement/parallel merge—we source it from its merged position, because the Work Space where it was originally built up has disappeared.

But the recovery of a phrase from somewhere within an already built-up structure for the purpose of remerge is not a trivial matter. The problems attendant on this operation have in fact been realized and commented on (occasionally!), but they have been largely ignored because there seemed to be no way to avoid

K.A. Jayaseelan (✉)
The English and Foreign Languages University, Hyderabad, India
e-mail: kajayaseelan11@gmail.com

G. Sengupta et al. (eds.), *Perspectives on the Architecture and Acquisition of Syntax*, DOI 10.1007/978-981-10-4295-9_5

them—if we wanted to keep Move at all in the Grammar.[1] But if we can say that the 'other' Work Spaces need not all be so ephemeral, but that they can stay and be used for remerge, we get a very different picture of Move: We can dispense with Internal Merge. In fact, the consequences for the organization of Grammar are immense. This is the main thesis of this chapter.[2]

This chapter is organized as follows. In Section "The Proposal", we state our proposal regarding remerge from parallel Work Spaces; we clarify some points regarding the content of these parallel Work Spaces and then discuss the problems of Internal Merge. In Section "Pied-Piping", we illustrate how our system works by showing how we handle pied-piping. In Sections "Successive-Cyclic Movement" and "Extraction Islands", we address two prima facie challenges to our proposal, namely successive-cyclic movement and extraction islands, and show how we can deal with them in our system. In Section "Parasitic Gaps", we discuss parasitic gaps. In Section "PIC, 'Partial' Spell-Out of Phases, and Other Matters", the conclusion, we argue that PIC, the "escape hatch," and 'partial' spell-out of phases can be dropped from the theory.

The Proposal

The Idea of Remerge from Parallel Work Spaces

Consider the situation of *L* merging to *K* (external merge). If *L* is a lexical item, it is a copy of a member of the Numeration. But if *L* is a phrase, it must have been built up in a different Work Space (Nunes and Uriagereka 2000; Collins 2002; Stroik 2009, and many others).[3] Currently, we think of it as being moved into a position in *K*′ (extension of *K*):

(1) (i) 

---

[1]See Koster (2007) for an awareness of the problems of Internal Merge. We examine these problems in Section "Recovering a Phrase for Remerge: The Problems of Internal Merge" (See also de Vries 2013: 146.)

[2]See Epstein et al. (2014) for important additional arguments for unifying External Merge and Internal Merge.

A clarification is possibly in order here. The movements that we plan to account for in our system are the "standard" A/A′ movements which are successive cyclic and long distance. (These are the movements that make use of the "edges" of phases in the system of Chomsky 2000.) But there are other types of phrasal movements that have been postulated in the literature, e.g., remnant movement, about which we have nothing to say. See fn. 16 for some remarks about these movements.

[3]We may assume that each such "derivational space" has its own Numeration or subarray.

But there is another way to conceptualize this operation: *L* is merged from the Work Space where it is built up, but this Work Space (containing *L*) can remain after the operation, so that *L* is still available for remerge from it. The operation of merge will look like this when we represent both Work Spaces simultaneously. (WS2 is the main derivation.)

(2)
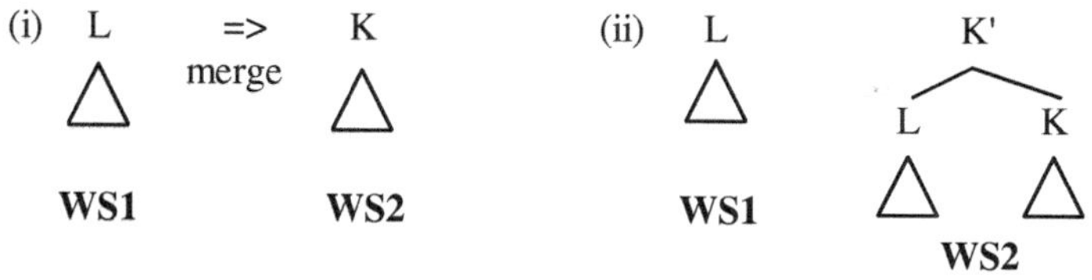

A picture of multiple merge (under this view) would be:

(3)
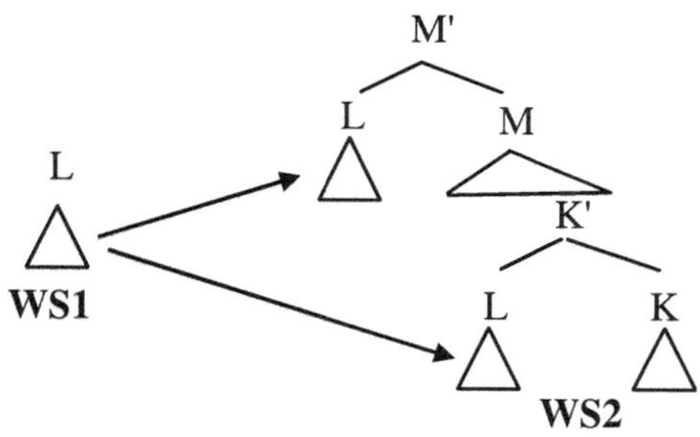

(3)—likewise (2)—invokes the Chomskyan notion of copy-merge (Chomsky 2003: 307; 2008: 140). But we are not forced to appeal to copies; we can as well merge *L* directly to multiple mother nodes as shown in (4)[4]:

[4]At a first glance, (4) may not look so very different from Internal Merge, especially if one were to argue that a "Work Space" is nothing more than the object created in it. But the difference of our system emerges very clearly when we consider a case like remerging an argument of an argument, in a configuration like (i) (where *A* is an argument of the main derivation and *B* is an argument of *A*):

(i) … [$_A$ … [$_B$ …] …] …

The Internal Merge theory will do subextraction here; i.e., it will remerge a term of A to the root of the tree. But in our system, B will also be in a parallel Work Space, the same as A, and B will be directly merged from its Work Space to the main derivation. Importantly, this will be a root-to-root merge and not a term-to-root merge which is what Internal Merge is. (This is illustrated in Section "Pied-Piping", in our account of pied-piping.)

(4)

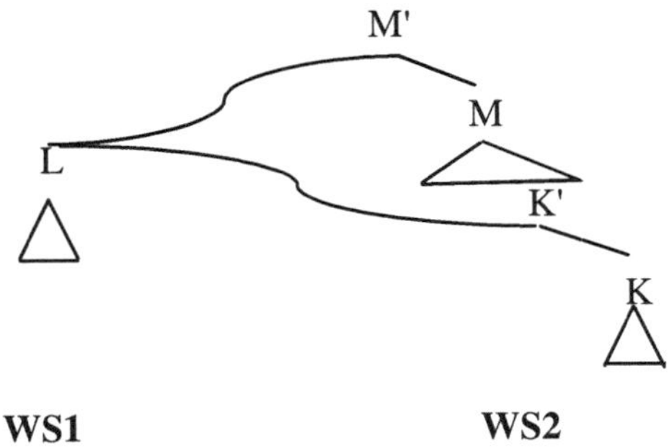

Let us make clear what (3)/(4) says about the way we conceptualize displacement. In early transformational grammar, displacement was conceived of as analogous to the physical movement of an object. But currently, and since a long time, the assumption is that when a constituent α is moved from Position A to Position B, it does not cease to be in Position A. While we assume this for Internal Merge (and for sideward movement/parallel merge), we still continue with the old conception of movement for External Merge. What (3)/(4) does is to do away with this anomaly and treat Internal Merge and External Merge alike. We can now maintain that there is only one type of displacement in natural language.

A question arises: Is *L* [in (3)/(4)] interpreted in all three positions? Let us say that *L* is already interpreted in WS1, i.e., the place where it is built up; but it is interpreted for its θ-related meaning in the first-merge position and for its discourse-related meaning (its "edge features," Chomsky 2008) in the criterial position, both of which are in WS2. (The derivation being in two Work Spaces simultaneously is not a problem: This is what we assume in the case of parallel merge.) The phrase will be linearized with respect to the rest of the derivation under either mother node.

The first noteworthy consequence of our proposal is the following:

(5) All merge is external merge

What would be the advantage of maintaining (5)?[5]

---

[5]The idea is not without antecedents. In fact, Chomsky (2008: 145–146) briefly considers, and rejects, this idea, but the execution he had in mind was in terms of generating the same phrase afresh for every merge, and he rightly says that this involves too much computation.

The implementation of "multiple Merge" that comes closest to our proposal is the "Survive Minimalism" of Stroik (1999; 2009) and Putnam and Stroik (2010). In this system, a phrase is merged in its base position from a Work Bench. If the phrase has a feature which is unchecked in the base position, it "will return to (i.e., be copied in) the Work Bench for Remerge" (Stroik 2009: 44–45). It will now be remerged to every new head that extends the derivation, until this feature is checked. So in a sense, every remerge has external merge as its last step.

The Content of Parallel Work Spaces

Before we proceed, let us make clear what syntactic objects we expect to find occupying parallel Work Spaces in a derivation. Obviously, the arguments and adjuncts of a derivation will be represented in such spaces, since these are built up separately and merged as chunks. (We are assuming that an argument that is a complement is no exception—it too is merged as a chunk from a different Work Space.[6] And so apparently are adjectival and nominal complements of main verb "be" which are not usually counted as arguments; these too—we must assume—are merged as chunks from a different Work Space, for they can be *wh*-moved, cf. *How beautiful is the rainbow*![7])

Now, are there any other elements that are built up and merged in this fashion? A little consideration will show us that there aren't. The heads that project the "skeleton" of the derivation are taken directly from the Numeration, and these never come to be in a parallel Work Space.[8] Similarly, the phrases that are built up in the derivation itself—i.e., in its own Work Space—also never come to be in a parallel Work Space. Some of these phrases will be intermediate projections; some of them may even be maximal projections, but no matter—the relevant fact is that they are not merged from a different Work Space. To illustrate: In the following structure:

(6)

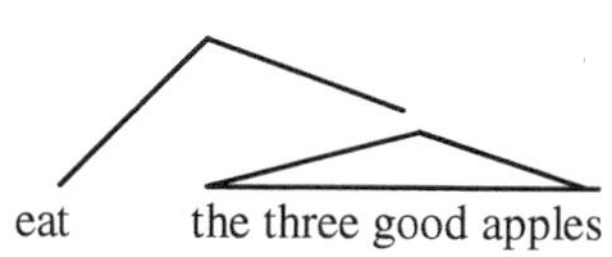

the three good apples will be represented in a parallel Work Space, since it is an argument, but neither *eat* nor *eat the three good apples* will be in such a space—the first is an element merged from the Numeration (Lexicon), and the second is a phrase built up internally (in this case, it happens to be a maximal projection, a VP).

This point deserves some elaboration. To put the matter more generally, neither heads of phrases, nor the phrases themselves *if they are not arguments or adjuncts* will be represented in a Work Space that coexists with the main derivation. As a corollary—and importantly—vP and TP will not be in such a space; for although they are maximal projections, they are not built up outside and merged as chunks but are built up in the derivation itself. What about CP? CP is a maximal projection

[6]For a contrary view, see Nunes and Uriagereka (2000).

[7]This last claim should not be too difficult to accept when we reflect that these complements can be quite complex, with arguments embedded in them, cf. *He is proud of his daughter*; *He is a member of every club*.

[8]Thus, we maintain a distinction between merge from the Numeration—ultimately from the Lexicon—and merge from a parallel Work Space. For a system that does not maintain this distinction, and which envisages a Numeration with "complex elements" (i.e., already-built-up phrases) in it, see Putnam and Stroik (2010); Stroik (2009: 44).

that can be merged as an argument or adjunct into another derivation; therefore, it will be in a parallel Work Space of *that* derivation. In sum, all and only the arguments and adjuncts of a derivation will be in the parallel Work Spaces associated with that derivation.[9,10]

These distinctions will become important in Section "Pied-Piping", where we shall see that they make exactly the right predictions about what phrases can, and what phrases cannot, be moved by pied-piping.

These distinctions may also be important for another reason. Note that it is only the elements taken directly from the derivation's own Numeration (and not from the Numeration of a different Work Space)—e.g., *eat* in (6)—that determine labels, i.e., project. It seems to be the case that phrases brought in from other Work Spaces, and their *heads*, are inert in the task of projection. (This is possibly because these phrases are treated as chunks and the derivation does not look inside them.) Thus, when V takes an internal argument, it is V that projects; again, when vP takes an external argument in its Spec position (using "Spec" only for expository purposes; see Starke 2004; Jayaseelan 2008; Chomsky 2013), the resulting structure is labeled "vP." (The same algorithm holds good in a VP which has two internal arguments: "put [on the table]" is a VP, and "[the book] [put on the table]" is also a VP, because "put" is the only element here which is taken from the derivation's own Numeration.)

We may contrast this very simple labeling algorithm with the one adopted in Chomsky (2008: 145, fn. 34). The Chomskyan algorithm is stated disjunctively with three subcases, each with its own solution. It says: For the output of binary merge {α, β}:

(i) If α is an LI, then α is the label;
(ii) If α is a phrase that is internally merged to β, i.e., sourced from within β, then the head of β is the label; and
(iii) If α is a phrase that is externally merged to β, then the head of either α or β can be the label, but the "wrong" choice will be filtered out at the C-I interface.[11]

[9] All that we say here applies equally to the derivation of the phrases in the parallel Work Spaces. Thus, an argument of an argument will be built up externally and merged as a chunk into the "parent" argument; see fn. 4 and Section "Pied-Piping".

[10] A possible query: A one-word argument or adjunct (e.g., "what" in "What did you see?") would appear to have the option of being merged directly from the Numeration without going through a parallel Work Space. Is this possible? We would say not, for the following reasons: An argument, we said, is initially interpreted in the place where it is built up and then interpreted again for its relational meanings in the positions where it is merged. Therefore, an argument that comes directly from the Numeration will not be fully interpreted. Also, this argument will not be able to move, given our account of remerge.

[11] There is actually also a fourth case, namely the merge of two LIs, which is how every derivation must start with. The Chomskyan solution is similar to that of case (iii): Either LI can be the label, and the "wrong" choice will be filtered out at the C-I interface. Note that this fourth case too presents no problem for our system, because one of the LIs must be an argument. Therefore, it must be merged from a parallel Work Space and will be inert in the matter of projection.

Chomsky also suggests (following Moro 2000) a different solution for case (iii): These structures are inherently unstable, and they are "rescued" by the raising of one of the phrases, say α. See Adger (2012, Chap. 2) for arguments showing why the Chomsky an algorithm is not viable. We can conclude that labeling still remains a problem in the current theory.

Recovering a Phrase for Remerge: The Problems of Internal Merge

Consider how Chomsky (1995: 243) describes the operation of Merge:

> Applied to two objects α and β, Merge forms the new object K, *eliminating* α and β. [emphasis added—KAJ][12]

If we take "eliminating" literally, α and β should no longer be available for a syntactic operation after K is formed. This is surely the simplest way to conceptualize Merge: After every merge operation, the derivation should be able to "forget" the earlier syntactic objects that it handled. But unfortunately this conception is not viable, for if we wish to remerge (say) α later in the derivation, we must be able to "reanimate" α. (Koster 2007 makes this point.) For this, the derivation must hold α and β in its memory. Since the remerging of α may take place after *n* operations of merge (of other elements), the derivation needs to remember syntactic objects that it handled *n* steps earlier. Also, if we continue with the idea that phrases may be built up in different derivational spaces and merged as chunks, α may have been merged with β in a different derivational space. Now, the main derivation must access the memory of *that* derivational space. In effect, the derivation must remember every term of every phrase in the tree (as it exists when the extraction of α is attempted). Now, some of these terms will be heads taken directly from the Numeration which project the "skeleton" of the derivation. Some of these terms will be phrases built *within* the derivation. The current system has no way of sorting these out from the phrases which have been built in other derivational spaces and merged as chunks. Reverting to our illustration (6), the derivation must hold in its memory *eat*, (each term of) *the three good apples*, and *eat the three good apples*. Therefore, in the current system with Internal Merge, the memory burden on the derivation is very great.

The phase theory of Chomsky (2000) is intended to limit this problem; its postulates are designed to yield the result that the derivation will need to remember only the current phase and the "left edge" of the earlier phase. But this does not help very much, for note that even within this delimitation, the derivation must

[12]The idea is repeated further down on the same page: "Suppose a derivation has reached state $\Sigma = \{\alpha, \beta, \delta_i \ldots \delta_n\}$. The application of an operation that forms *K* [where $K = \{\gamma, \{\alpha, \beta\}\}$, γ the label—KAJ] … converts Σ to $\Sigma' = \{K, \delta_i \ldots \delta_n\}$, including *K* but not α, β."

remember every term without exception—even though many (or most) of these terms are not eligible to move. (An example would be intermediate projections, not only of the "skeleton" of the derivation but of every argument and adjunct in the phase. Their nonmoveability is stipulated, but the derivation still has to remember them.) In our system, as we shall see, the derivation has to hold in its memory only the phrases in parallel Work Spaces and these too only as "chunks". That is, it must remember just the potentially moveable elements.

But the real problem (for the current theory) is that the derivation *cannot* have those memories, because all those memories have been wiped out—this wiping out being done by our assumption that when a phrase is merged from a different Work Space, that Work Space disappears. The phrase now exists only in its merged position. The problem with this way of doing things becomes clear when we look at an element that we are seeking to move which is multiply embedded. We examine this problem in the next section.

Pied-Piping

Consider a *wh*-element which is multiply embedded. (7) is a "premovement" structure represented in terms of the current theory that assumes Internal Merge:

(7) The newspapers want [pictures of [the wedding of [[which] celebrity]]]

The grammar allows the movement of any of the bracketed elements except the innermost one. The D^0 element *which* cannot move by itself.

Given our proposal about simultaneously present parallel Work Spaces, (7) will have the representation (8) in our theory:

(8)

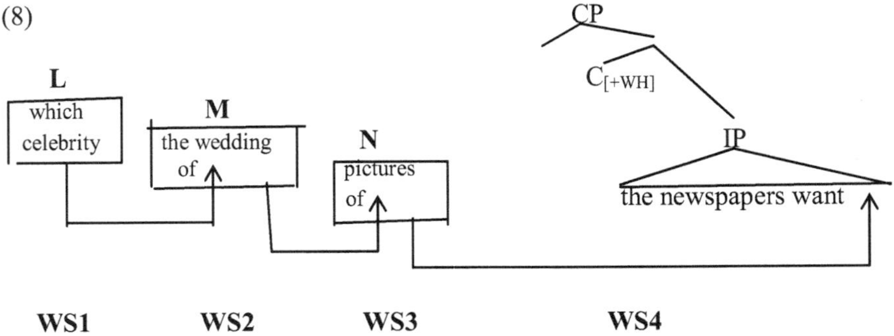

For ease of reference, we have labeled the phrases on the left of the main derivation *L*, *M*, and *N*. *L* is built up in a separate Work Space prior to *M*; similarly, *M* is built up prior to *N*. It is *N* which is base-merged in the main derivation.

If Work Spaces 1, 2, and 3 may coexist with Work Space 4, the "default" expectation—i.e., assuming that no stipulation is introduced to somehow prohibit such an operation—is that either *L*, or *M*, or *N* can be merged in Work Space 4 to satisfy $C_{[+WH]}$'s need for a *wh*-phrase in its specifier position. And this is indeed right, cf. the three results[13]:

(9) a. Which celebrity do the newspapers want pictures of the wedding of?
b. The wedding of which celebrity do the newspapers want pictures of?
c. Pictures of the wedding of which celebrity do the newspapers want?

Note that there is no notion of extracting a smaller phrase from a larger phrase in our system; i.e., there is no such thing as subextraction. The only possibility is that of giving a phrase that exists in a parallel Work Space a new mother node; this is our implementation of phrasal movement.

Our method is cognitively simpler, because it restricts its operations to roots. By contrast, subextraction involves many complications. Consider (7), which has a deeply embedded *wh*-word *which*. The dominant line of thinking about *wh*-movement is that a $C^0_{[+WH]}$ acts as a probe that seeks to match its [+WH] feature with an element in its domain (Chomsky 2000: 101, 119).[14] Strictly, the matching is with a *wh*-feature, but since a feature cannot be moved by itself, a larger syntactic object that contains the *wh*-feature is moved. The mechanism that determines how large this syntactic object should be is the core of any account of pied-piping.

The earliest idea in this regard was feature percolation (Chomsky 1973): The *wh*-feature is copied upward from the *wh*-word to the phrases that contain it. But the problematic nature of the copying involved here has long been recognized. The feature must travel not only along the spine of the derivation, but must be able to "jump" from specifier to head, cf. (10) (see Heck 2009: 99 for a discussion of the problems of this movement); also, it must be able to span adjunct island boundaries, cf. (11):

(10) [Whose book] did you read?
(11) [The books which WHO wrote] were they unhappy about?

But the most damaging evidence against feature percolation (to my mind) is that the copying must be discontinuous—because VP and TP cannot be pied-piped,[15] whereas CP can be. These well-known facts about pied-piping are illustrated below:

(12) * [Want pictures of which celebrity] do the newspapers?
(13) * [The newspapers had pictures of which celebrity] did you say that?
(14) [That WHO came] did you find surprising?

---

[13](9b) and (9c) would be considered instances of heavy pied-piping. We comment on how we can deal with the differing acceptability judgments about heavy pied-piping later in this section.

[14]We comment on the "free movement" idea of Chomsky (2013) later.

[15]VP can be displaced by other types of operations than pied-piping, see fn. 16; but TP-movement (stranding C) is not possible at all.

CP pied-piping is not considered very felicitous in English, which in fact "dis-prefers" heavy pied-piping, but many languages—e.g., Basque (Ortiz de Urbina 1990) and Malayalam (Jayaseelan 2001)—standardly pied-pipe an embedded CP containing a *wh*-phrase to a position in the matrix clause, in order to give the *wh*-phrase matrix scope.

Note that the Internal Merge theory, which essentially seeks to move a phrase containing the *wh*-feature, has no way of distinguishing between VP/TP and CP. On the other hand, our system *predicts* this distinction. In Section "The Content of Parallel Work Spaces", we explained that VP and TP will not be represented in a parallel Work Space of the derivation because they are structures built up *internally* to the derivation and that they contrast (in this respect) with arguments and adjuncts which are built up externally and merged as chunks. CP (on the other hand) can be merged as an argument or adjunct into another derivation and then will be represented in a parallel Work Space of *that* derivation. The crucial difference here is that VP and TP are not arguments or adjuncts, but an embedded CP is.

The same considerations should explain why, in a structure like (7), the *wh*-word *which* cannot be moved by itself. This functional word is merged directly from the Numeration (subarray) of *which celebrity* when that phrase is being built up and therefore will not be represented in any parallel Work Space; what the relevant parallel Work Space will have is the entire argument *which celebrity*. But if *which* were the entire argument, it would indeed be able to move, cf. *Which do you prefer?* (Recall that our options for A/A′ movement are strictly limited to giving a new mother node to a structure that exists in a parallel Work Space.)[16]

---

[16]Let us glance at this juncture at some other types of movements that need to be distinguished from pied-piping. *N*-to-*D* movement or *V*-to-*T* movement—head movement, more generally—obviously does not fall within the purview of pied-piping. It is easy to differentiate this type of movement—which has its own very distinct properties: It is morphologically motivated, strictly local, and can induce "roll-up"—from phrasal movement of the type that we are concerned with (Jayaseelan 2010b).

We said (fn. 15) that VP can be displaced by other types of movements than pied-piping. We can think of at least two such movements. One is remnant VP-movement (Kayne 1998). This controversial type of movement has been sought to be explained as a "repair strategy" (Müller 2000), or as a movement necessitated by the need to bring together the verb and its inflexion (Jayaseelan 2010a). It is strictly local. A second type of movement is VP-fronting or more generally predicate fronting:

(i) Kiss her, I didn't.
(ii) Innocent, he is not.

A fronted VP/predicate needs—at least in English—a linguistic antecedent (Phillips 2003); it is in this respect like VP-deletion. It is interesting that both remnant VP-movement and VP-fronting are operations that remove a constituent from the "bottom of the tree." And they certainly do not move a constituent from Spec-to-Spec. It should be obvious that these movements have nothing to do with the types of movements that Chomskyan checking theory and EPP try to account for, and which we usually have in mind when we speak of Internal Merge.

There have been notable attempts to do pied-piping without feature percolation, e.g., Heck (2009), Cable (2010). Heck's system explains pied-piping by a "local agree" condition, the essential idea being that the pied-piping movement seeks to minimize the number of XP boundaries that separate the probe ($C^{0}_{[+WH]}$) and the goal (the *wh*-word). The inadmissibility of cases like VP pied-piping is put down to a constraint: "Pied-piping of β by α is possible only if movement of α from β is blocked" (p. 92). But this does not explain why CP pied-piping is possible—perhaps infelicitously or marginally in a language like English but quite standardly in some other languages.[17]

In Cable (2010)'s system, it is not the *wh*-word itself that is probed by the interrogative C head, but a Q(uestion)-particle that adjoins to, or takes as complement, a phrase containing the *wh*-word. *Wh*-fronting is a secondary effect of the movement of the Q-particle to $C^{0}_{[+WH]}$. The Q-particle can be generated above any phrase that contains the *wh*-word. Therefore, this system cannot explain the "cut" between VP/TP and CP: Why can't the Q-particle take VP or TP as complement when it can take CP as complement? Cable in fact notes this problem: "[T]he data from Tlingit are consistent with a generalization that the language permits pied-piping only of DP, PP and CP, a generalization that also seems applicable to languages like English and does not obviously follow from the Q-based account" (p. 581: fn. 20).

So we see that our account of pied-piping is the only one in the literature that makes the right distinction between VP/TP and CP in a principled way. This is strong support for our way of implementing phrasal movement.

Let us conclude this section with an account of heavy pied-piping. Clearly, the "orthodoxy" in the vast literature on pied-piping is that pied-piping is perfect only when the *wh*-word is at the left edge of the pied-piped phrase (Webelhuth 1992;

---

[17]It can be easily shown that in these latter languages, TP pied-piping is completely impossible. Cf. the following Malayalam data, showing the completely normal (and standard) CP pied-piping and an attempted TP pied-piping:

(i) *CP pied-piping to cleft focus*

[$_{CP}$ John AAR-e kaNDu ennə] aaNə nii t_{CP} paRaññ-atə?
John who-ACC saw COMP COP you said-NOM
Lit. '(It) is that John saw WHO, that you said?' (='Who did you say that John saw?')

(ii) *TP pied-piping to cleft focus*

** [$_{TP}$ John AAR-e kaNDu] aaNə nii t_{TP} enn paRaññ-atə?
John who-ACC saw COP you COMP said-NOM

Extraction of a *wh*-phrase from an embedded clause (by Spec-to-Spec movement) is not possible in Malayalam; this fact may appear to support Heck's constraint. But then, why can't the derivation be saved by TP pied-piping to the cleft focus?

Grimshaw 2000; Horvath 2007, and many others); this claim has even been formalized as an "edge generalization" (see, e.g., Heck 2009: 89). Cable (2010), who was trying to account for Tlingit pied-piping where this generalization certainly does not hold, faced the same dilemma as we ourselves face, namely that our basic mechanisms of pied-piping do not distinguish between phrases in which the *wh*-word is at the left edge and phrases in which it is not. Cable draws a distinction between what he calls "limited pied-piping languages" (like English) and languages that are not similarly limited (like Tlingit); the former class of languages are the ones in which "pied-piping past adjunct islands and pied-piping past lexical categories is not permitted" (p. 581). He accounts for this constraint as follows: In the English-type languages—but not in the Tlingit-type languages—there is a requirement that the Q-particle must agree with the *wh*-word, and if this agreement is to take place, the *wh*-word "cannot be dominated in the sister of *Q* by adjunct islands or lexical categories" (p. 584; see Cable 2010 for the feature-checking mechanism that implements this constraint). We can readily adapt Cable's proposal and use it in our system, although we do not postulate a Q-particle. We can say that in English-type languages, $C^{0}_{[WH]}$ must agree with the *wh*-word in the phrase that is sought to be merged in its Spec position. The other details of Cable's proposal can be kept intact. The way this constraint will work with the sentences of (9) is the following: (9a) is fine because the *wh*-word is not dominated by any lexical category, but (9b) and (9c) will be marked as unacceptable because the *wh*-word is dominated by one or more nouns.[18]

Successive-Cyclic Movement

Chomsky (2000; 2001) implemented successive-cyclic movement by using two devices, both embedded in the idea of a "phase." CP and vP are taken to be the phases. At the end of each phase, the complement of the head of the phase—i.e., the complement of C^0 or v^0—is "transferred" to spell-out and semantic interpretation; thereafter, this part of the structure is inaccessible to operations like extraction. This postulate is called the "Phase Impenetrability Condition" (PIC). A consequence of PIC is that any phrase that needs to move out of the phase eventually should have

[18]There is more to be said about heavy pied-piping in the Germanic languages. First of all, the judgments are gradient; even within English, there are speakers who find examples of heavy pied-piping completely acceptable—e.g., (famously) Ross (1967). Also (as is well-known), heavy pied-piping is better in matrix questions than in embedded questions, and in non-restrictive relative clauses than in restrictive relative clauses, which suggests that there are factors like sentence stress at play here. Again, there are many rather complicated differences *within* the Germanic family, between English, Dutch, and German (see de Vries 2005). All this suggests that the constraints on heavy pied-piping—whatever they are—should not be part of the "core" account of pied-piping. In our system, there is no special rule of pied-piping. Pied-piping is simply an instance of the completely normal operation of remerge of phrases from parallel Work Spaces.

already moved to the "edge" of the phase—Spec, CP or Spec, vP—before the end of the phase.

But PIC by itself does not force movement. Movement is actually implemented by Chomsky's second device: Every intermediate C^0 and v^0 in the path of a long movement is given an EPP feature, and this enables the C^0/v^0 to pull up the phrase to its Spec.

In the system of Chomsky (2000; 2001), EPP targets a phrase because it contains an uninterpretable feature ('uF') that makes it "active." For A-movement, Chomsky assumes the uF to be Case; for *wh*-movement, it is a [+WH] feature. But the system of Chomsky (2008; 2013) dispenses with any uF on phrases which move (Chomsky 2008: 151). The suggestion in Chomsky (2008) is that the EF of the phase head can "indiscriminately" pull up any phrase in its domain to the edge position of the phase; the interpretation of the moved phrase will depend on the final position it reaches. An interrogative *wh*-phrase will be labeled by an *interpretable* interrogative *wh*-feature, and if this phrase does not reach the Spec position of an interrogative C, it will simply be interpreted as deviant. The system of Chomsky (2013) proposes "free Merge."

It should be fairly clear that implementing successive-cyclic movement in our system presents no particular problem. If an intermediate phase head has an EF that induces merge, it can induce the merge of a phrase that exists independently in a parallel Work Space even more easily than of a phrase in an embedded position.

In the "free Merge" proposal of Chomsky (2013), so far as I understand the system, what drives successive-cyclic movement appears to be only PIC. But if PIC is dropped from the theory (a move which has been argued for; see, e.g., Stjepanović and Takahashi 2001), what can implement successive-cyclicity? Let us see whether we can obtain the effects of EFs on phase heads in a manner that would be consistent with "free Merge." (The EFs—or the earlier EPP features—were simply diacritics and were unexplanatory.) It is reasonable to assume that a phrase that was merged/remerged recently is more active in the derivational memory—and therefore more "accessible"—than a phrase merged/remerged earlier. This would explain Superiority effects in our system, such as is illustrated in: "Who bought what[19]?/* "What did who buy?" (This new formulation would replace the idea of "distance" in the tree measured in terms of the number of intervening nodes, which was natural in a system with Internal Merge.) In the same spirit, let us say that a phrase that needs to maintain itself as active in the derivational memory, such as a long-moving phrase, seeks to remerge at the end of each phase, merge being "free." So it is a need of the derivational memory that implements successive-cyclic merge. Note that this is a "third factor" explanation as much as the current explanation in terms of "shortest steps."

[19]In the framework of Chomsky (2008), all operations in a phase, including the movement of the Subject, must be driven by a feature inherited from the phase head. See also Rizzi (2005).

Extraction Islands

After Ross's (1967) discovery of some syntactic configurations that resist extraction from within them, there have perhaps been two main approaches to explaining this phenomenon. The early approach was in terms of "bounding nodes" (which were variously defined). The idea was that a phrase trying to come out of one of these opaque domains was "stopped" by a bounding node. The main exemplars of this approach were the Subjacency idea of Chomsky (1973) and its subsequent reworkings up to the "barriers" idea of Chomsky (1986). Takahashi (1994) is a latter-day variation of (essentially) the "bounding node" idea. This type of explanation is peculiarly dependent on there being Internal Merge in the theory.

While Chomsky's later work in the minimalist framework did not come back to the question of extraction islands, there has more recently been a very different type of proposal about this problem, which appeals to the organization of the Grammar. The idea of the new proposal is that a constituent resists extraction from within it because it has already been spelt-out at the time of the attempted extraction. See Uriagereka (1999), Epstein (1999), Nunes and Uriagereka (2000). Nunes and Uriagereka (2000) make the following claims:

A. Phrases in specifier positions are already spelt-out: They have been spelt-out prior to being merged in these positions.
B. All phrases that have moved have already been spelt-out, or in other words, phrases are spelt-out before they are moved.
C. Adjuncts are spelt-out before they are merged in the main derivation.

In effect, only a complement can be subextracted from, because this is the only constituent in a tree that has not been spelt-out.

The Nunes–Uriagereka proposal seeks to subsume the left-branch condition (A), the freezing principle (B), and the Adjunct Island Condition (C). Huang's (1982) Condition on Extraction Domain (CED), which was an attempt to give a unified explanation of adjunct islands and subject islands—more generally, of noncomplements as islands—is also subsumed by this proposal.

Recently, it has been argued that adjunct islands and subject islands should not be unified (Stepanov 2001a; 2007). The most compelling reason for saying this is that there appear to be languages which allow extraction out of subjects, whereas the Adjunct Condition is universal.

In our present proposal here, we do not group together Subject and Adjunct. Instead, we group Subject with Topic and Focus. All three are known to be islands for extraction (Ross 1967; Lasnik and Saito 1992). Cf. (15), (16) and (17):

(15) *Subject Island*

a. [Which politician]$_i$ would the voters like [a picture of t_i]?
b. * [Which politician]$_i$ would [a picture of t_i] please the voters?

(16) *Topic Island*

a. I think (that) [a picture of Peter]$_i$ Mary would like t_i.
b. * Who$_j$ do you think (that) [a picture of t_j]$_i$ Mary would like t_i?

(17) *Focus Island*

a. It is [a picture of Peter]$_i$ that Mary wants t_i.
b. * Who$_j$ is it [a picture of t_j]$_i$ that Mary wants t_i?

What Subject, Topic, and Focus have in common is that they are all exemplars of an "edge property" (Chomsky 2008).[20] And what we have in the sentences exemplifying the Subject/Topic/Focus Condition is a "nested" structure as regards edge properties. Thus, in (15b), *a picture of which politician* is Subject, and *which politician* (a proper term) is [+WH].

Why is this "nesting" of edge properties problematic? A plausible reason is that this creates a difficulty of interpretation. While nothing prevents a phrase as a whole having two edge properties—thus a phrase can be both Subject and Topic, cf. *This book$_i$, I don't believe [t_i has been read t_i]*—the assignment of distinct edge properties to a phrase and a proper subpart of it appears to be difficult. Our claim (then) is that the problem here is one of the interpretational mechanisms of the grammar, and not something purely syntactic.

Coming to adjuncts, traditionally taken to be opaque domains for extraction, we may need to speak about different types of adjuncts (see Cattell 1976; Stepanov 2007 for a discussion). Thus, instrumental adverbials, which are thematically adjuncts, are transparent for subextraction (cf. *What did you break the glass with*?). So are infinitival adjuncts of purpose (cf. *Who did she come here to look for*?). But time/place adverbials and adverbials of cause are opaque (cf. * *Who did you see a snake near*?; * *Who did you arrive after*?; * *Who did she cry, because you hit*?). For our purposes, we don't need to investigate this question in any depth. (See Boeckx 2008: Sect. 1.3.2 for a wide-ranging discussion.) We can adopt any of the current proposals to explain the opacity of adjuncts, none of which conflicts with our basic proposal. Takahashi (1994) suggests that opaque adjuncts represent a kind of coordination structure. Another proposal is that adjuncts are late insertions: They are merged acyclically (or postcyclically); see Lebeaux (1988), Uriagereka (1999), Stepanov (2001a, b; 2007). Their late insertion could be the reason why adjuncts (or at least some types of adjuncts) cannot make available a proper term of it to the main derivation.[21] (However, as we shall see directly, the main derivation can make available a proper term of it to an adjunct.)

---

[20]Note that this would be a "third factor" explanation (in the sense of Chomsky 2005) of the opacity of adjuncts, unlike the bounding node idea.

[21]A traditional claim in the literature on parasitic gaps is that a parasitic gap cannot be inside an extraction island properly contained in an adjunct (or subject)—this was the main supporting evidence for an operator movement account of this phenomenon (Chomsky 1986). Cf.

(i) * Which book$_i$ did you like t_i [after meeting the man who wrote t_i]?

Parasitic Gaps

For any framework that assumes that movement begins from a position in the tree, the parasitic gap construction—illustrated in (18)—presents a problem:

(18) a. Which paper$_i$ did you read t_i [before filing t_i]?
b. Which politician$_i$ would [a picture of t_i] please t_i?

How can a chain have two base positions in the tree? Or if there are two chains, how do they "coalesce," such that there is only one chain-head? A natural solution—given this way of formulating the problem—was in terms of "chain-composition," which was proposed in Chomsky (1986). Another noteworthy attempt to solve the problem appeals to "across-the-board" movement (Williams 1990).

The solution that we find most interesting (and which is closest to our proposal) is one in terms of "sideward movement" (Nunes 2001; 2004; 2013; Nunes and Uriagereka 2000). The essential idea here is that an adjunct and the main derivation are built up simultaneously and "in parallel", and a phrase merged in the adjunct can be copied and merged in the main derivation. This "sideward movement" from one PS tree to another must be done (importantly) *before* the adjunct is merged with the main derivation; because when the adjunct is so merged, it has already been spelt-out and is now opaque to extraction (see our account of the Nunes–Uriagereka proposal in Section "Extraction Islands"). The new copy in the main derivation can be moved unproblematically—say, to Spec, CP. And the deletion of traces gives us the parasitic gap construction.

But the following sentence is equally bad although there is no extraction island inside the adjunct:

(ii) * Which book$_i$ did you like t_i [after your wife said that she liked t_i]?

A number of unclear factors seem to impinge on the acceptability of parasitic gaps. It is perhaps correct to say that a parasitic gap is "perfect" only when the adjunct that contains it is nonfinite and has a PRO-subject, or at least if the subject of the adjunct is the same as the subject of the main clause; cf.:

(iii) a. Which books$_i$ do you read t_i before buying t_i?
b. Which books$_i$ do you read t_i, before you buy t_i?
c. * Which books$_i$ do you read t_i, before your students buy t_i?

Consider the following example from Chomsky and Lasnik (1993) (cited by Nunes 2004: 115)

(iv) * The book was filed without my reading first.

Chomsky and Lasnik cite this sentence as evidence that a trace of A-movement cannot license a parasitic gap, but this cannot be the right explanation, cf. (v) which has an operator trace to license the parasitic gap:

(v) * Which book did you file without my reading first?

Nunes's explanation (ibid.) of (iv) is that *the book* in the subject position of the main clause and its copy in the object position of *reading* cannot form a chain "because of the intervention of *my*." This explanation might be on the right track, for it seems to me that the gradient judgments about parasitic gaps are due to factors of interpretation and not of phrasal movement per se.

From our new perspective in this chapter, we can see that the parasitic gap problem is an artifact of Internal Merge. If merge is from a parallel Work Space, we can say that a phrase that is present in a parallel Work Space can be merged in an adjunct as easily as in the main derivation. If adjuncts are built up late in the derivation, this makes a nice prediction: The arguments of the main derivation are already in place in parallel Work Spaces when the adjunct is being built up. Why is the gap in the adjunct "parasitic" on a gap in the main derivation? If the main derivation is already "completed" when the adjunct's derivation is attempted, a phrase built up in a parallel Work Space of the adjunct will be unable to merge into a matrix position. (The claim, in other words, is that it is the "timing difference" between the derivation of the matrix and the adjunct—the first completed before the second is begun—that is responsible for the one-way dependency: It is always an argument of the matrix that is "borrowed" by the adjunct, and not the other way round.)

Again, a subject island violation as in (18b) is not a problem at least for the syntax (although there could still be an interpretation problem): The subject argument can be "got ready" later than the object argument; the latter can be already present in a parallel Work Space, and it can be merged as a subphrase when the subject argument is being built up.

PIC, "Partial" Spell-Out of Phases, and Other Matters

The Phase Impenetrability Condition (PIC) is usually sought to be justified in terms of third factor considerations: At the end of a phase, the complement of the phase head is transferred to spell-out and semantic interpretation; after this, the derivation can "forget" this part of the structure, thereby reducing its memory burden. PIC also has another reason for its existence: It does half the work of implementing successive-cyclic movement, the other half being done by EPP. But in a system that dispenses with EPP and movement is "free" (Chomsky 2013),[22] PIC—as far as I can see—is left to shoulder the entire burden of successive-cyclic movement.

We should bear in mind that PIC is predicated on a close identification of spell-out and Pronunciation. This identification itself is very clear; e.g., consider Chomsky's (2004) suggestion that movement can be ordered before or after spell-out and that the ordering gives us overt or covert movement. The idea is that if α has not moved at the time of spell-out, there is only one copy of α, and so this copy is spelt-out—and therefore pronounced. But if α has moved, there are two copies of α, and the lower copy is not spelt-out—and therefore not pronounced. (Chomsky 1995: 228 says that it is marked as "invisible at the interface.") This assumes that what is spelt-out must be pronounced, and what is pronounced has

[22]See also Epstein et al. (2014) for a discussion of this new conception of remerge, which the authors call "simplest Merge."

been earlier spelt-out. Also note that the "deletion" of traces is done—or at least determined—by spell-out, at the level of the phase.

This identification of spell-out and Pronunciation has many disadvantages. One problem is that there is also discourse-dependent deletion, e.g., VP-deletion, and obviously, spell-out cannot do this deletion. So in the current theory, trace deletion and discourse-dependent deletion cannot be unified.

But of course it could be argued that discourse-dependent deletion is another *type* of deletion and should not be unified with trace deletion. While this is plausible enough, note that phase-wise deletion of traces is problematic in itself: It gives rise to "look ahead" in the multiple *wh*-construction in English. Consider (19):

(19)
a. Who(m)$_i$ does John think that he is in love with t_i?
b. Who thinks that he is in love with whom?

In (19b), *whom* should not start to move to Spec, vP in the embedded vP-phase; but this decision is dependent on whether or not there is another *wh*-phrase merged in the higher vP-phase.

Let us say (instead) that all copies of a phrase are spelt-out (Bobaljik 2002, a.o.). And that deletion is done by Pronunciation—late in the derivation. This enables us to unify the two kinds of deletion and to avoid the look-ahead problem. Adapting this proposal to systems (like ours) that assume multi-dominance—i.e., the idea that a phrase can have many mother nodes—is straightforward: We can say that a phrase can be pronounced under any of its mother nodes, the choice of the mother node being a late decision.

This way of looking at things naturally gets rid of the old "escape hatch" idea (Chomsky 1973), which has its latest implementation as the "partial" spell-out of phases. Much dissatisfaction has been felt about this last-mentioned idea, cf. Boeckx and Grohmann (2007), Richards (2011).

But let us ask the question: Can the economy argument for phases still be retained? I believe it can. We suggested (in Section "The Proposal") that a phrase is already interpreted—and let us now say, spelt-out—in the parallel Work Space where it is built up. Let us say that in the main derivation, each phase (similarly) is interpreted and spelt-out, as and when it is completed.

References

Adger, D. 2012. *A Syntax of Substance*. Linguistic Inquiry Monograph, 64. Cambridge, MA: The MIT Press.
Bobaljik, J. 2002. A-chains at the PF-interface: Copies and 'covert' movement. *Natural Language and Linguistic Theory* 20 (2): 197–267.
Boeckx, C. 2008. *Bare Syntax*. Oxford: Oxford University Press.
Boeckx, C., and K. Grohmann. 2007. Putting phases in perspective. *Syntax* 10: 204–222.
Cable, S. 2010. Against the existence of pied-piping. *Linguistic Inquiry* 41: 553–594.
Cattell, R. 1976. Constraints on movement rules. *Language* 52: 18–50.
Chomsky, N. 2013. Problems of projection. *Lingua* 130: 33–49.

Chomsky, N. 2008. On phases. In *Foundational issues in linguistic theory*, ed. R. Freidin, C. P. Otero, and M.L. Zubizarreta, 133–166. Cambridge, MA: MIT Press.
Chomsky, N. 2005. Three factors in language design. *Linguistic Inquiry* 36: 1–22.
Chomsky, N. 2004. Beyond explanatory adequacy. In *Structures and beyond: The cartography of syntactic structures*, ed. A. Belletti, 104–131. Oxford: Oxford University Press.
Chomsky, N. 2003. Replies. In *Chomsky and His Critics*, ed. Louise M. Antony, and Norbert Hornstein, 255–328. Oxford: Blackwell.
Chomsky, N. 2001. Derivation by phase. In *Ken Hale: A Life in Language*, ed. M. Kenstowicz, 1–52. Cambridge, MA: MIT Press.
Chomsky, N. 2000. Minimalist inquiries: The framework. In *Step by Step*, ed. R. Martin, D. Michaels and J. Uriagereka, 89–155. Cambridge, MA: MIT Press.
Chomsky, N. 1995. Categories and transformations. In *The Minimalist Program*, ed. N. Chomsky, 219–394. Cambridge, MA: MIT Press.
Chomsky, N. 1986. *Barriers*. Cambridge, MA: MIT Press.
Chomsky, N. 1973. Conditions on transformations. In *A Festschrift for Morris Halle*, ed. S. Anderson & P. Kiparsky, 232–286. New York: Holt, Rinehalt, and Winston.
Chomsky, N., and H. Lasnik. 1993. The theory of principles and parameters. In *Syntax: An international handbook of contemporary research*, ed. J. Jacobs, A. von Stechow, W. Sternefeld, and T. Vennemann, 506–569. Berlin: Walter de Gruyter.
Collins, C. 2002. Eliminating labels. In *Derivation and explanation in the minimalist program*, ed. S.D. Epstein, and T.D. Seely, 42–64. Oxford: Blackwell.
de Vries, M. 2013. Unconventional mergers. In *Ways of structure building*, ed. Myriam Uribe-Etxebarria, and Vidal Valmala, 143–166. Oxford: Oxford University Press.
de Vries, M. 2005. Possessive relatives and (heavy) pied-piping. *Journal of Comparative Germanic Linguistics* 9: 1–52.
Epstein, S.D., H. Kitahara, and T.D. Seely. 2014. Labeling by minimal search: Implications for successive-cyclic A-movement and the conception of the postulate 'phase'. *Linguistic Inquiry* 45 (3): 463–481.
Epstein, S.D. 1999. Un-principled syntax: The derivation of syntactic relations. In *Working Minimalism*, ed. S. D. Epstein and N. Hornstein. Cambridge, MA: The MIT Press.
Grimshaw, J. 2000. Locality and extended projection. In *Lexical specification and insertion*, ed. P. Coopmans, M. Everaert, and J. Grimshaw, 115–133. Amsterdam: John Benjamins.
Heck, F. 2009. On certain properties of pied-piping. *Linguistic Inquiry* 40: 75–111.
Horvath, J. 2007. Pied-piping. In *The Blackwell syntax companion*, ed. M. Everaert, and H. van Riemsdijk, 569–630. Oxford: Blackwell.
Huang, C-T.J. 1982. *Logical relations in Chinese and the theory of grammar*. Doctoral dissertation, MIT, Cambridge, MA.
Jayaseelan, K.A. 2010a. Stacking, stranding and pied-piping: A proposal about word order. *Syntax* 13:4, 298–330.
Jayaseelan, K.A. 2010b. On two types of movements. Paper Presented at GLOW-in-Asia VIII, Beijing Language and Culture University, August 12–14, 2010.
Jayaseelan, K.A. 2008. Bare phrase structure and specifier-less syntax. *Biolinguistics* 2 (1): 87–106.
Jayaseelan, K.A. 2001. IP-internal topic and focus phrases. *Studia Linguistica* 55 (1): 39–75.
Kayne, R. 1998. Overt vs. covert movement. *Syntax* 1: 128–191.
Koster, J. 2007. Structure preservingness, internal merge, and the strict locality of triads. In *Phrasal and Clausal Architecture: Syntactic Derivation and Interpretation* (Linguistik Aktuell/Linguistics Today 101), ed. Simin Karimi, Vida Samiian and Wendy K. Wilkins, 188–205. Amsterdam: John Benjamins.
Lasnik, H., and M. Saito. 1992. *Move α*. Cambridge, MA: MIT Press.
Lebeaux, D. 1988. *Language Acquisition and the Form of the Grammar*. Doctoral dissertation, University of Massachusetts, Amherst.
Müller, G. 2000. Shape conservation and remnant movement. In *Proceedings of NELS 30*, ed. M. Hirotani, A. Coetzee, N. Hall, and J.-Y. Kim, 525–539. Amherst, MA: GLSA Publications.

Nunes, J. 2013. Sideward movement: Triggers, timing, and outputs. In *Ways of Structure Building*, ed. Myriam Uribe-Etxebarria and Vidal Valmala, 114–142.
Nunes, J. 2004. *Linearization of Chains and Sideward Movement*. Cambridge, MA: MIT Press.
Nunes, J. 2001. Sideward movement. *Linguistic Inquiry* 32: 303–344.
Nunes, J. and J. Uriagereka. 2000. Cyclicity and extraction domains. *Syntax* 3: 20–43. Oxford: Oxford University Press.
Ortiz de Urbina, J. 1990. Operator feature percolation and clausal pied-piping. In *MIT Working Papers, vol. 13: Papers on Wh-Movement*, ed. L. Cheng and H. Demirdash, 193–208.
Phillips, C. 2003. Linear order and constituency. *Linguistic Inquiry* 34: 37–90.
Putnam, M., and T. Stroik. 2010. Syntactic relations in survive-minimalism. In *Exploring crash-proof grammars*, ed. M. Putnam, 143–166. Amsterdam: John Benjamins.
Richards, M. 2011. Deriving the edge: What's in a phase? *Syntax* 14: 74–95.
Rizzi, L. 2005. On some properties of subjects and topics. In *Contributions to the thirtieth "Incontro di Grammatica Generativa"*, ed. L. Brugé, G. Giusti, N. Munaro, W. Schweikert, G. Turano, 203–224. Università Ca' Foscari Vanezia.
Ross, J.R. 1967. *Constraints on variables in syntax*. Doctoral dissertation, Cambridge, MA: MIT Press.
Starke, M. 2004. On the inexistence of specifiers and the nature of heads. In *The Cartography of Syntactic Structures*, vol. 3: Structures and Beyond (Oxford Studies in Comparative Syntax), ed. A. Belletti, 252–268. New York: Oxford University Press.
Stepanov, A. 2007. The end of CED? Minimalism and extraction domains. *Syntax* 10 (1): 80–126.
Stepanov, A. 2001a. *Cyclic domains in syntactic theory*. Ph.D. dissertation, University of Connecticut, Storrs.
Stepanov, A. 2001b. Late adjunction and minimalist phrase structure. *Syntax* 4: 94–125.
Stjepanović, S., and S. Takahashi. 2001. Eliminating the phase impenetrability condition. Paper Presented at the Workshop on 'Motivating Movement: Explaining the Displacement Property of Natural Language'. University of Ulster.
Stroik, T.S. 2009. *Locality in minimalist syntax*. Cambridge, MA: MIT Press.
Stroik, T.S. 1999. The survive principle. *Linguistic Analysis* 29: 278–303.
Takahashi, D. 1994. Minimality of Movement. Doctoral dissertation, University of Connecticut.
Uriagereka, J. 1999. Multiple spell-out. In *Working Minimalism*, ed. S.D. Epstein and N. Hornstein, 251–82. Cambridge, MA: The MIT Press.
Webelhuth, G. 1992. *Principles and parameters of syntactic saturation*. Oxford: Oxford University Press.
Williams, E. 1990. The ATB theory of parasitic gaps. *The Linguistic Review* 6: 265–279.

Part II
Architecture of Syntax: Focus and the VP domain

Chapter 6
Argument Doubling in Japanese with VP-Internal Focus

Mamoru Saito

Introduction

This chapter consists of two notes on Japanese sentences with argument doubling. The following example is from Kuroda (1988), which considered those sentences in depth for the first time:

(1) [$_{CP}$ Masao-ga Hanako-o but-ta no]-wa hoho(-o) da
Masao-NOM Hanako-ACC hit-Past COMP-TOP cheek-ACC is
'It is on the cheek that Masao hit Hanako'

The simple sentence corresponding to this cleft example is as in (2) and is ungrammatical.

(2) *Masao-ga Hanako-o hoho-o but-ta
Masao-NOM Hanako-ACC cheek-ACC hit-Past
'Masao hit Hanako on the cheek'

But Kuroda argues that this is because of a surface constraint that prohibits two accusative (or dative) phrases in a simple sentence, and that the grammaticality of (1) demonstrates that (2) is allowed when we abstract away from this surface constraint. He points out further that both *Hanako* and *hoho* "cheek" receive the

I am happy to contribute this paper to the volume in honor of Prof. Amritavalli, who has been a wonderful leader and has provided constant inspiration to the younger scholars in the linguistic community in Asia.

M. Saito (✉)
Nanzan University, Nagoya, Japan
e-mail: saito@nanzan-u.ac.jp

G. Sengupta et al. (eds.), *Perspectives on the Architecture and Acquisition of Syntax*, DOI 10.1007/978-981-10-4295-9_6

theme role from the verb *but* "hit" in (1). This raises doubts on the θ-criterion, which implies that a θ-role is assigned to one and only one argument.

Building on Kuroda's insights, I argue in the first note that examples of this kind are found extensively in Japanese and provide solid evidence against the θ-criterion. In the second note, I suggest that in examples like (1)–(2), one of the accusative arguments is construed as a focus and the other serves to specify the set of alternatives for the focus, in the sense of Rooth (1992). Before I present the two notes, I briefly compare examples like (1) with the more widely discussed multiple nominative and multiple accusative sentences so that their special properties become clear.

A Comparison with Major Subjects and Accusative Adverbials

It is well known that Japanese allows multiple subject sentences. A celebrated example from Kuno (1973) is shown in (3).

(3) [$_{TP}$ Bunmeikoku-ga [$_{TP}$ dansei-ga [$_{TP}$ heikin-zyumyoo-ga mizika-i]]]
civilized.country-NOM male-NOM average-life.span-NOM short-Pres.
'It is in civilized countries that the male population has a short life-span'

In this type of examples, the lowest nominative phrase is interpreted as the subject of the predicate. What is short is the average life span and not civilized countries or their male population. The higher subjects, which Kuroda calls major subjects, are in some sort of predication relation with their sister TPs.[1]

Multiple accusative sentences like (4) have also been widely discussed since Harada (1973) and Kuroda (1978).

(4) ??Hanako-ga gakusei-o san-nin hamabe-o hasir-ase-ta
Hanako-NOM student-ACC three-CL beach-ACC run-make-Past
'Hanako made three students run on the beach'

The example is marginal due to the ban on multiple accusative phrases mentioned above. (5a, b), where one of the accusative phrases is dislocated, are perfect.

[1]When the matrix predicate is individual level, the sentence-initial nominative phrase is interpreted as the focus, as shown in the translation of (3). This holds for the subsequent examples although I do not always indicate this in the translations. See Kuno (1973) and Heycock (2008) for detailed discussion on this interpretive property of matrix sentences with individual-level predicates.

(5) a. [$_{CP}$ Hanako-ga gakusei-o san-nin hasir-ase-ta no]-wa hamabe-o da
Hanako-NOM student-ACC three-CL run-make-Past COMP-TOP beach-ACC is
'It is on the beach that Hanako made three students run'

b. [$_{CP}$ Hanako-ga hamabe-o hasir-ase-ta no]-wa gakuse-o san-nin da
Hanako-NOM beach-ACC run-make-Past COMP-TOP student-ACC three-CL is
'It is three students that Hanako made run on the beach'

In (4), *gakusei-o* "student-ACC" is the causee argument, whereas *hamabe-o* "beach-ACC" expresses a location or a path. Hence, the example is consistent with the θ-criterion.

The situation is different with (1), repeated below as (6).

(6) [$_{CP}$ Masao-ga Hanako-o but-ta no]-wa hoho(-o) da
Masao-NOM Hanako-ACC hit-Past COMP-TOP cheek-ACC is
'It is on the cheek that Masao hit Hanako'

Kuroda (1988) argues that the two accusative phrases in this example receive the same θ-role from the verb. (6) says that Masao hit Hanako, and more specifically, her cheek. Kuroda confirms this with the ungrammaticality of (7).

(7) *[$_{CP}$ Masao-ga Hanako-o ot-ta no]-wa yubi-o ni-hon da
Masao-NOM Hanako-ACC break-Past COMP-TOP finger-ACC two-CL is
'It is on the cheek that Masao hit Hanako'

This example is ungrammatical because one can break fingers but not a person as shown in (8a, b).

(8) a. Masao-ga Hanako-no yubi-o ni-hon ot-ta
Masao-NOM Hanako-GEN finger-ACC two-CL break-Past
'Masao broke two of Hanako's fingers'

b. *Masao-ga Hanako-o ot-ta
Masao-NOM Hanako-ACC break-Past
'Masao broke Hanako'

Then, the verb *but* "hit" in (6) assigns the theme role to both *Hanako* and *hoho* "cheek" in violation of the θ-criterion. In the following section, I demonstrate that this kind of argument doubling is widely observed in Japanese.

Argument Doubling as a General Phenomenon

It should be noted first that Kuroda (1988) already presents an example similar to (6) with two dative arguments. It is shown in (9).

(9) [$_{CP}$ Masao-ga Hanako-ni kisusi-ta no]-wa hoho-ni da
Masao-NOM Hanako-DAT kiss-Past COMP-TOP cheek-DAT is
'It is on the cheek that Masao kissed Hanako'

In this example, *Hanako* and *hoho* "cheek" are both thematic arguments of *kisus* "kiss." This can be confirmed with the following contrast:

(10) a. [$_{TP}$ Taroo-ga [$_{TP}$ musume-ga totemo kasiko-i]]
Taroo-NOM daughter-NOM very wise-Pres.
'Taroo is such that his daughter is very wise'

b.*[$_{CP}$ Masao-ga Taroo-ni kisusi-ta no]-wa musume-ni da
Masao-NOM Taroo-DAT kiss-Past COMP-TOP daughter-DAT is
'*Lit.*: It is on his daughter that Masao kissed Taroo'

(10a) is a typical example of the major subject construction. It says that Taroo's daughter is wise (or more precisely, Taroo is such that his daughter is wise), but does not imply that Taroo is. The discourse can continue with the utterance "But Taroo himself isn't wise at all" without any contradiction. On the other hand, (10b) makes sense only if kissing Taroo's daughter automatically means kissing Taroo, which is not true.

This kind of argument doubling is observed not only with accusative and dative arguments but with PPs as well. A relevant example is shown in (11).

(11) a. ??Nihon-kara Hirosima-kara(-dake) sankasya-ga at-ta
Japan-from Hiroshima-from-only participant-NOM be-Past
'*Lit.*: There were participants only from Hiroshima from Japan'

b. [$_{CP}$ Nihon-kara sankasya-ga at-ta no]-wa Hirosima-kara(-dake) da
Japan-from participant-NOM be-Past COMP-TOP Hiroshima-from-only is
'*Lit.*: It is (only) from Hiroshima that there were participants from Japan'

(11b) is fine, although the source argument is doubled in the example.[2] The examples in (12) point to the same conclusion.

---

[2]The degraded status of (11a) indicates that there is a surface constraint against multiple occurrences of a postposition in a simple sentence, similar to the ban on multiple accusative and multiple dative phrases. I return to this in the following section.

(12) a. *Hanako-ga Yooroppa-e Doitu-e san-kai(-dake) it-ta
Hanako-NOM Europe-to Germany-to three-CL-only go-Past
'*Lit.*: Hanako went only to Germany three times to Europe'

b. [CP Hanako-ga Yooroppa-e it-ta no]-wa Doitu-e san-kai(-dake) da
Hanako-NOM Europe-to go-Past COMP-TOP Germany-to three-CL-only is
'*Lit.*: It is (only) three times to Germany that Hanako went to Europe'

In (12b), the goal argument is doubled, but the sentence is perfectly grammatical. In addition, there is evidence that the external agent argument can also be doubled. Let us first consider the following examples with major subjects:

(13) a. [TP Taroo-ga [TP musume-ga hito-ri(-dake) totemo kasiko-i]]
Taroo-NOM daughter-NOM one-CL-only very wise-Pres.
'Taroo is such that only one of his daughters is very wise'

b. ??[TP Taroo-ga [TP musume-ga hito-ri(-dake) sono kaigi-de hatugensi-ta]]
Taroo-NOM daughter-NOM one-CL-only that meeting-in speak.up-Past
'Taroo is such that (only) one of his daughters spoke up in the meeting'

As Kuno (1973) observes the major subject construction is most natural with an individual-level predicate, as the inner TP describes a property attributed to the major subject. Thus, (13b) is degraded compared with (13a). Further, a lower subject cannot be dislocated to a position above a higher subject in this construction. (14) is totally ungrammatical.

(14) *[CP Taroo-ga totemo kasiko-i no]-wa musume-ga hito-ri(-dake) da
Taroo-NOM very wise-Pres. COMP-TOP daughter-NOM one-CL-only is
'*Lit.*: It is (only) one of his daughers that Taroo is very wise' (cf. (13a))

Let us now consider (15) in the light of this background.

(15) a. ?*Gakusei-ga itinensei-ga san-nin(-dake) sono kaigi-de hatugensi-ta
student-NOM freshman-NOM three-CL-only that meeting-in speak.up-Past
'*Lit.*: The students are such that only three freshmen spoke up in the meeting'

b. [CP Gakusei-ga sono kaigi-de hatugensi-ta no]-wa itinensei-ga
student-NOM that meeting-in speak.up-Past COMP-TOP freshman-NOM
san-nin(-dake) da
three-CL-only is
'*Lit.*: It is (only) three freshmen that students spoke up in the meeting'

(15a) is degraded. When interpretation is forced, it sounds like a major subject sentence with a wrong kind of predicate. On the other hand, (15b) is fine. This cleft example cannot be derived from a major subject sentence by placing *itinensei-ga san-nin(-dake)* "freshman-NOM three-CL(-only)" in the focus position. (14) shows that it would result in total ungrammaticality. Then, why is (15b) grammatical?

There is one outstanding difference between (13a) and (15a). The former does not say that Taroo is smart, as mentioned. On the other hand, (15a) implies that students spoke up in the meeting. Thus, (15a) need not be a regular major subject sentence but can be an instance of thematic subject doubling. The example is degraded even under this reading because it is a simple sentence containing two thematic nominative arguments. But this surface effect is avoided when one of the nominative arguments is displaced as in (15b). If this analysis is correct, then (15b) shows that an agentive subject can also be doubled in Japanese.

In this section, I argued, building on Kuroda's (1988) lead, that any thematic argument can be doubled in Japanese. This demonstrates that the θ-criterion should be eliminated as a verb can assign the same θ-role to more than one argument quite generally.[3] One question that remains is why (13a), for example, cannot be construed as an example of thematic subject doubling. If it could be, (14) should be grammatical. I simply stated above that the example does not convey that Taroo is very smart, and hence, must be an instance of the major subject construction. But the fact indicates that there is a restriction on argument doubling that forces the major subject interpretation of (13a). I turn to this in the following section.

Argument Doubling as a Focus Construction

The following simple examples show that argument doubling is not quite free:

(16) a. *Hanako-ga Taroo-o gakusei-o san-nin sikat-ta
Hanako-NOM Taroo-ACC student-ACC three-CL scold-Past
'*Intended*: Hanako scolded Taroo and three students'

b. *[$_{CP}$ Hanako-ga Taroo-o sikat-ta no]-wa gakusei-o san-nin da
Hanako-NOM Taroo-ACC scold-Past COMP-TOP student-ACC three-CL is
'*Lit.*: It is three students that Hanako scolded Taroo'

[3]This raises the question why argument doubling does not obtain in many languages, including English. Although I do not discuss this question in this chapter, a possible answer is given in Saito (2014). There, I mainly consider the major subject construction and argue that the labeling algorithm, in the sense of Chomsky (2013), accounts for why it is possible in Japanese and not in English. As far as I can see, the account extends to the cases of argument doubling discussed in this chapter.

Then, what makes the grammatical examples of argument doubling possible? I consider this question in this section.

Kuroda's (1988) examples in (6) and (9), repeated below as (17a) and (17b), suggest that the doubled arguments should have a whole-part relation with body parts.

(17) a. [$_{CP}$ Masao-ga Hanako-o but-ta no]-wa hoho(-o) da
Masao-NOM Hanako-ACC hit-Past COMP-TOP cheek-ACC is
'It is on the cheek that Masao hit Hanako'

b. [$_{CP}$ Masao-ga Hanako-ni kisusi-ta no]-wa hoho-ni da
Masao-NOM Hanako-DAT kiss-Past COMP-TOP cheek-DAT is
'It is on the cheek that Masao kissed Hanako'

However, the other examples discussed above show that the requirement is not so specific. (11b), repeated below as (18), has nothing to do with body parts.

(18) [$_{CP}$ Nihon-kara sankasya-ga at-ta no]-wa Hirosima-kara(-dake) da
Japan-from participant-NOM be-Past COMP-TOP Hiroshima-from-only is
'*Lit.*: It is (only) from Hiroshima that there were participants from Japan'

Another relevant example is shown in (19).

(19) a. ?*Hanako-ga kudamono-o ringo-o hito-tu tabe-ta
Hanako-NOM fruit-ACC apple-ACC one-CL eat-Past
'Hanako ate fruits, and it was an apple'

b. [$_{CP}$ Hanako-ga kudamono-o tabe-ta no]-wa ringo-o hito-tu(-dake) da
Hanako-NOM fruit-ACC eat-Past COMP-TOP apple-ACC one-CL-only is
'*Lit.*: It is only one apple that Hanako ate fruits'

Let us first look into the properties of (19) to see what sort of relation is required between the two accusative theme objects. First, the example clearly implies that Hanako ate fruits and that Hanako ate an apple. Thus, the two accusative arguments both receive the theme role from the verb *tabe* "eat," as Kuroda observed. Secondly, (19a) improves as focus is placed on the second accusative argument. (20) with the focus particle *-dake* "only" on this argument is already better than (19a).

(20) ??Hanako-ga kudamono-o ringo-o hito-tu-dake tabe-ta
Hanako-NOM fruit-ACC apple-ACC one-CL-only eat-Past
'Hanako ate fruits, but what she ate was only one apple'

And when the argument is placed in the focus position of a cleft sentence, the example becomes perfect as (19b) shows.

A similar effect can be achieved by making the first argument a topic. Thus, (21b) is far better than (21a).[4]

(21) a. *Hanako-ga Yooroppa-e Doitu-e san-kai it-ta
Hanako-NOM Europe-to Germany-to three-CL go-Past
'*Lit.*: Hanako went to Germany three times to Europe'

b. ?Yooroppa-e-wa Hanako-ga Doitu-e san-kai it-ta
Europe-to-TOP Hanako-NOM Germany-to three-CL go-Past
'*Lit.*: To Europe, Hanako went to Germany three times'

Then, argument doubling seems to require that the second argument be a focus. This descriptive conclusion is confirmed further by the fact that the first argument cannot be placed in focus. (22a) is totally ungrammatical in clear contrast with (12b), repeated in (22b).

(22) a. *[$_{CP}$ Hanako-ga Doitu-e san-kai it-ta no]-wa Yooroppa-e da
Hanako-NOM Germany-to three-CL go-Past COMP-TOP Europe-to is
'*Lit.*: It is to Europe that Hanako went to Germany three times'

b. [$_{CP}$ Hanako-ga Yooroppa-e it-ta no]-wa Doitu-e san-kai(-dake) da
Hanako-NOM Europe-to go-Past COMP-TOP Germany-to three-CL-only is
'*Lit.*: It is (only) three times to Germany that Hanako went to Europe'

Given this, I suggest in the remainder of this section that the first argument in argument doubling must serve to specify the set of alternatives for the focus, in the sense of Rooth (1992). Rooth proposes that a focus generates a set of alternatives. Let us consider (23) for an illustration.

(23) a. John saw MARY
b. {Bill, Susan, Mary, ...}
c. {John saw Bill, John saw Susan, John saw Mary, ...}

(23a) places focus on *Mary*. (23b) is the set of alternatives for *Mary*, that is, the set of people that John could see. Then, roughly speaking, (23a) asserts that 'John saw Mary' is the true sentence among those in the set (23c). Consequently, it is interpreted as "It is Mary that John saw." Rooth assumes that the set of alternatives that a focus generates is determined by the context.

This analysis of focus provides an insight into the interpretation of (19b), repeated in (24a).

---

[4]An example of PP doubling is employed here because an NP topic may be licensed by the "aboutness" relation as Kuno (1973) demonstrates, and hence, it is not clear that it participates in argument doubling.

(24) a. [CP Hanako-ga kudamono-o tabe-ta no]-wa ringo-o hito-tu(-dake) da
Hanako-NOM fruit-ACC eat-Past COMP-TOP apple-ACC one-CL-only is
'*Lit.*: It is only one apple that Hanako ate fruits'

b. [CP Hanako-ga tabe-ta no]-wa ringo-o hito-tu(-dake) da
Hanako-NOM eat-Past COMP-TOP apple-ACC one-CL-only is
'*Lit.*: It is only one apple that Hanako ate fruits'

This example states that an apple is the only fruit that Hanako ate. In particular, it does not mean that an apple is the only thing that Hanako ate. She could have eaten some vegetables and meat in addition. The interpretation absent with (24a) obtains when the first accusative argument *kudamono-o* "fruit-ACC" is missing as in (24b). Then, this accusative argument serves in (24a) to restrict the set of alternatives to fruits as in (25).

(25) {one orange, two bananas, five peaches, one banana, one apple, ...}

(24a) indeed means that it is only *one apple* among the members of the set in (25) that Hanako ate.

Recall that *kudamono-o* "fruit-ACC" in (24a) is interpreted as a theme. So, the sentence implies (26).

(26) Hanako-ga kudamono-o tabe-ta
Hanako-NOM fruit-ACC eat-Past
'Hanako ate fruits'

At the same time, this accusative argument specifies the set of alternatives for the second accusative object. Then, it is only natural that it is indefinite. If it were "all fruits," for example, it could still specify the set of alternatives, but would lead to a contradiction because the sentence would imply that Hanako ate all fruits, not just an apple.

This analysis is still at an informal stage, but extends to the other examples discussed so far. Let us consider again Kuroda's (1988) (17b), repeated in (27).

(27) [CP Masao-ga Hanako-ni kisusi-ta no]-wa hoho-ni da
Masao-NOM Hanako-DAT kiss-Past COMP-TOP cheek-DAT is
'It is on the cheek that Masao kissed Hanako'

Hanako here can be construed as "Hanako's body parts." Then, it specifies the set in (28).

(28) {Hanako's hand, Hanako's head, Hanako's cheek, ...}

The example states that it is *Hanako's cheek* among the members of the set in (28) that Masao kissed. The ungrammaticality of (16b), repeated below as (29), is also expected under this analysis.

(29) *[$_{CP}$ Hanako-ga Taroo-o sikat-ta no]-wa gakusei-o san-nin da
Hanako-NOM Taroo-ACC scold-Past COMP-TOP student-ACC three-CL is
'*Lit.*: It is three students that Hanako scolded Taroo'

Taroo-o "Taroo-ACC" simply fails to specify the set of alternatives for *gakusei-o sann-nin* "three students."

I suggested in this section that in argument doubling, the second argument must be a focus and the first must serve to specify its set of alternatives. This provides a partial answer for why good examples of argument doubling involve the dislocation of one of them. The dislocation must help establish the required relation between the two arguments by putting the second in focus. Before I close this section, I would like to briefly speculate on why this specific relation is required between doubled arguments.

The main conclusion of Section "Argument Doubling as a General Phenomenon" was that a verb can assign a single θ-role to two arguments. This implies that an argument need not have a unique role in the predicate argument structure. When it is interpreted as the theme, for example, there may be another theme argument in the sentence. However, the informal analysis in this section suggests that each argument must have a unique role in the wider semantic interpretation. In (27), *hoho-ni* "cheek-DAT" shares the θ-role with *Hanako-ni*, but is unique as a focus. *Hanako-ni*, on the other hand, has the unique role of specifying the set of alternatives for the focus. Although this is merely a speculation at this point, a version of the θ-criterion that is generalized beyond thematic roles may be at work as part of Full Interpretation.

Conclusion

In this chapter, I examined argument doubling in Japanese, extending Kuroda's (1988) observations. I argued that the phenomenon is quite general and provides solid evidence against the θ-criterion. At the same time, I arrived at the conclusion that argument doubling requires one of the arguments to be a focus and the other to specify the set of alternatives for the focus. I speculated at the end that although the θ-criterion seems untenable, there may be a more general requirement that each argument plays a unique role in semantic interpretation.

References

Chomsky, N. 2013. Problems of projection. *Lingua* 130: 33–49.

Harada, S.-I. 1973. Counter equi NP deletion. *Annual bulletin* 7: 113–147. Research Laboratory of Logopedics and Phoniatrics, University of Tokyo.

Heycock, C. 2008. Japanese -wa, -ga and Information Structure. In *The oxford handbook of Japanese linguistics*, ed. Shigeru Miyagawa, and Mamoru Saito, 54–83. New York: Oxford University Press.

Kuno, S. 1973. *The structure of the Japanese language*. Cambridge, Mass.: MIT Press.

Kuroda, S.-Y. 1988. Whether we agree or not: A comparative syntax of english and Japanese. *Linguisticae Investigationes* 12: 1–47.

Kuroda, S.-Y. 1978. Case-marking, canonical sentence patterns and counter equi in Japanese. In *Problems in Japanese syntax and semantics*, ed. John Hinds, and Irwin Howard, 30–51. Kaitakusha: Tokyo.

Rooth, M. 1992. A theory of focus interpretation. *Natural language semantics* 1: 75–116.

Saito, M. 2014. Case and labeling in a language without φ-feature agreement. In *On Peripheries*, ed. Anna Cardinaletti, Guglielmo Cinque, and Yoshio Endo, 269–297. Hituzi Syobo: Tokyo.

Chapter 7
Self and *Only*: A Comparative Study of Reflexive Adverbials in Squliq Atayal and Mandarin Chinese

Wei-Tien Dylan Tsai

The Puzzle

In Squliq Atayal, an Austronesian language spoken in the central part of Taiwan, there is a rather peculiar modifier-like expression, i.e., *nanak*, that can be construed either as a focus adverb, as exemplified by (1a, b), or as an adnominal reflexive, as exemplified by (2a, b):

(1) a. yaqih   na-Temu   **nanak**   qu-Tali.
NAV.hate   Obl-Temu   only   Nom-Tali
'Only Temu hates Tali'

b. yaqih   **nanak**   na-Temu   qu-Tali.
NAV.hate   only   Obl-Temu   Nom-Tali
'Only Temu hatesTali'

(2) a. yaqih   na-Temu   qu-hiya-**nanak**.
NAV.hate   Obl-Temu   Nom-3S-self
'Temu hates himself'

b. nyux   m-lahang   squ-hiya-**nanak**   qu-Temu.
Prg   AV-protect   Dat-3S-self   Nom-Temu
'Temu is protecting himself'

This chapter is a tribute to Professor Amritavalli for her dedication to our cause over the years. I am grateful for the help and comments from Lisa Cheng, Sihwei Chen, Gennaro Chierchia, Daniel Hole, Chris Hsieh, James Huang, Jennifer Huang, Audrey Li, and Tanya Reinhart. The research leading to this article is funded by the National Science Council of Taiwan (NSC 89-2411-H-007-045, NSC 94-2411-H-007-020, and NSC 96-2411-H-007-026).

W.-T.D. Tsai (✉)
National Tsing Hua University, Hsinchu, Taiwan
e-mail: wttsai@mx.nthu.edu.tw

G. Sengupta et al. (eds.), *Perspectives on the Architecture and Acquisition of Syntax*, DOI 10.1007/978-981-10-4295-9_7

The adverbial *nanak* very often gets an exclusive reading, akin to *only* in English (Kiss 1998), and its distribution is relatively free. By contrast, when attached to an argument, *nanak* has a much more restricted distribution, and its reading is distinctively reflexive, very much like *-self* in English. Interestingly enough, there is also a gray area between the two construals, where *nanak* occupies an adjunct position, while sporting a variety of reflexive and contrastive readings, as illustrated below:[1]

(3) a. s<m>oya **nanak** m-aniq siam qu-Tali.
AV-like self AV-eat pork Nom-Tali
'Tali ate the pork out of his own liking. (Don't blame the others!)'

b. s<m>oya m-aniq **nanak** siam qu-Tali.
AV-like AV-eat self pork Nom-Tali
'Tali likes to eat pork alone. (So don't disturb him!)'

c. s<m>oya m-aniq siam **nanak** qu-Tali.
AV-like AV-eat pork self Nom-Tali
'Tali likes to eat the pork in private. (He won't share it with others)'

This chapter proposes to investigate the peculiar syntax and semantics of *nanak* in a cross-linguistic context. Our inquiry is twofold: The first part is to deal with the issue whether there is a conceptual connection between *self* and *only*, especially in view of a strong resemblance from *ziji* "self" in Mandarin Chinese, which behaves very much like an intensifier before negation, as in (4a), while serving as a reflexive adverbial after negation, as in (4b).

(4) a. Akiu **ziji** bu kai zhe-bu che. ta dou jiegei bieren kai.
Akiu self not drive this-CL car he all lend others drive
'Akiu himself does not drive this car. He always lends it to others'

b. Akiu bu **ziji** kai zhe-bu che. you yi-ge siji bang ta kai.
Akiu not self drive this-CL car have one-CL chauffeur help him drive
'Akiu does not drive this car in person. There is a chauffeur driving for him'

The typological comparison is done in Sections "The Delimiting Factors" and "Adverbial Self in Comparative Perspective". The second part of our inquiry is to

[1]The abbreviations used in this paper are glossed as follows: Acc: accusative case; AV: agent/actor voice; CL: classifier; Inc: inchoative aspect; Nom: nominative case; Obl: oblique case; Prf: perfective aspect; Prg: progressive aspect; PV: patient voice; Top: topic marker.

find an interpretive procedure which aims to capture the generalization behind various construals of *nanak* and *ziji*, which task is carried out throughout Sections “Simplex Self as a Reflexive Focus Marker”, “Inner Self and Anti-comative Semantics” and “Outer Self and Anti-causal Semantics”. The Section “Concluding Remarks” concludes this chapter.

The Delimiting Factors

Pseudocleft Constructions

To begin with, it is instructive to examine some basic patterns of the behavior of *nanak*, which is typically interpreted as “only” when associated with predicate nominals in the sentence-initial position, as shown below (AV: actor voice marker):

(5) a. **nanak** Tali qu-[m-aniq siam].
only Tali Nom AV-eat pork
‘Only Tali eats pork’

b. Tali **nanak** qu-[m-aniq siam].
Tali only Nom AV-eat pork
‘Only Tali eats pork’

Here the structure needs a bit more explanation: Squliq Atayal is a typical VOS language, so the proper name *Tali* in (5a, b) is actually a predicate nominal followed by a headless relative in the subject position (also cf. Potsdam 2006), as indicated by the nominative case marker *qu-* that marks the boundary between the predicate and the subject, as illustrated below ([e]: empty category):

(6) [$_{predicate}$ Tali] [$_{subject}$ qu-[[e]$_k$ [m-aniq siam [e]$_k$]]
Tali Nom AV-eat pork
‘[(The one who) eats pork] (is) Tali’

Here the actor voice marker *m-* picks an actor argument to serve as the subject of the relative clause, which is further related to the empty head noun either by raising or by matching (cf. Aoun and Li 2003). This analysis provides the reason why it is the agent of the eating event that appears as the predicate of this pseudocleft-like (equational) construction. A similar analysis has already been proposed for Kavalan by Tsai (1997) and for Malagasy by Potsdam (2006) (a concealed pseudocleft in his terms).

Exactly the same treatment applies to the following nonactor voice construals as well (PV: patient voice marker):

(7) a. **nanak** siam qu-[niq-un na-Tali].
only pork Nom eat-PV Obl-Tali
'Tali eats only pork'

b. siam **nanak** qu-[niq-un na-Tali].
pork only Nom eat-PV Obl-Tali
'Tali eats only pork'

Here the patient voice marker *-un* picks a theme argument as the subject of the relative clause. As a result, the main predicate is identified instead with the theme of the eating event, i.e., *siam* "pork". In both the actor and nonactor voice constructions, *nanak* may appear either before or after the main predicates, serving as an exclusive focus adverb.

By contrast, *nanak* is interpreted as "self" when appearing within the subject headless relative, as evidenced by the reflexive adverbial construals in (8a, b):

(8) a. Tali qu-[m-aniq **nanak** siam].
Tali Nom AV-eat self pork
'Tali ate the pork alone/by himself'

b. Tali qu-[m-aniq siam **nanak**].
Tali Nom AV-eat pork self
'Tali had the pork to himself while eating'

c. siam qu-[niq-un **nanak** na-Tali].
pork Nom eat-PV only Obl-Tali
'Tali eats only pork'

d. siam qu-[niq-un na-Tali **nanak**].
pork Nom eat-PV Obl-Tali only
'Tali eats only pork'

Moreover, while the reflexive usage requires an agentive subject, the focus usage does not. This can be seen by employing the patient voice, which picks the theme argument *siam* "pork" instead as the relative subject, as in (8c, d). As a result, *siam* "pork" is located in the predicate nominal position (i.e., the sentence-initial position), and the interpretation of *nanak* has become "only" again.

Inner Self Versus Outer Self

The adverbial reflexive *nanak* can be further divided into two groups according to their syntactic distribution. Let us take the pair of control sentences in (9a, b) for examples:

(9) a. s<m>oya [m-aniq siam qu-Tali].
AV-like AV-eat pork Nom-Tali
'Tali likes to eat pork'

b. syon [m-aniq na-Tali qu-siam].[2]
like.PV AV-eat Obl-Tali Nom-pork

We can place *nanak* immediately after the control verb *smoya* "like," as in (10a) ((3a) repeated here), which produces a kind of voluntary reading. We will call this occurrence an outer self construal. By contrast, when *nanak* appears within the control complement, either before the object *siam* "pork," as in (10b) ((3b) repeated here), or after it, as in (10c) ((3c) repeated here), its interpretation is distinctively exclusion of any companies or partners. Since here *nanak* is much lower than its counterpart in (10a), we will label it an inner self instead. Finally, it is instructive to note that adverbial *nanak* can never appear after the subject, as evidenced by (10d):

(10) a. s<m>oya **nanak** [m-aniq siam qu-Tali]. (outer self)
AV-like self AV-eat pork Nom-Tali
'Tali eats pork out of his own liking (i.e., without coercion from others)'

b. s<m>oya [m-aniq **nanak** siam qu-Tali]. (inner self)
AV-like AV-eat self pork Nom-Tali
'Tali likes to eat pork alone (i.e., without the company of others)'

c. s<m>oya [m-aniq siam **nanak** qu-Tali]. (inner self)
AV-like AV-eat pork self Nom-Tali
'Tali likes to eat the pork in private (i.e., without sharing it with others)'

d. *s<m>oya [m-aniq siam qu-Tali **nanak**].
AV-like AV-eat pork Nom-Tali self

The same pattern holds for a pseudocleft construction such as (11a, b), where *nanak* serves as a typical focus adverb expressing exclusiveness when associated with the predicate nominal in the main clause:

(11) a. **nanak** Tali qu-[s<m>oya m-aniq siam].
only Tali Nom AV-like AV-eat pork
'Only Tali likes to eat pork'

b. Tali **nanak** qu-[s<m>oya m-aniq siam].
Tali only Nom AV-like AV-eat pork
'Only Tali likes to eat pork'

On the other hand, when *nanak* appears within the headless relative, it again behaves like a reflexive adverbial observing the above inner–outer distinction. (12a) shows that *nanak* receives a voluntary reading when preceded by the AV control verb *smoya* "like." By contrast, it receives a "lone wolf" reading when embedded in the control complement, as evidenced by (12b, c):

(12) a. Tali qu-[s<m>oya **nanak** [m-aniq siam]]. (outer self)
Tali Nom AV-like self AV-eat pork
'Tali eats pork out of his own liking (i.e., without coercion from others)'
Lit. 'The one who eats pork out of his liking is Tali'

b. Tali qu-[s<m>oya [m-aniq **nanak** siam]]. (inner self)
Tali Nom AV-like AV-eat self pork
'Tali likes to eat pork alone (i.e., without company of others)'
Lit. 'The one who likes to eat pork alone is Tali'

c. Tali qu-[s<m>oya [m-aniq siam **nanak**]]. (inner self)
Tali Nom AV-like AV-eat pork self
'Tali likes to eat the pork in private (i.e., without sharing with others)'
Lit. 'The one who likes to eat the pork in private is Tali'

Even when we replace the AV control verb with its PV counterpart *syon*, as in (13a, b), the same inner–outer dichotomy re-emerges, as illustrated by (14a, b). Here the theme argument is picked as the subject of the headless relative, which, as mentioned above, is in turn identified by the main predicate *siam* "pork":

(13) a. **nanak** siam qu-[syon m-aniq na-Tali].
only pork Nom like.PV AV-eat Obl-Tali
'Tali likes to eat only pork'

b. siam **nanak** qu-[syon m-aniq na-Tali].
pork only Nom like.PV AV-eat Obl-Tali
'Tali likes to eat only pork'

(14) a. siam qu-[syon **nanak** [m-aniq na-Tali]]. (outer self)
pork Nom like.PV self AV-eat Obl-Tali
'Tali eats pork out of his own liking (i.e., without coercion from others)'

b. siam qu-[syon [m-aniq **nanak** na-Tali]]. (inner self)
pork Nom like.PV AV-eat self Obl-Tali
'Tali likes to eat pork by himself (i.e., without company of others)'

Finally, the postsubject position is again not available for adverbial *nanak*, as shown by the ungrammaticality of (15):

(15) * siam qu-[syon [m-aniq na-Tali **nanak**]].
pork Nom like.PV AV-eat Obl-Tali self

Outer Self as Reflexive of Nature

The most curious case concerns the interaction between an inanimate subject and *nanak*, where an external force (often appearing in the form of a topic) is required to license the adverbial usage. (16a) expresses that, with the water-pouring event as a trigger, it is just natural that the water will flow as a result. Here the outer reflexive construal has shifted from "voluntarily" to "by nature," the reason being that, in absence of animacy, *nanak* seems to invoke a causal relation that ascribes the current event to a higher cause through the law of physics, i.e., gravity in this case. The same analysis applies to the rock-throwing event of (16b) and the walking-over event of (16c), where kinetics and automation are at work, respectively:

(16) a. tkuran qsya ga, m-qlui' **nanak** qu-qsya.
pour water Top AV-flow self Nom-water
'Pour the water, and it will flow by nature'

b. m-uling tunux ga, m-turuy **nanak** qu-tunux.
AV-throw rock Top AV-roll self Nom-rock
'Throw the rock, and it will roll by nature'

c. m-usa-saku ga, g-m-yah **nanak** qu-blihun.
AV-go-1S Top AV-open self Nom-door
'I walk over, and the door will open by nature (of its built-in mechanism)'

Interestingly enough, if there is no external force present in the context, then very often the outer selfhood is ascribed to a supernatural cause, as shown in (17a–c):

(17) a. m-qlui' **nanak** qu-qsya. cyux ki'an utux!
AV-flow self Nom-water Pst.there with ghost
'The water flowed by itself. There must be a ghost!'

b. m-turuy **nanak** qu-tunux. cyux ki'an utux!
AV-roll self Nom-rock Pst.there with ghost
'The stone rolled by itself. There must be a ghost!'

c. m-t-gyah **nanak** qu-blihun. cyux ki'an utux!
AV-T-open self Nom-door Asp with ghost
'The door opened by itself. There must be a ghost!'

Adverbial Self in Comparative Perspective

Reflexive Adverbial Vs Adnominal Intensifier

With the basic patterns of *nanak* being sorted out, we are now in a position to address the "self" vs "only" distinction from a comparative point of view. First, it is not difficult to see that the focus semantics is at the heart of both construals. As shown by (18a), when *himself* appears in the VP-adjunct position, it receives an "alone" reading. Namely, Akiu is the sore participant of this Taipei-going event. By contrast, when *himself* serves as an adnominal to the subject, as in (15b), it receives an "in person" reading, which means none other than Akiu himself is active in the event.

(18) a. Akiu went to Taipei **himself** yesterday (reflexive adverbial)
b. Akiu **himself** went to Taipei yesterday (adnominal intensifier)

This focus connection obtains for Mandarin as well, as evidenced by the distinct semantic interpretations of (19a, b). In fact, our observation seems to hold across languages (cf. Bickerton 1987; Tang 1989; Siemund 2000; König 2001; Gast 2002; Hole 2002; Gast and Siemund 2004; among many others).

(19) a. Akiu zuotian **ziji** qu-le Taibei. (reflexive adverbial)
Akiu yesterday self go-Prf Taipei
'Akiu went to Taipei by himself yesterday'

b. Akiu **ziji** zuotian qu-le Taibei. (adnominal intensifier)
Akiu self yesterday go-Prf Taipei
'None other than Akiu himself went to Taipei yesterday'

Furthermore, the peculiar behavior of *ta-ziji* "him-self" in (20a) also lends some support to our analysis. As a complex reflexive, it cannot function as an adjunct except in an adnominal position, as illustrated by the deviance of (20b, c). More importantly, here the reading is distinctively "in person," akin to identity functional readings in the sense of Eckardt (2001), Gast (2002):

(20) a. Akiu **ta-ziji** changchang hui qu Taibei. (adnominal intensifier)
Akiu him-self often will go Taipei
'Akiu himself went to Taipei yesterday'

b. * Akiu changchang **ta-ziji** hui qu Taibei.
Akiu often him-self will go Taipei

c. * Akiu changchang hui **ta-ziji** qu Taibei.
Akiu often will him-self go Taipei

What we do not quite expect in this context is the presence of the inner–outer dichotomy of the reflexive adverbials in question, whose interpretations vary with respect to the type of syntactic projections they modify (cf. Tsai 2015a, b, 2016). First, take the following minimal pair for example:

(21) a. Akiu **ziji** ken chuli zhe-jian shi.
Akiu self willing handle this-CL matter
'Akiu is willing to handle this matter on his own initiative'

b. Akiu ken **ziji** chuli zhe-jian shi.
Akiu willing self handle this-CL matter
'Akiu is willing to handle this matter by himself'

(21a) has the reflexive adverbial *ziji* in front of the volitional modal *ken* "willing," and the sentence is true if Akiu is willing to handle this matter without others' persuasion. (21b), on the other hand, has *ziji* following *ken* instead, and the sentence is true if Akiu is willing to handle this matter without others' company or help. So (21a) can be true while (21b) is false, as in the scenario where Akiu is willing to handle this matter voluntarily, but he did ask for help. Equally, (21b) can be true when (21a) is false, as in the scenario where Akiu is willing to handle this matter alone only after someone persuaded him to do so.

As a result, we may take premodal *ziji* to be an instance of outer self, and therefore receives an anti-causal reading, in that it excludes all possible causes or causers except for Akiu himself. By contrast, postmodal *ziji* should be classified as inner self, hence the anti-comitative construal, where all possible comitants or help are excluded except for Akiu himself.

Now recall the inner vs outer distinction of adverbial *nanak* in (10), (12), and (14). There is actually a direct parallel in Mandarin Chinese, as exemplified by the following control sentences containing *jihua* "plan" and *dasuan* "intend":

(22) a. Akiu **ziji** jihua [qu Taibei]. (outer self)
Akiu self plan go Taipei
'Akiu plans to go to Taipei on his own initiative'

b. Akiu jihua [**ziji** qu Taibei]. (inner self)
Akiu plan self go Taipei
'Akiu plans to go to Taipei alone'

(23) a. Akiu **ziji** dasuan [qu Taibei]. (outer self)
Akiu self intend go Taipei
'Akiu intends to go to Taipei of his own accord'

b. Akiu dasuan [**ziji** qu Taibei]. (inner self)
Akiu intend self go Taipei
'Akiu intends to go to Taipei alone'

Here everything works pretty much the same as in Squliq Atayal, except that the reflexive adverbials are on the other side of the predicates they modify (presumably due to the word order typology of the two languages). Namely, when *ziji* precedes the control verb, the reading is distinctively anti-causal; when it follows the control verb (hence embedded within the control complement), the reading is anti-comitative. Sometimes the distinction could be rather subtle, but one careful look at relevant truth conditions would usually do the trick. Consider the following minimal pair, which may sound alike to some people:

(24) a. Akiu **ziji** yao [shui na-zhang chuang].
Akiu self want sleep that-CL bed
'Akiu wants to sleep on that bed exclusively'

b. Akiu yao [**ziji** shui na-zhang chuang].
Akiu want self sleep that-CL bed
'Akiu wants to sleep on that bed alone'

Nonetheless, (24a) is true if Akiu does not want others to sleep on that bed at all, whereas (24b) is true if Akiu does not want others to share that bed while he is sleeping. The typical voluntary reading is suppressed in this case probably because the control verb *yao* "want" encodes this property by default. When forced, one can employ the *shi ... de* construction to bring out the reading with emphasis, as evidenced by the following example:

(25) Akiu shi **ziji** yao [shui na-zhang chuang] de.
Akiu be self want sleep that-CL bed DE
'It is out of his own liking that Akiu wants to sleep on that bed'

This again shows that selfhood and exclusiveness are closely related but still not exactly the same thing.

Furthermore, it is worthwhile to note that the inner–outer dichotomy is attested in German as well, except that the outer self receives an additive focus interpretation (cf. Siemund 2000; König 2001):

(26) Der Koch hat **selbst** schon mal Blaubeeren gepflückt. (outer self)
the cook has himself alreadyonce blueberries picked
'The cook has himself picked blueberries before'

(27) Der Koch hat die Blaubeeren **selbst** gepflückt. (inner self)
the cook has the blueberries himself picked
'The cook has picked the blueberries himself'

(26) expresses that the cook, too, has picked blueberries; while according to (27), the cook has picked the blueberries without any help.

Delimitating Factors Revisited

Presumably due to its word order and robust analyticity (cf. Huang 2015), Chinese modals appear in the same side of adverbials. As a result, just like control verbs, they are able to separate outer self in (28) from its inner counterpart in (29):

(28) tamen **ziji** yinggai/bixu chuli zhe-jian shi. (outer self)
they self should/must handle this-CL matter
'They should/must handle this matter on their own initiative'

(29) tamen yinggai/bixu **ziji** chuli zhe-jian shi. (inner self)
they should/must self handle this-CL matter
'They should/must handle this matter in person'

As expected, (28) is true if they should/must handle this matter without others' persuasion, while (29) is true if they should/must handle this matter without asking others to do it.

The same observation applies to negation such as *mei* "have.not." As illustrated in (30), an emphatic/contrastive construal becomes available when *ziji* appears above the negation (cf. Tang 1990), while *ziji* below the negation generally receives an "in person" reading, as in (31):

(30) Akiu **ziji** mei jiao qian, you jiao bieren ye bu yao jiao. (outer self)
Akiu self have.not pay money again ask others also not want pay
'Not only Akiu himself did not pay the money, but he also asked others to do the same'

(31) Akiu mei **ziji** jiao qian, shi jiao bieren dai-jiao de. (inner self)
Akiu have.not self pay money be ask others acting-pay DE
'Akiu did not pay the money in person, but asked others to do that for him'

Not surprisingly, sentential adverbs also do the same trick, as shown by the interpretive contrast between the outer self in (32) and its inner counterpart in (33):

(32) tamen **ziji** changchang/henshao/congbu chuli zhe-zhong shi. (outer self)
they self often/seldom/never handle this-kind matter
'They themselves often/seldom/never handled this kind of matters'

(33) tamen changchang/henshao/congbu **ziji** chuli zhe-zhong shi. (inner self)
they often/seldom/never self handle this-kind matter
'They often/seldom/never handled this kind of matters in person'

All in all, a systematic distinction is shown to exist between the two types of reflexive adverbials both in terms of their syntactic distribution and semantic interpretations.

Subject Agentivity

In this section, we continue to examine a rather peculiar agentivity restriction on inner self, which may further set them apart from their outer counterpart. First note that predicate types have a close bearing on the distribution of Chinese reflexive adverbials. Inner self is consistently blocked when its subject is not an agent, as is the case with the passive construal of (34b):

(34) *passives:*
na-ge xuesheng **ziji** bei pian-le, hai xiang pian bieren.
that-CL student self BEI cheat-Inc still want cheat others
a. 'That student himself was cheated, and he still wants to cheat others'
b. 'That student alone was cheated, and he still wants to cheat others'

The same pattern shows up with unaccusatives, locative-existentials, psyche-verbs, as well as unergative sentient verbs, as illustrated by the fact that all the inner self readings of (35b), (36b), (37b), and (38b) are ruled out without exception:

(35) *unaccusative verbs:*

wo hai mei zhao, na-ben shu jiu **ziji** chu-xian le.
I still have.not search that-CL book then self show-up Inc

a. 'I have not looked for it yet. Then the book showed up spontaneously'
b.# 'I have not looked for it yet. Then the book showed up alone'

(36) *locative-existential verbs:*

cong faguo **ziji** lai-le san-ge gongchengshi.
from France self come-Prf three-CL engineer

a. 'From France came three engineers without invitation'
b.# 'From France came three engineers by themselves'

(37) *psych verbs:*

Akiu **ziji** xihuan hua, jiu guli dajia zhong.
Akiu self like flower then encourage people plant

a. 'Akiu likes flowers out of his own liking. He then encouraged people to plant them'
b.# 'Akiu alone likes flowers. He then encouraged people to plant them'

(38) *non-agentive unergative verbs:*

bu **ziji** zenme de, Akiu ziji ku-le qilai.
not know how DE Akiu self cry-Inc up

a. '(I) don't know how (that happened). Akiu started to cry without cause'
b.# '(I) don't know how (that happened). Akiu started to cry alone'

By contrast, predicates with an agentive subject allows both outer and inner reflexive interpretations, as evidenced by the ambiguity of (39a, b):

(39) *agentive unergative verbs:*
bu zhi zenme de, Akiu **ziji** pao-le chuqu.
not know how DE Akiu self run-Inc out
a. '(I) don't know how (that happened). Akiu ran out on his own initiative'
b. '(I) don't know how (that happened). Akiu ran out by himself'

Now recall that, in Squliq Atayal, an outer self associated with an inchoative ergative may receive a "by nature" reading given that an external force is available in the context. This is exactly what happens in (37a) and (38a), where an inner self would be totally out of place, since it does not involve a cause–effect relationship in any way, as evidenced by (40b) and (41b):

(40) a. diu-xia-qu, shitou **ziji** hui gun.
throw-down-go stone self will roll
'Throw it down, and the stone by nature will roll'

b.?? diu-xia-qu, shitou hui **ziji** gun.
throw-down-go stone will self roll
'??Throw it down, and the stone will roll by itself'

(41) a. da ge dong, chuan **ziji** hui chen.
punch CL hole ship self will sink
'Punch a hole, and the ship naturally will sink'

b.?? da ge dong, chuan hui **ziji** chen.
punch CL hole ship will self sink
'??Punch a hole, and the ship will sink by itself'

In cases where there is no external cause at work, an inner reflexive construal suddenly becomes possible with a supernatural reading of the rolling/sinking event, as shown below:

(42) a. shitou hui **ziji** gun. you gui!
stone can self roll have ghost
'The stone can roll by itself. There must be a ghost!'

b. chuan hui **ziji** chen. zhe zhenshi jian gui le!
ship can self sink this really see ghost Inc
'The ship can sink by itself. I must be seeing a ghost!'

Note that here the modal force of *hui* has changed into ability (hence much lower in cartographic terms, which is again a sure indication for the inner selfhood (cf. Tsai 2015a, b)).

Simplex Self as a Reflexive Focus Marker

To solve the mystery surrounding the hybrid nature of reflexive adverbials, it is noted by Tsai (2016) that they may well combine properties from an adnominal intensifier and an anaphors. As a result, they carry an identificational focus while triggering argument reduction. More specifically, the complex reflexive *ta-ziji* "him-self" heads an argument DP, specializing in contrasting an individual (i.e., the subject *Akiu* in (20a)) against possible alternatives. The simplex reflexive *ziji*, on the other hand, functions as an adverbial, hence contrasting a proposition/eventuality against possible alternatives (cf. Rooth 1985; 1992, among others). Another piece of evidence comes from Gast and Siemund (2004), where it is pointed out that, in Tetelcingo Nahuatl, *sie* plus a pronoun serves as an adnominal intensifier, while *sa... siel* together function as an adverbial intensifier:

(43) a. pos **sie yaha** David kɪhtoa ipa inu libro de Salmos ...
well one he David he.says in Det book of psalms
'and David himself saith in the book of Psalms'

b. **sa** **i-siel** okɪchɪhchɪ i-kal.
only 3.Poss-Int he.built 3.Poss-house
'He built his house himself'

By extending Reinhart and Reuland's (1993) version of Binding Principle to reflexive adverbials, reflexive-marking can be taken to be a mechanism of reducing peripheral arguments. That is, by reflexive-marking *v*P instead of V, inner self reduces an applicative argument rather than a core argument (i.e., coargumental self in the object position):

(44) A reflexive predicate must be reflexive-marked

By the same token, the proposed identificational focus is now operating on the *v*P level, shifting its alternatives from an individual to an eventuality. In terms of syntax, it is situated at the edge of *v*P, presumably an applicative projection (ApplP) in the *v*P periphery (cf. Tsai 2015b), where inner *ziji* serves to reflexive-mark the main predicate, resulting in the anti-comitative reading mentioned above. Outer *ziji*, by contrast, is introduced by a causative projection (CauP) above ModP, hence reflexive-marking the modal projection. As a result, the anti-causal interpretation emerges accordingly.

In the event that *ziji* merges to a even higher functional projection (presumably in the upper lay of the CP domain), *ziji* may be engaged in the role of a logophor, situated in the Spec of a Source Phrase (SrcP) (cf. Huang and Liu 2000). We are therefore in a position to spell-out the whole spectrum of selfhood in cartographic terms, where reflexive adverbials can be seen as a missing link between logophors and anaphors with respect to their "height of interpretation" in the order of logophoricity (speaker-orientedness) > causality (eventuality) > comitativity (applicativity) > anaphoricity (transitivity). A tentative visualization of this selfhood spectrum is given in the following diagram:

(45)

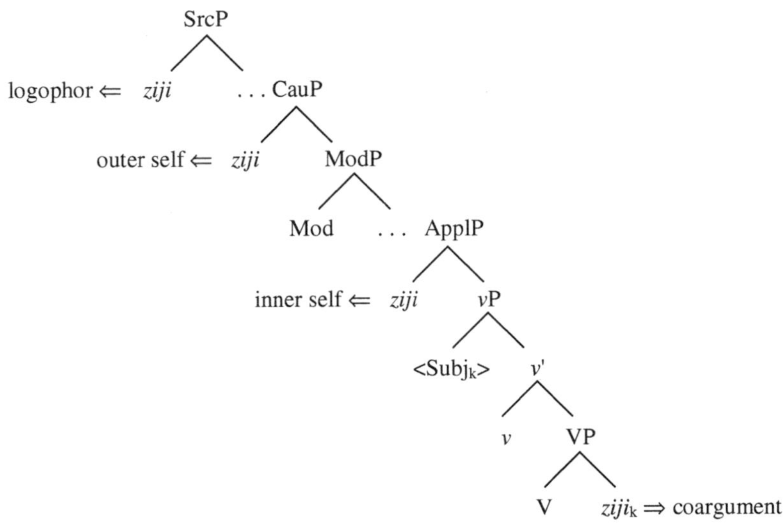

Inner Self and Anti-comitative Semantics

In light of the analysis presented above, we would like to propose a natural extension of the reductionist view of reflexives. Namely, inner reflexive-marking reduces an applicative argument instead of a theme argument. For one thing, inner reflexive-marking actually allows two types of interpretations: one is comitative, as in (46a); the other is instrumental, as in (46b):

(46) Akiu ken **ziji** chuli zhe-jian shi.
Akiu willing self handle this-CL matter
a. 'Akiu is willing to handle this matter without others' company' (comitative)
b. 'Akiu is willing to handle this matter without others' help' (instrumental)

An illuminating view on the applicativity of the instrument role can also be found in the following quote from Reinhart (2002):

"In standard agent verbs… an instrument is always allowed optionally, but it is not directly selected by the verb. (This is a general entailment licensed by the agent role, which need not be listed for each individual entry.)"

One way to think of this issue is to group instrumental and comitative arguments together under a proto-comitant role in the spirit of Dowty (1991), as illustrated by the closely related usages of *with* and *by* below:

(48) a. Akiu left with his friends (comitant)
b. Akiu left with a limousine (instrument)
c. Akiu left with apparent ease (manner)

(49) a. Akiu stands by his friends (comitant)
b. Akiu came by the highway (path, method)
c. Akiu was killed by a knife (instrument)

Parsons (1995) defines an instrument role as a relation between an event e and an individual x such that e is with x. In light of this definition, one may take this proto-(applicative) argument to be someone or something in a comitative relation to an event, which can easily translate into an instrumental, path, or manner relation. It then becomes clear from Reinhart's remarks that the proto-role in question must be licensed by an agentive subject, and subject to (applicative) argument reduction in presence of inner self. This in turn provides a straightforward account of why predicates with a non-agentive subject do not get along with inner reflexive-marking, as we have seen in both Mandarin Chinese and Squliq Atayal.

Now recall the inner *nanak*-construals of (50a, b) ((10b, c) repeated here). One may well represent their basic ingredients with the Neo-Davidsonian formula (51) along the line of Parsons (1990; 1995):

(50) a.

s<m>oya	[m-aniq	**nanak**	siam	qu-Tali].	(inner self)
AV-like	AV-eat	self	pork	Nom-Tali	

‘Tali likes to eat pork by himself (i.e., without the company of others)’

b.

s<m>oya	[m-aniq	siam	**nanak**	qu-Tali].	(inner self)
AV-like	AV-eat	pork	self	Nom-Tali	

‘Tali likes to eat the pork in private (i.e., without sharing it with others)’

(51) $\text{Self}\ (\lambda x\ \exists e\ (\textit{maniq}\ (e)\ \&\ \text{Agent}(x, e)\ \&\ \text{Theme}(\textit{siam}, e)\ \&\ \text{Comitant}(x, e)))\ (\textit{Tali})$

Here θ-roles are viewed as thematic relations between arguments and an underlying event, and an adjunct is treated as a conjunct of the main predicate, both predicating upon the event argument. Since there is an agent subject in the sentence, a proto-comitant is introduced. Reflexive-marking is triggered by the inner self-operator NANAK then applies to reduce the comitative role, while the identification focus excludes all the possible alternatives except for the agent himself, as shown by the following derivations:

(52) $\text{NANAK}\ (\lambda x\ \exists e\ (\textit{maniq}(e)\ \&\ \text{Agent}(x, e)\ \&\ \text{Theme}(\textit{siam}, e)\ \&\ \text{Comitant}\ (x, e)))\ (\textit{Tali})$

$\Rightarrow \lambda x\ \exists e\ (\textit{maniq}(e)\ \&\ \text{Agent}(x, e)\ \&\ \text{Theme}(\textit{siam}, e)\ \&\ \cancel{\text{Comitant}\ (x, e)}$
$\&\ {\sim}\exists y\ (y \neq x\ \&\ \text{Comitant}(y, e)))\ (\textit{Tali})$

$\Rightarrow \exists e\ (\textit{maniq}(e)\ \&\ \text{Agent}(\textit{Tali}, e)\ \&\ \text{Theme}(\textit{siam}, e)\ \&\ {\sim}\exists y\ (y \neq \textit{Tali}\ \&\ \text{Comitant}(y, e)))$

Outer Self and Anti-causal Semantics

The question remains as to how the outer selfhood may be characterized in such a way that the anti-causal reading of (53) ((10a) repeated here) may be related to the syntactic position of outer *nanak*:

(53)

s<m>oya	**nanak**	[m-aniq	siam	qu-Tali].	(outer self)
AV-like	self	AV-eat	pork	Nom-Tali	

‘Tali eats pork out of his liking (i.e., without coercion from others)’

First assume that there is a causal relation underpinning every eventuality, whether it is a state or an event. We then distinguish the following three types of causal relation between two events, based on the insights from Shen (1985):

(54) a. Enable: One event is a necessary condition for the other.
(e.g., Max entered the pool, and then he drowned.)

b. Cause: One event is a sufficient condition for the other.
(e.g., Xiaodi gave an order, so Akiu will handle this matter.)

c. Motivate: One event either enables or causes the other, mediated by a mental state. (e.g., Max wanted to eat, so he started to cook.)

To break down the above construal of outer *nanak*, we propose that, for every eventuality, there is a causative argument licensed by the relation Cause specified in (54b). The outer self-operator NANAK again reduces the cause role, while introducing the identificational focus responsible for the anti-causal interpretation, as illustrated below:

(55) NANAK ($\lambda x\ \exists e$ (Cause(x, e) & *smoya-maniq*(e) & Experiencer(x, e) & Theme(*siam*, e))) (*Tali*)

$\Rightarrow$ $\lambda x\ \exists e$ (~~Cause(x, e)~~ & *smoya-maniq*(e) & Experiencer(x, e) & Theme(*siam*, e) & $\sim\exists y$ ($y \neq x$ & Cause(y, e))) (*Tali*)

$\Rightarrow$ $\exists e$ (*smoya-maniq*(e) & Experiencer(*Tali*, e) & Theme(*siam*, e) & $\sim\exists y$ (y≠*Tali* & Cause(y, e))

The resulted semantics goes as follows: There is a mental state of *like-to-eat* such that Tali is the experiencer, and the pork the theme, and there is no other cause except for Tali himself.

It then follows that the common properties shared by adverbial reflexive-marking and the *only*-construals of (56a, b) ((1a, b) repeated here) can be captured by the Neo-Davidsonian semantics given in (57), based on the classic analysis of Horn (1969):

(56) a. yaqih na-Temu **nanak** qu-Tali.
NAV.hate Obl-Temu only Nom-Tali
'Only Temu hates Tali'

b. yaqih **nanak** na-Temu qu-Tali.
NAV.hate only Obl-Temu Nom-Tali
'Only Temu hates Tali'

(57) Only (λx ∃e (*yaqih*(e) & Experiencer(*Temu*, e) & Theme(x, e))) (*Tali*)
a. Presupposition: ∃e (*yaqih*(e) & Theme(*Tali*, e) & Experiencer(*Temu*, e))
b. Assertion: ∃e (*yaqih*(e) & Theme(*Tali*, e) & ~∃y (y≠ *Temu* & Experiencer(y, e)))

As stated in the assertion part (57b) of *nanak* as a pure focus operator, no one else but Temu is the holder of the mental state of Tali-hating. Here we see the convergence of the alternative semantics invoked by self and *only*, which in turn explains the variety of interpretations associated with *nanak* in Squliq Atayal.

Moreover, if our analysis presented above is on the right track, then it would not be surprising to find other types of focus construal of adnominal/adverbial self across languages. This point is best illustrated by *selbst* "self" in German. As we have already seen in (26), it receives an additive reading as outer self. As a matter of fact, it can be construed either as an intensifier in (58a) or as *even* in (58b):

(58) Einstein selbst weiß das nicht.
Einstein self know this not
a. Literal meaning with *selbest* stressed: 'Einstein himself does not know this'
b. New meaning with *Einstein* stressed: 'Even Einstein does not know this'

According to Eckardt (2002), this *even* interpretation of *selbest* can be characterized by adopting the following alternative semantics:

(59) a. Contextually derivable: A set of alternatives to Einstein

b. Presupposition: The alternative propositions 'x does not know this' are ordered on a scale according to probability, and 'Einstein does not know this' is at the most improbable end of the scale. All alternative propositions hold true

c. Assertion: 'Einstein does not know this' holds true as well

Finally, questions still remain as to when and how outer self is turned into a reflexive of nature, where a causal relation is no doubt involved. With an external cause available in the context, the reflexive adverbial in question elects instead to substantiate the cause–effect relation by predicating upon the external cause. Consequently, it fails to reduce a causative argument, and no focus interpretation is ever detected in the Squliq example (16a–c) and the Mandarin examples (40a) and (41a).

Concluding Remarks

In this chapter, we build upon Horn's (1969) classic analysis of *only* and characterize reflexive adverbials as focus operators involving a set of alternatives. As a result, a unified account of *self* and *only* can be offered in the following form:

(61) $F(x) \& \sim(\exists y)\ (y \neq x \ \& \ F(y))$

Depending on the locus of reflexive adverbials, F may stand for a variety of thematic relations such as experiencer, cause, instrument, or comitant. In the case of Squliq Atayal, when *nanak* is associated with the external argument, it is interpreted as "only." When the focus is placed upon a peripheral argument, *nanak* is interpreted as "self" instead, resulting in the inner–outer dichotomy (i.e., anti-comitative vs anti-causal). In the case of Mandarin, *ziji* lacks the option of focusing on the external argument. On the other hand, Chinese does distinguish significantly more layers of verbal projection due to its robust analyticity (cf. Huang 2015). This typological feature thus creates a spectrum of selfhood through reflexive-marking, stemming from anaphoricity all the way to logophoricity, just as we have seen in the topography illustrated in (45).

All in all, we have shown that it is imperative to substantiate the focus semantics of reflexive adverbials through cross-linguistic comparisons. The distinction between inner self and outer self also follows from our cartographic analysis of *nanak* and *ziji* with respect to their "height of interpretation," At the end, we have put forward an explicit theory of reflexivity across the board, which hopefully will lead us to a deeper understanding of how a focus interacts with reflexive-marking in human languages.

References

Aoun, Joseph, and Yen-hui Audrey Li. 2003. *Essays on the Representation and Derivational Nature of Grammar: The Diversity of Wh-constructions*. Cambridge: MIT Press.
Bickerton, Derek. 1987. He himself—Anaphor, pronoun, or…? *Linguistic Inquiry* 18: 345–348.
Dowty, David. 1991. Thematic proto-roles and argument selection. *Language* 67 (3): 547–619.
Eckardt, Regine. 2001. Reanalyzing selbest. *Natural Language Semantics* 9: 371–412.

Eckardt, Regine. 2002. Semantic change in grammaticalization. In *Proceedings of the 6th Annual Meeting of Gesellschraft für Semantik*, ed. by Graham Katz, Sabine Reinhard, and Philip Reuter, 133–150.

Gast, Volker and Peter Siemund. 2004. *Rethinking the relation between Intensifiers and Reflexives*. Ms. Freie Universität Berlin and Universität Hamburg.

Gast, V. 2002. *The Grammar of Identity—Intensifier and Reflexives as Expressions of an Identity Function*. PhD diss., Free University of Berlin.

Hole, Daniel. 2002. Agentive Selfbest in German. In *Proceedings of the 6th Annual Meeting of Gesellschraft für Semantik*, ed. by Graham Katz, Sabine Reinhard, and Philip Reuter, 133–150. University of Osnabrück.

Horn, Larry. 1969. *A Presuppositional Theory of Only and Even*. CLS 5, Chicago Linguistic Society.

Huang, C.-T. James. 2015. On syntactic analyticity and parametric theory. In *Chinese syntax in a cross-linguistic Perspective*, ed. by Li, Y.-H. Audrey, Andrew Simpson, and W.-T. Dylan Tsai, 1–48. New York: Oxford University Press.

Huang, C.-T. James, and Luther C.-S. Liu. 2000. Logophoricity, attitudes and *Ziji*at the interface. In *Syntax and semantics 33: Long-distance reflexives*. ed. by Peter Cole, Gabriella Hermon and C.-T. James Huang, 141–195. New York: Academic Press.

Kiss, Katalin. 1998. Indentificational focus vs informational focus. *Language* 71: 245–273.

König, Ekkehard. 2001. Intensifiers and reflexive pronouns. Language typology and language universals: an international handbook, vol. 1, ed. by Martin Haspelmath, Ekkehard König, Wulf Oesterreicher and Wolfgang Raible, 747–60. Berlin/New York: Walter de Gruyter.

Parsons, Terence. 1995. Thematic relations and arguments. *Linguistic Inquiry* 26: 635–662.

Parsons, Terence. 1990. *Events in the Semantics of English: a Study in Subatomic Semantics*. Cambridge: MIT Press.

Potsdam, Eric. 2006. More concealed pseudoclefts in Malagasy and the clausal typing hypothesis. *Lingua* 116: 2154–2182.

Reinhart, Tanya. 2002. The theta system–an overview. *Theoretical Linguistics* 28(3).

Reinhart, Tanya, and Eric Reuland. 1993. Reflexivity. *Linguistic Inquiry* 24: 657–720.

Rooth, Mats. 1992. A theory of focus interpretation. *Natural Language Semantics* 1: 75–116.

Rooth, Mats. 1985. *Association with Focus*. PhD diss., University of Massachusetts at Amherst.

Shen, Yeshayahu. 1985. *The Structure of Action in the Short Narrative Text*. PhD diss., Tel Aviv University.

Siemund, Peter. 2000. *Intensifiers—A Comparison of English and German*. London: Routledge.

Tang, C.-C.Jane. 1989. Chinese reflexives. *Natural Language & Linguistic Theory* 7: 93–121.

Tsai, Wei-Tien Dylan. 2016. Causality, Commitativity, Contrastivity, and Selfhood. To appear in *Interfaces in Grammar*, ed. by Jianhua Hu. John Benjamins.

Tsai, Wei-Tien Dylan. 2015a. On the topography of Chinese modals. In *Beyond Functional Sequence*, ed. Ur Shlonsky, 275–294. New York: Oxford University Press.

Tsai, Wei-Tien Dylan. 2015b. A tale of two peripheries: Evidence from chinese adverbials, light verbs, applicatives and object fronting. In *The Cartography of Chinese Syntax*, ed. by Wei-Tien Dylan Tsai, 1–32. New York: Oxford University Press.

Tsai, Wei-Tien Dylan. 1997. Indefinite Wh-Construals in Formosan languages: A comparative study of Kavalan, Tsou, and Seediq, Tsing Hua. *Journal of Chinese Studies New Sieries* 27 (4): 381–422.

Chapter 8
Getting the Identical Infinitives Filter in Bangla Under Control

Probal Dasgupta

An infinitival construction in Bangla can contain an embedded infinitive, as illustrated in (1)—the infinitival format is **Verb-*te***:

(1) ram SomeSke bonnar kOtha bolte dite caYni
Ram Somesh.DAT flood.GEN about tell.Inf let.Inf want.Pa.NEG
'Ram didn't want to let Somesh talk about the flood'

But such strings become bizarre when the two verbs are identical—we are using the special double ampersand symbol to mark the status "bizarre for reasons that remain to be conceptualized"; later in the chapter, we will unpack the content of such flagging:

(2) &&ram SomeSke bonnar kOtha bolte bolte caYni
Ram Somesh.DAT flood.GEN about tell.Inf tell.Inf want.Pa.NEG
'Ram didn't want to tell Somesh to talk about the flood'

En route to descriptive adequacy, let us encode this observation in the form of a filter, continuing to use the noncommittal double ampersand flag:

This research was supported by the Indian Statistical Institute under the "biaxial syntax of inflected clauses in Assamese and Bangla" project. The help received from Gitanjali Bez mentioned in the text is to be understood in the context of this project. Input from an anonymous reviewer, from audiences at the University of Hyderabad and at Adam Mickiewicz University (Poznań, Poland), and from Priyanka Biswas, Dustin Chaco, Noam Chomsky, and Devarati Jana is gratefully acknowledged. The usual disclaimers apply.

P. Dasgupta (✉)
Indian Statistical Institute, Kaberi 1st Floor, 123A Purbachal Kalitala Rd,
Kolkata 700078, India
e-mail: probal53@gmail.com

G. Sengupta et al. (eds.), *Perspectives on the Architecture and Acquisition of Syntax*, DOI 10.1007/978-981-10-4295-9_8

(3) The Identical Infinitives Filter
&& ...[...[...V1.Inf] V2.Inf]..., where V1 = V2

As usual, the phenomenon does not wear its heart on its sleeve. In order to approach it, one juxtaposes it with related facts, triangulating toward a clearer view.

In some sentences, a word is repeated on purpose as a matter of grammar. They fall into two subclasses. Consider first (4), an example whose reduplication we characterize as *contingent* because the grammar of the conjunctive participle per se does not compel the verb to be reduplicated:

(4) rita *diye* *(diye)* klanto hoYe gEche, Ekhon nite caY
Rita *give*.Cjv *(give*.Cjv*)* tired become has, now take.Inf wants
'Rita has given and given and is tired, now she wants to take'

In contrast, (5) counts as an example of *essential* reduplication because the progressive participle per se does insist—(6), where the participle stands unreduplicated, is marked with a crosshatch to indicate that it cannot be interpreted as a progressive participle:

(5) buddhoke paYeS *dite* *dite* Sujatar mone poRlo hironnokoSipur gOlpo
Buddha.Dat payasam *serving serving* Sujata.Gen recall Aux Hiranyakasipu's story
'While serving payasam to the Buddha, Sujata recalled the story of Hiranyakasipu'

(6) #buddhoke paYeS *dite* Sujatar mone poRlo hironnokoSipur gOlpo
Buddha.Dat payasam *serving* Sujata.Gen recall Aux Hiranyakasipu's story
Cannot have the reading 'While serving payasam to the Buddha, Sujata recalled the story of Hiranyakasipu'
Does have the irrelevant reading 'When somebody else (whose identity is contextually recoverable) served payasam to the Buddha, Sujata recalled the story of Hiranyakasipu'

In what way do these remarks contribute to the work of analysis? To see where they become pertinent, consider a compound verb in which the vector and the pole happen to be the same verb:

(7) dilip bibekke kapoR diye dilo
Dilip Bibek.Dat clothes give.Cjv gave
'Dilip gave the clothes away to Bibek'

In (7), the pole of the compound verb appears in a finite tense, the Past. Suppose we choose instead the conjunctive inflection, so that the pole and the vector carry the same ending. Such a string admits of two readings, as shown in the glosses for (8):

(8) bibekke kapoR diye diye diliper apSoS holo
Bibek.Dat clothes give.Cjv give.Cjv Dilip.Gen repentance Aux
a. 'Having given the clothes away to Bibek, Dilip repented'
b. 'Having given clothes away to Bibekagain and again, Dilip repented'

It is the sequence of identical conjunctives in *diye diye* that is ambiguous. One can parse this sequence as a compound verb whose vector happens to carry conjunctive inflection, (8a); or one can parse it as a case of contingent reduplication, with the characteristic iterated-action interpretation, (8b). The two readings are sharply different. Contextual factors play a role in deciding which of the readings counts as salient, to be sure; but even after taking them into account, one concludes that the string is systematically amenable to both interpretations in principle.

In contrast to the state of affairs involving such contingent reduplication of the conjunctive verb form *diye*, the essential reduplication skeleton of the progressive participle exemplified in *dite dite* "while giving" does not give rise to any ambiguity within the range of participial readings. What about ambiguity across the participial-infinitival boundary, however? The unacceptable identical infinitives in example (2), given its lexical content, cannot be shunted into a participial parse to rescue the string. But the ingenuity of psycholinguists will no doubt produce experiment-worthy examples. Coming up with a pertinent string is only half the battle; even a mere grammarian can solve that problem by coming up with (9), for instance, where Verb-*te*, glossed as *Verb-TE*, is ambiguous between the infinitival ending and the progressive participial ending, and where *bOl*, glossed as *BOL*, is ambiguous between "say" and "tell":

(9) bibekke dilip kapoR dite dite bOleni
Bibek.Dat Dilip clothes give.*TE* give.*TE* *BOL*.Aux.Neg
a. double infinitival reading: &&'Dilip didn't tell Bibek to let [someone] give clothes away'
b. participle plus infinitive reading: 'Dilip didn't say X while giving clothes to Bibek [X contextually recoverable]'

The real challenge that an experimental psycholinguist must face has to do with constructing a plausible prior context that enables subjects to postulate a null complement and arrive at parse (9b). We are cautiously optimistic that challenge can be met and that experimental work will indeed be done on this front.

Sharpening the issues as we await such psycholinguistic inquiry, we turn now to identical infinitives that involve a "composite verb" (in the sense in which Dasgupta 1990 uses this term). Consider first a composite verb without any doubling, such as *baron kOra* "to forbid" as in (10):

(10) dilip bibekke krikeT khelte baron korbe na
Dilip Bibek.Dat cricket to.play forbid Aux Neg
'Dilip won't forbid Bibek to play cricket'

Is there any problem if the embedded verb itself, instead of *khEla* "to play," is another instance of *baron kOra* "to forbid"? No, there is not:

(11) bibek eTa SeTa baron kore bERacchilo; dilip, baddho hoYe,
Bibek this that forbid Aux.Cjv was.going.around; Dilip, compelled being,
oke SOb bEparei baron korte baron korlo
him all matters.Loc forbid Aux.Inf forbid Aux
'Bibek had been going around forbidding this and forbidding that;
Dilip, perforce, forbade him to do any forbidding at all'

Now, we construct an example where the matrix composite verb itself is in the infinitival form, (12); again, the result is perfectly well-formed:

(12) bibeker bokami dekheo dilip oke tobu SOb bEparei *baron*
Bibek's silliness seeing.Foc Dilip him still all matters.Loc *forbid*
korte baron korte caYni
Aux *.Inf forbid* Aux.*Inf* didn't.want
'Even in the face of Bibek's silliness, Dilip still didn't want to
forbid him to do any forbidding at all'

The crucial point here is that this sequence of identical infinitival composite verbs, *baron korte baron korte* "forbid Aux.Inf forbid Aux.Inf," is distinct from the progressive participle form—which, as illustrated at (13), iterates only the infinitivally inflected auxiliary word *korte*, not the entire two-word sequence *baron korte*:

(13) bibek *baron korte korte* bhule jaY kake ki bolche
Bibek *forbid* Aux.*ing* Aux.*ing* forget.Cjv Aux to.whom what is.saying
'Bibek, when he is busy forbidding, tends to forget what he is
saying to whom'

At the heart of the phenomenon we are addressing in this study, then, lies the issue of whether a particular identical infinitives sequence does or does not coincide with the corresponding progressive participle. Where the two fail to coincide, the identical infinitives construction comes across as unproblematic. Where the two do coincide, it counts as anomalous and gets flagged with a double ampersand for which we had promised a fuller unpacking. On our way to that unpacking, we just have one more empirical point to make.

In a sentence that embeds one infinitival under another infinitival, if the lower infinitival is endowed with a focus particle, as in (14), the sentence sounds normal:

(14) ram SomeSke bonnar kOtha bolteo bolte ce Yechilo
Ram Somesh.Dat flood.Gen about tell.Inf.Foc tell.Inf want.Pa
'Ram wanted to tell Somesh to also talk about the flood'

This fact reinforces what we have observed so far. The template **Verb-*te*-Focus Verb-*te*** precludes a progressive participle reading, because a participle, even a two-word participle, brooks no interruption. In the absence of lateral pressure from the participle construction, it becomes easy to parse the structure in terms of two infinitives; hence, the non-anomalous status of (14). The point is not confined to focus particles. Any interruptor has the same effect, as we see at the equally readily intelligible sentence (15), where it is an adverb that interrupts the sequence of verbs:

(15) ram SomeSke bonnar kOtha bolte tahole bolte ce Yechilo
Ram Somesh.Dat flood.Gen about tell.Inf then tell.Inf want.Pa
'Ram wanted, then,to tell Somesh to talk about the flood'

With that empirical point in place, we can now look at (2) again, calling it (16) to stop the numbering fairy from scowling at us—

(16) &&ram SomeSke bonnar kOtha bolte bolte caYni
Ram Somesh.Dat flood.Gen about tell.Inf tell.Inf want.Pa.Neg
'Ram didn't want to tell Somesh to talk about the flood'

—and at last unpack the "&&" notation, by which we mean we have to now choose between the two obvious options. Option one is to give that double ampersand symbol "&&" a permanent place in our toolkit. Option two is to get rid of that special notation after translating it into whatever elaborate explanation we can provide now but did not wish to provide in the first few paragraphs because at that stage we had not yet had a chance to make the background clear.

Please forgive us for wanting to have our cake and eat it too, but we would actually like to do both. Exercising option one, we do wish to retain && as a permanent symbol for general use, as a sort of observational level joker. We propose that the symbol should always be taken to mean "there is something wrong with this sentence, but we have no immediate basis for identifying it either as a case of syntactic ill-formedness, or of semantic ill-formedness, or of a severe processing difficulty." At the same time, exercising option two, we are indeed about to translate && into an elaborate explanation for the case under review; in other words, we will eliminate this particular use of the double ampersand.

Our elaborate explanation begins by noting that native speakers exposed to a **Verb-*te* Verb-*te*** sequence react differently, depending on whether they encounter a particular identical infinitives sequence in a **written** stimulus or in a **spoken** stimulus. Facing a **written** stimulus featuring the problem sequence, the reader invariably tries the progressive participial construal first; the ultimate outcome depends on whether this effort is successful or not, and on subsequent strategies that the reader adopts. In contrast, a **speaker** uttering such a string typically intones it in a way that encourages one particular construal. Thus, the intonation leads the listener to parse a potentially ambiguous token either as an embedded infinitival or as a progressive participial construction.

In the case of example (16) = (2), the upshot is that the string sounds acceptable when uttered with an intonation that elicits the infinitival embedding reading (e.g., placing a higher pitch on the second occurrence of **Verb-*te***). However, the string comes across as unacceptable in its written form. Readers compelled to process the string do not easily recover from the garden path experience; even after they arrive at the embedded infinitival parse and discover that only this construal is viable, they remain uncomfortable. Correspondingly, such strings are either nonexistent or vanishingly infrequent in spontaneous speech and writing.

In other words, the double ampersand here can be replaced by the elaborate unpacking "basically unacceptable in the written mode; acceptable in the spoken mode only if the speaker chooses an intonation that leads to the right parse." This unpacking can be improved upon. For instance, if the prior context in a written passage makes an embedded infinitival reading for (16) plausible, then a properly clued in reader may arrive at that parse without special effort and may thus find the sentence acceptable. It is to subsume such details that our unpacking uses the hedge word "basically."

The reason for wishing to nonetheless retain && as a reporting device becomes clear when we consider parallel phenomena pertaining to adjectives. In Bangla, a classifier language with a tenuous phi-feature system, one strategy for expressing semantic plurality is to reduplicate an adjectival word, as in (17); note that when the adjective is modified by an adverb, such reduplication, illustrated in (18), targets only the adjectival word proper—(19) exemplifies the fact that reduplication of the entire adjectival projection is unacceptable:

(17) rakeS prottek bar bORo bORo alu niye aSe
Rakesh every time big big potato bring Aux
'Every time, Rakesh brings big potatoes'

(18) rakeS prottek bar bhiSon bORo bORo alu niye aSe
Rakesh every time awfully big big potato bring Aux
'Every time, Rakesh brings awfully big potatoes'

(19) *rakeS prottek bar bhiSon bORo bhiSon bORo alu niye aSe
Rakesh every time awfully big awfully big potato bring Aux

With these observations about adjectival reduplication in place, now consider (20) and (21), which are terminal string identical:

(20) mukeS [kOYekTa SOccho [SOccho plasTike moRa] camoc] kineche
Mukesh [a.few transparent [transparent plastic packed] spoons] has.bought
'Mukesh has bought a couple of transparent spoons wrapped in transparent plastic'

(21) mukeS [kOYekTa SOccho SOccho [plasTike moRa] camoc] kineche
Mukesh [a.few transparent transparent [plastic packed] spoons has.bought
'Mukesh has bought a couple of transparent spoons wrapped in plastic'

The written string, presented to unprepared subjects, is likely to elicit reading (21), not (20). The spoken token can only be intoned in a way that has the effect of disambiguating the string and eliciting one parse at a time. In this adjectival excursus, we find a replication of the verbal pattern explored in the main body of this chapter. The string unpacked in two different ways at (20) and (21) is ambiguous; but following its lead, we can readily come up with a string such as (22), which was designed for the embedded identical adjective parse, but which resists this reading and thus comes out anomalous:

(22) &&amra [moTa [moTa cheleTar mapmOton] jama] kinte cay
we [thick [fat the.boy's size.fitting] shirts] to.buy want
'We want to buy thick shirts that fit the fat boy'

The parallel between the material in this adjectival excursus and the verbal story that we have been narrating is so clear that we need not make all the details explicit. Why draw the parallel, then? Are we only illustrating the utility of the double ampersand as a reporting device?

Surely the astute reader will have noticed that in the adjectival excursus, as well as in the verbal headline narrative, the reduplicated construction whose paradigmatic impact makes the embedded interpretation unavailable most of the time crucially involves a **single word** being reduplicated—a single Verb-*te* or a single adjective—and never targets two-word sequences such as a composite verb or an adverb-adjective structure. This fact is not a quirky feature of the two examples considered in this study. More generally, reduplication can target either a word or some entity smaller than a word (such as a CV sequence), but never a construction larger than a word.

Some day, formal theories of language that eschew semiotic considerations will, no doubt, offer a purely formalistic account of this general fact about reduplication processes. Once they do, serious theory comparison will become possible. Until that moment, those of us who work with the substantivist approach—which (a) regards facts of speech and of writing as equally pertinent to a theory of language, (b) takes the paradigmatic axis entirely seriously in the calculus of economy, (c) privileges the word as a salient unit on the syntagmatic and paradigmatic axes, (d) constructs biaxial descriptions that crucially refer to both axes in the same breath, (e) deploys the mechanisms of WWM (Whole Word Morphology) as part of these descriptions and (f) offers semiotic explanations for the salience of the word and related phenomena—are likely to regard this upper limit on the applicability of reduplication as part of the evidence that (to slightly tweak what philosophers used to say about clarity some decades ago) formalism is not enough. We do not offer an actual substantivist account here, given the fact the overwhelming majority of linguists have avoided acquiring basic literacy regarding substantivist tools. Experience shows that the amount of substantivist pedagogy that can be carried out on the margins of one paper is insufficient to ensure efficient communication. This is one of the contexts where silence is golden.

It would be remiss of us not to report, however, that Gitanjali Bez has looked at Assamese equivalents to our non-finite verb examples and found that there are no ampersand strings. It turns out that Assamese infinitival and progressive participles are morphologically quite distinct. The same holds for several eastern dialects of Bangla. The search is on for other languages in which anomalous strings involving inflectional homonymy are available and can be compared with the data of this case study. While we run that search, perhaps colleagues can be persuaded to look at adjectival reduplication in other languages, compare their results with ours, and come up with a theoretically interesting take of their own.

To bring some closure to our little narrative: have we indeed managed to bring the identical infinitives filter under control? We have now taken a look at yet another domain in which the double ampersand plays a role, and in which the phenomena of interest cluster around a constraint closely resembling the identical infinitives filter. This bit of triangulating helps us to see that this type of constraint appears on the surface wherever a syntactic derivation proper is affected by a paradigmatically adjacent grammatical process that reduplicates a word. Heuristically speaking, we will want to state such a filter, or a filter-like constraint, as the first step in our analytical procedure—as a diagnostic first step. Once we have identified some new phenomenon as part of this syndrome, perhaps with even a double ampersand as part of the paraphernalia, we then retrace the now familiar itinerary and go on to specify the particular paradigmatic adjacency responsible for the particular effect that we have diagnosed.

To the extent that we have found our identical infinitives filter to be just the tip of an interesting iceberg and have found at least one other iceberg with a similar tip, we have been able to expand the scope of the observations that our narrative started out with. This perhaps is as far as a descriptively adequate account can hope to go. Readers who wish to go further, in this electronic day and age, hardly need such old-fashioned crutches as bibliographies that scholars were once addicted to. Given the ubiquity of search engines and other supplements, surely the explicit presentation of bibliographic entries should restrict itself to items that the standard search engines cannot be expected to track down. If we continue to maximize redundancy at the level of our scholarly practices, then the paradigmatic impact of that wastefulness will contaminate the pursuit of economical solutions within the confines of formal linguistics, will it not? Is that not one of the morals to be drawn from the material examined in this study?

Reference

Dasgupta, Malasree. 1990. Composite verbs in Bangla. *Indian Journal of Linguistics* 17:1.1–31.

Part III
Architecture of Syntax: The Syntax-Semantics Interface

Chapter 9
Binding Theory, Scope Reconstruction, and NPI Licensing Under Scrambling in Hindi

Utpal Lahiri

It is an old observation that displaced elements—quantifier phrases in particular—are sometimes interpreted in their premovement position. An obvious example in English is the case of a quantified NP/DP that raised out of a clausal complement of a raising predicate, as in the following example:

(1) A car seems to be approaching

A sentence like (1) is standardly assumed to have an LF like (2):

(2) [A car]$_i$ seems [t$_i$ to be approaching]

The sentence in (1) can be interpreted in one of two ways: on one reading, it means that there is a car that seems to the speaker to be approaching; this is the so-called wide scope reading; on the other, "narrow scope" reading, the sentence can mean that it seems to the speaker that a car is approaching, a reading compatible with a situation in which no car may, in fact, be approaching, perhaps because the speaker has seen something which appears to her to be a car, even though it is in fact something else. Similarly, a sentence like (3) can be interpreted in one of two ways: a "wide scope" reading and a "narrow scope reading":

(3) How many books is John likely to read?

(4) a. What is the number n such that John is likely to read n number of books? (Narrow Scope reading)

b. What is the number n such that there are n books that John is likely to read? (Wide Scope reading)

U. Lahiri (✉)
The English and Foreign Languages University, Hyderabad, Telangana, India
e-mail: lahiri1963@gmail.com

G. Sengupta et al. (eds.), *Perspectives on the Architecture and Acquisition of Syntax*, DOI 10.1007/978-981-10-4295-9_9

The wide scope readings of (1) and (3) are relatively straightforward to derive in any theory of the syntax-semantic interface. The derivation of the narrow scope readings, however, requires special stipulations. (The narrow scope readings of sentences such as (1) and (3) are often called the *reconstructed* readings, for reasons that should be obvious.) One approach to deriving the narrow scope readings is called *syntactic reconstruction*: this involves assuming that the whole or part of the syntactically moved phrase is reconstructed or moved back either to the base position or some intermediate position within the clause that the quantified phrase moved from (presumably one of those intermediate positions that the moved phrase moved through, e.g., a Spec, C of an embedded clause or an adjoined position in the embedded clause). In the specific examples mentioned above, the theory of interpretation via syntactic reconstruction assumes that the LFs corresponding to the narrow scope readings of (1) and (3) would look something like:

(5) a. seems [[a car][be approaching]]
(alternatively, seems [[a car]$_i$ [t$_i$ be approaching]])
b. wh$_1$ John is likely [[n$_1$ many books]$_2$ [to read t$_2$]]
(abstracting away from the raising of "John")

The usual semantic interpretation rules that everyone needs to assume yield the narrow scope readings when applied to LFs in (5) without further stipulations. Cases like (5a) are said to represent "full reconstruction," as the entire moved phrase is moved back in order to be interpreted, whereas cases like (5b) are said to represent "partial reconstruction" as only a part of the moved phrase is moved back. Interpretation via syntactic reconstruction has been argued for in many works: for a representative sample, see Fox (2000) and Romero (1998) and the references cited therein. An alternative to this account is a family of approaches that might be called interpretation via *semantic reconstruction*, which assume that the moved phrases are interpreted in their postmovement position, but that the narrow scope reading is derived semantically, either by raising the semantic type of an interpreted trace (see, e.g., Cresti 1995; Rullmann 1993; Sharvit 1999) or various other constituents and predicates (an example of such an approach, working within a theory that does not assume the existence of traces, would be Jacobson (1999; 2000). To give an example, the narrow scope reading of (1), e.g., might be derived by assuming that the trace of the raised phrase in (2), rather than being of type e as would normally be assumed, can also have the interpretation of a variable of the type of generalized quantifiers, corresponding to something like (6), which can then yield the narrow scope reading by the usual operations of variable binding and function application:

(6) a. A car seems [Q to be approaching]
b. λQ [seem' (Q to be approaching')] (a car')
c. seem' ((a car')(be approaching'))

To derive the narrow scope reading of (3), one could raise the type of an intermediate phrase, presumably, one in the Spec, C position to that of a generalized quantifier: for details, see Cresti (1995), for example. Many researchers have defended interpretation by syntactic reconstruction for the relevant cases by pointing to evidence from English and some other languages, involving the application of Binding Theory in reconstructed readings. This involves both Principle C (see Fox 2000; Romero 1998; Elbourne and Sauerland 2002); and Principle A (Fox and Nissenbaum 2004). The two generalizations that underlie this argument can be summarized as follows: (a) an r-expression inside a moved phrase that has moved out of a clause cannot be anaphorically dependent on (i.e., coindexed with) a pronoun in the matrix clause on the narrow scope reading (though it might on the wide scope reading); (b) an BT-anaphor inside a moved phrase that has moved out of a clause (a local domain for Principle A) cannot be coindexed with a DP in the matrix clause on the narrow scope reading (though it might on the wide scope reading). These two generalizations are stated as follows:

(7) a. * [… r-expression$_1$ …]$_2$[$_{\text{Clause1}}$ … pronoun$_1$ … [$_{\text{Clause2}}$ … t$_2$ …]]
(on the narrow scope reading)
b. * [… anaphor$_1$ …]$_2$ [DP$_1$ … [$_{\text{Local Domain}}$ … t$_2$ …]]
(on the narrow scope reading)

For reasons that should be obvious, I will call (7a) Generalization C and (7b), Generalization A. On the interpretation by syntactic reconstruction view, Generalizations C and A follow because the moved phrases are reconstructed back to the moved position at LF on the narrow scope reading, and hence lead to violations of Principles C and A, respectively, on the assumption that BT principles apply at LF and LF alone (as is assumed in much current work):

(8) a. * [$_{\text{Clause1}}$ … pronoun$_1$ … [$_{\text{Clause2}}$ … [… r-expression$_1$ …]…]]
(Principle C violation)
b. * [DP$_1$ … [$_{\text{Local Domain}}$ … [… anaphor$_1$ …] …]] (Principle A violation)

This follows naturally on the syntactic reconstruction view, but needs further explanation on the view that the narrow scope readings are derived by semantic reconstruction. The purpose of this article is to present data from NPI licensing under across-the-clause scrambling in Hindi that provide counterexamples to both generalizations C and A. The data seems to suggest that semantic reconstruction should be an available, though possibly marked, option. If binding principles are assumed to hold at LF, and only at LF, the data from reciprocal binding would suggest that both syntactic and semantic reconstruction should be available options. Reconciling the Hindi and the English data is beyond the scope of this work, but at the very least, the data presented here should be part of the debates in work on the syntax-semantics interface.

Basic Facts About NPI Licensing and Scrambling in Hindi

The major class of Negative Polarity Items (NPIs) in Hindi consists of an indefinite and a particle *bhii* that means "also" or "even." Examples of such NPIs are expressions such as *koi bhii* ("anyone," consisting of *koi* "some/a," and *bhii* "even"), *ek bhii* ("even one," consisting of *ek* "one," and *bhii* "even"), and others like these combinations (for the detailed relevant evidence on the entire series and the distribution, see the standard work on the topic, Lahiri 1998). Two examples below show the NPI behavior of these items:

(9) * ek bhii aadmii aayaa.
one even person came
'* Even one person came'

(10) ek bhii aadmii nahiiN aayaa.
one even person neg came
'Not even one person came'

In the rest of this squib, I will use examples involving *ek bhii* as the points made carry over to all the other NPIs of the relevant series. As pointed out in Lahiri (1998), the NPI behavior of these expressions follow if we simply assume that the meaning of these expressions is simply composed of the meaning of the parts, plus generally made assumptions about the pragmatic/semantic behavior of indefinites in general, and numerals in particular. I will not go into the details here: the reader interested in the details may wish to consult the above mentionedwork. However, I would like to mention briefly the assumptions about the LF-syntax that need to be made about sentences containing *even* or *bhii*. One could assume, following Rooth's reinterpretation of prior work by Karttunen and Peters (Rooth 1985; Karttunen and Peters 1977) that *even/bhii* is a scope taking sentential operator that simply associates with a focussed element, and that moreover, can take scope over other elements, negation being the obvious one. This means that the LF-syntax corresponding to (9) and (10) would be (11) and (12), respectively, (in a very schematic form, abstracting away from Hindi word order and lexicon):

(11) *bhii/even* $_C$ [[one]$_F$[person] came]

(12) *bhii/even* $_C$ [neg [[one]$_F$[person] came]]

An alternative to the Rooth-Karttunen and Peters assumptions might be to assume the proposal of Krifka (1995), which does not analyze *even* directly, but uses an operator that he calls the Emph(atic) Assert(ion) (EmphAssert) operator to analyze emphatic statements like the sentences that contain lexical items like *even* as well as strong NPIs. According to his proposal, words like *even* are a lexical realization of the EmphAssert operator. We could adapt this idea to say that lexical items like *even/bhii* are not meaningful in themselves, but are required to appear in structures that contain an EmphAssert operator. On this proposal, *even/bhii* are not required to move themselves, but the scopal interactions can be captured by the relative scope of the EmphAssert operator and the other scope-bearing element. In other words, the LFs corresponding to (9) and (10) would be something like (13) and (14), respectively:

(13) EmphAssert $_C$ [[even[one]$_F$[person]]came]

(14) EmphAssert $_C$ [neg [[even[one]$_F$[person]]came]]

I will assume for the rest of this squib that this adaptation of Krifka's idea is the right one for the analysis of the phenomena we are looking at: as we shall see, proposals for either syntactic or semantic reconstruction of scrambled NPIs become considerably simpler under these assumptions.

Let me also briefly mention the basic facts about Hindi scrambling. Hindi is an SOV language, and NP/DPs may be freely moved to the left. Rightward scrambling is possible, but more constrained: for a recent discussion of these phenomena, see Bhatt and Dayal (2007) and the references cited therein. The most detailed recent discussion of leftward scrambling can be found in Kidwai (2000). DPs can be scrambled to the left across clauses, as the following examples show:

(15) a. Ramesh-ko maiN-ne kahaa ki [siitaa-ne t dekhaa]
Ramesh-acc I-erg said that Sita-erg saw
'I said that Sita saw Ramesh'

b. ek aadmii-ko maiN-ne kahaa ki [siitaa-ne t dekhaa]
one person-acc I-erg said that Sita-erg saw
'I said that Sita saw someone' (ambiguous, both wide and narrow scopes of the scrambled existential quantifier possible)

Keeping this in mind, one may note that NPIs can also be scrambled out of a clause, licensed by a negation in the embedded clause, as the following example shows:

(16) ek bhii pikcar, siitaa kahtii hai ki [saritaa-ne t nahiiN li]
one even picture Sita says that Sarita-erg not take
'Sarita says that Sarita didn't take even a single photograph'

Clearly, given that this is a scrambled NPI that is "licensed" by the negation in the embedded clause, it only has the narrow scope reading, and as mentioned earlier, this narrow scope reading can be derived either by syntactic reconstruction, or by semantic reconstruction. On the syntactic reconstruction account, the scrambled NPI would be moved back in the embedded clause in an intermediate position (presumably IP-adjoined), yielding an LF that would schematically look something like (17) (as before, abstracting away from Hindi word order and lexicon):

(17) Sita said [EmphAssert $_C$ not [[one$_F$ even picture]$_i$ [Sarita t_i took]]]

The standardly assumed semantic rules would apply to yield the proper interpretation of this sentence, without further stipulations. The semantic reconstruction account would assume on the other hand that a trace in an adjoined IP position that the scrambled NPI moved through would be interpreted as a generalized quantifier variable, and semantic interpretation would proceed accordingly, i.e., the LF-syntax looks something like (18):

(18) a. [one$_F$ even picture]$_i$ Sita said [EmphAssert $_C$ not [[-]$_{i,F}$ [Sarita t$_i$ took]]

b. [one$_F$ even picture]$_i$ Sita said [EmphAssert $_C$ not [[Q]$_{i,F}$ (λx[Sarita took x])]

c. λQ$_i$[Sita said [EmphAssert $_C$ not [[Q]$_{i,F}$ (λx[Sarita took x])]]([one$_F$ even picture])

d. Sita said [EmphAssert $_C$ not [[one$_F$ even picture]$_{i,F}$ (λx[Sarita took x])]

In interpreting (18), the trace "-" gets interpreted as a variable of type e, whereas the trace "-" gets interpreted as a variable of type <et, t>. On these assumptions, semantic interpretation is straightforward when some technical details are filled in; for example, one has to make sure that the intermediate trace contains focus features in order for the EmphAssert to apply correctly. The only nontrivial assumption is the interpretation of the intermediate trace: on some theories of the syntax-semantics interface, like that of Bittner (1994), this is prohibited (in her theory intermediate traces get no translation, effectively making semantic reconstruction impossible), but this must be the case for theories of semantic reconstruction to work.

Scrambled NPIs and Principle C

To choose between the two alternatives sketched above, the place to look for is the evidence that is usually presented to argue that syntactic reconstruction is the right theory for cases like the one mentioned above, where a syntactically moved element is interpreted as having narrow scope inside a clause it moved from. In recent work, Rajesh Kumar (Kumar 2006) looks at examples like the following (italics indicate coindexation in the following examples):

(19) raajiiv-ne kah-aa ki [aisii ek bhii pikcar jo *saritaa*-ne lii]
Rajiv said that such one even pictures which Sarita took
usko pasand nahiiN hai
she like not
'Rajiv said that she doesn't like any pictures that Sarita took'

(20) * raajiiv-ne kah-aa ki *usko* pasand nahiiN hai [aisii ek bhii pikcar
Rajiv said that she like not such one even pictures
jo *saritaa*- ne lii]
which Sarita took

He concludes from the contrast between (19) and (20) that scrambled NPIs are not interpreted via (syntactic) reconstruction, as moving the scrambled NPI to the base position would lead to a violation of Principle C. However, these are not the right examples to illustrate the point. While some of the earlier syntactic work on reconstruction assumed that reconstruction involves moving elements to the base position, the more recent work on the syntax-semantics interface that is informed by formal semantic theory recognizes that that position is untenable. For example, everyone recognizes that the "narrow scope" reading of *how many*-questions does not involve moving the quantifier back to the base position, but rather to an intermediate Spec or adjoined position (cf. examples 4b. and 5b. above, also Romero (1998) for a careful discussion of these points). For the same reason, also irrelevant are examples like the contrast between the following sentences:

(21) [aisii ek bhii pikcar jo *saritaa*-ne lii] raajiiv-ne kah-aa ki *usko*
such one even picture which Sarita took Rajiv said that she
pasand nahiiN hai
like not
'Rajiv said that she doesn't like any pictures that Sarita took'

(22) *raajiiv-ne kah-aa ki *usko* pasand nahiiN hai [aisii ek bhii pikcar
Rajiv said that she like not such one even pictures
jo *saritaa*-nelii]
which Sarita took

Again, syntactic reconstruction does not require the scrambled NPI to be moved back to the base position: all one needs is for it to move to a position that is in the scope of negation, but above the subject pronoun in the embedded clause, and such a position is available for (21). The relevant examples (as pointed out in her discussion of reconstructed wh-phrases in English by Romero (1998), now applied to scrambled Hindi NPIs) are examples like the following:

(23) aisii ek bhii pikcar jo *saritaa*-ne lii, *vo* kahtii hai ki
such one even pictures which Sarita took she says that
rajiiv-ko pasand nahiiN hai
Rajiv like not
'Sarita said that Rajiv doesn't like any pictures that she took'

(24) aisii koii bhii pikcar jo *saritaa-ne lii, vo* kahtii hai ki
such some even pictures which Sarita took she says that
rajiiv-ko pasand nahiiN hai
Rajiv like not
'Sarita said that Rajiv doesn't like any pictures that she took'

Examples like (23) are indeed possible and acceptable, thus casting doubt on generalization C mentioned in the introduction. Rajesh Bhatt (p.c.) points out that there is a contrast between (23) and (25), where the r-expression in the scrambled NPI is inside an argument rather than in a relative clause, as in (23):

(25) ?? *saritaa* kii ek bhii pikcar, *vo* kahtii hai ki rajiiv-ko pasand nahiiN hai
Sarita-gen one even picture she says that Rajiv like not
'Sarita says that Rajiv doesn't like a single picture of hers'

While I agree with the judgement, note that the following sentence is quite acceptable:

(26) *saritaa*-ke do baccoN-kii ek bhii pikcar, *vo* kahtii hai ki
Sarita's two children's one even picture she says that
rajiiv-ko pasand nahiiN hai
Rajiv like not
'Sarita says that Rajiv doesn't like a single picture of her two children'

Whatever the reason for the contrast between (23) and (25), it cannot be simply because the r-expression is in an argument position in the scrambled NPI. Thus, the evidence presented here would seem to be genuine counterexamples to generalization C.[1] Moreover, as we see below in the following discussion of Principle A, the argument/adjunct distinction is not relevant for the phenomena at hand.

Scrambled NPIs and Principle A

We can now look for evidence from Principle A and see whether we can decide between syntactic and semantic reconstruction accounts for these phenomena. The configuration we need to look at is the following (7b, repeated here as 27, the "generalization A"):

(27) $*\ [\ldots\ \text{anaphor}_1\ \ldots]_2\ [\text{DP}_1\ \ldots\ [_{\text{Local Domain}}\ \ldots\ t_2\ \ldots]]$

[1]Under standard assumptions, it is unclear why the adjunct-argument distinction should matter in the first place in scope reconstruction anyway. The standard argument for late merger of adjuncts involves wh-movement, like the contrast between (a) "Guess which argument that supports *John's* theory *he* adopted" and (b) "??Guess which argument that *John's* theory is correct *he* adopted". On the copy theory of movement, for example, the copy that is eventually deleted phonologically would be the one violating Principle C in both cases if there was no late merger. The standard account is that the relative clause is not present in (a) before wh-movement, and so the copy that gets deleted in the phonology is simply *which argument*, thus not violating Principle C. The relative clause gets merged late, i.e., after wh-movement. This option is not available with the nominal complement clause in (b), which cannot be merged late, and thus the oddity of (b), taken to be a violation of Principle C. However, in the scope reconstruction cases, the relative clauses have to be present at LF (simply in order to be interpreted) and if binding principles apply at LF, a principle C violation must result. Trying to get an argument-adjunct distinction in the scope reconstruction cases would require late merger of adjuncts *after* covert movement, and not just overt movement. For discussion and other independent arguments against allowing late merger after covert movement, see Fox (2003).

Examples corresponding to the configuration in (27) would look like the following, at a first glance:

(28) a. *ek duusre*-kii ek bhii pikcar, *vo* kahte haiN ki un
each other's one even picture, they say that those
logoN-ko pasand nahiiN hai.
people like not
'*They* say that those people do not like *each other*'s pictures'

b. *ek duusre*-kii ek bhii pikcar, *vo* socte haiN ki un
each other's one even picture, they think that those
logoN-ko pasand nahiiN hai.
people like not
'*They* think that those people do not like *each other*'s pictures'

c. *ek duusre*-kii ek bhii pikcar, *rameS aur siitaa* kahte haiN ki
each other's one even picture, Ramesh and Sita say that
un logoN-ko pasand nahiiN hai.
those people like not
'*Ramesh and Sita* say that those people do not like *each other*'s pictures'

While these examples might at first glance seem to be counterexamples to generalization A, the argument has to be made carefully. Fox and Nissenbaum (2004), discussing earlier work by Sportiche, Brody and others argue that a potential confound in the data is the existence of a logophoric interpretation of reflexives and reciprocals. They note that this would explain apparent counterexamples to generalization A, as in the following English examples (Fox's (22)):

(29) a. How many songs about *each other* did *John and Mary* say Bill should compose?

b. *John and Mary* wonder how many songs about *each other* Bill should compose.

(29a), e.g., allows a scope reconstructed reading where coindexation between *each other* and the DP *John and Mary* is perfectly possible. These examples also conflict with other data presented in Fox and Nissenbaum (2004) that they take to exemplify generalization A in cases involving scope reconstruction of *how many*-questions. Fox and Nissenbaum suggest that these acceptable readings arise because reciprocals and reflexives can also have logophoric readings, following earlier work by Pollard and Sag. They note, e.g., that a subject antecedent can sometimes bind reciprocals and reflexives across local domains, as the example (29b) shows. They note that once the antecedent is changed to an object, the sentences corresponding to (2) become unacceptable (Fox and Nissenbaum's (23)):

(30) a. * How many songs about *each other* did you tell *John and Mary* Bill should compose?

b. * I told *John and Mary* how many songs about *each other* Bill should compose.

They argue that in (29), the antecedent is licensed by a Logophor-Licensing Condition, and that under their hypothesis, "an anaphor that is exempt from the binding theory (a logophor) is licensed only if it refers to a sufficiently salient individual (or is bound by an NP that quantifies over such individuals)." They argue that "subjects (but not objects) of predicates like *say*, *believe*, *ask,* and *tell* refer to individuals that are salient enough for anaphors to corefer with …". As they point out, these considerations also explain the contrasts in (31)–(32) (their (24)–(25)):

(31) a. ?*John and Mary* think Bill should compose five songs about *each other.*

b. *I told John and Mary that Bill should compose five songs about each other.

(32) a. ?*John and Mary* wondered whether Bill composed any songs about *each other.*

b. * I asked *John and Mary* whether Bill composed any songs about *each other.*

If their basic point about logophor licensing is correct, it would seem then that (28) does not counterexemplify generalization A. It is entirely possible, therefore that in (28), the reciprocal *ek duusre* is licensed by the logophor licensing condition. One could further support this hypothesis by noting that if the potential antecedents in the examples in (28) are changed from the subject of the matrix clause to the object, the resulting sentences are bad.[2]

(33) **ek duusre* kii ek bhii pikcar, rameS-ne *suniil aur afzal*-se kahaa ki ramaa-ko pasand nahiiN haiN.
each other's one even picture, Ramesh-erg Sunil and Afzal-instr said that Rama like not.
'*Ramesh told *Sunil and Afzal* that Rama doesn't like any pictures of *each other*'

Moreover, scrambling the object plural DP across the subject does not improve the sentence, as shown in (34):

[2]The object of the verb kah- "tell" is marked with the instrumental in the western dialects of Hindi.

(34) **ek duusre* kii ek bhii pikcar, *suniil aur afzal*-se rameS-ne kahaa ki ramaa-ko pasand nahiiN haiN.
each other's one even picture, Sunil and Afzal Ramesh-erg said that Rama like not.
'*Ramesh told *Sunil and Afzal* that Rama doesn't like any pictures of *each other*'

Note, however, that scrambling the object further across the moved NPI makes the sentence acceptable:

(35) *suniil aur afzal*-se, *ek duusre* kii ek bhii pikcar, rameS-ne kahaa ki ramaa-ko pasand nahiiN haiN.
Sunil and Afzal each other's one even picture, Ramesh-erg said that Rama like not.
'*Ramesh told *Sunil and Afzal* that Rama doesn't like any pictures of *each other*'

This is puzzling, if logophoric licensing is all that is going on in these examples. For one, this would mean that when the matrix object is scrambled across the matrix subject, it does not count as "salient" to be a possible antecedent for a logophor, unless it is also clause-initial, in which case it would become a possible antecedent. This is not plausible for the following reason: one can reproduce contrasts like the English contrasts in (31) and (32), but where scrambling the object to a clause-intial position does not improve matters:

(36) a. ?? suniil aur afzal socte haiN ki rameS-ne ek duusre-kii pikcar lii
Sunil and Afzal think that Ramesh-erg each other's pictures took
'?Sunil and Afzal think that Ramesh took each other's photograph'

b. * maiN-ne suniil aur afzal-se kahaa ki rameS-ne ek duusre-kii pikcar lii
I-erg Sunil and Afzal say that Ramesh each other's picture took
'* I told Sunil and Afzal that Ramesh took each other's photograph'

c. *suniil aur afzal-se maiN-ne kahaa ki rameS-ne ek duusre-kii pikcar lii

It does seem then, that (35) is a genuine counterexample to generalization A. What is going on here? Let us assume that reciprocals can indeed, following Fox and Nissenbaum, be licensed either by Binding Theory or by logophoric licensing. Licensing by binding theory requires strict c-command by the antecedent at LF. This is why (33) and (34) are ungrammatical, whereas (35) is acceptable, as the scrambled clause-initial matrix object in (35) strictly c-commands the anaphor, but the matrix object in (33) and (34) do not. The anaphors in (28) are indeed licensed by logophoric licensing, following Fox and Nissenbaum. I take it that licensing of logophors does not require strict c-command. This is the best explanation of the entire range of Hindi facts reviewed above, but this leads us to conclude that generalization A does not hold for Hindi scrambling of NPIs.

Final Remarks

The facts reviewed above lead us to conclude that generalizations A and C do not hold in Hindi for NPIs licensed in an embedded clause scrambled across a matrix clause. If binding principles are taken to hold at LF, this means that semantic reconstruction should at least be a possibility, if only as a marked option.[3]

References

Bhatt, Rajesh, and Veneeta Dayal. 2007. Rightward scrambling as rightward remnant movement. *Linguistic Inquiry* 38: 287–301.
Bittner, Maria. 1994. Cross-linguistic semantics. *Linguistics and Philosophy* 17: 53–108.
Cresti, Diana. 1995. Extraction and reconstruction. *Natural Language Semantics* 3: 79–122.
Fox, Danny. 2003. On logical form. In *Minimalist Syntax*, ed. Randall Hendricks. London: Routledge.
Fox, Danny. 2000. *Economy and Semantic Interpretation*. Cambridge: MIT Press.
Fox, Danny, and Jon Nissenbaum. 2004. Condition A and scope reconstruction. *Linguistic Inquiry* 35: 475–485.
Jacobson, Pauline. 2000. Paycheck pronouns, Bach-Peters sentences, and variable-free semantics. *Natural Language Semantics* 8: 77–155.
Jacobson, Pauline. 1999. Toward a variable-free semantics. *Linguistics and Philosophy* 22: 117–184.
Karttunen, Lauri, and Stanley Peters. 1977. Conventional implicature. In *Syntax and Semantics 11: Presupposition*, ed. C.K. Oh, and D.A. Dineen. New York: Academic Press.
Kidwai, Ayesha. 2000. *XP-Adjunction in Universal Grammar: Scrambling and Binding in Hindi-Urdu*. New York: Oxford University Press.
Krifka, Manfred. 1995. The semantics and pragmatics of polarity items. *Linguistic Analysis* 25: 209–258.
Kumar, Rajesh. 2006. *The Syntax of Negation and the Licensing of Negative Polarity Items in Hindi*. London: Routledge.
Lahiri, Utpal. 1998. Focus and negative polarity in Hindi. *Natural Language Semantics* 6: 57–125.
Romero, Maribel. 1998. Focus and reconstruction effects in Wh-phrases. Doctoral Dissertation, University of Massachusetts at Amherst, Amherst.
Rooth, Matts. 1985. Association with focus. Doctoral Dissertation, University of Massachusetts at Amherst, Amherst.
Rullmann, Hotze. 1993. Scope ambiguities in *how many*-questions. Paper presented at the Linguistic Society of America meeting, 1993.
Sauerland, Uli, and Paul Elbourne. 2002. Total reconstruction, PF movement, and derivational order. *Linguistic Inquiry* 33: 283–319.
Sharvit, Yael. 1999. Connectivity in specificational sentences. *Natural Language Semantics* 7: 299–339.

[3]While I do not discuss the relevant examples in the main body of the paper, I should note that a reciprocal inside a scrambled NPI can also be bound by a NP/DP in the embedded clause that the NPI scrambled out of: thus in example (28), *ek duusre* "each other" can also be bound by *un logoN* "those people-obl." This means that if one sticks to the simplest semantics for reciprocals and reflexives, syntactic reconstruction is also allowed in Hindi. Alternatively, one can assume a more complex semantics for these items (as would be assumed in the Jacobson works referred to in the text) and just stick to a semantic reconstruction account for these cases as well: this well requires a very different binding theory. Alternatively, one could mimic the semantics of reciprocals via appropriately typed interpretations of traces of the reciprocal operators in the embedded clause, which would obviate the need for syntactic reconstruction at all for these readings.

Chapter 10
Prima La Musica, Dopo Le Parole? A Small Note on a Big Topic

Josef Bayer

Introduction

For a linguistic contribution, the choice of my title needs an explanation. The question *prima la musica, dopo le parole?* ("the music first, the words later?") plays the central role in Richard Strauss' (1864–1949) last opera, *Capriccio*, first performed in 1942. The work is superficially about a love triangle in which a poet (*Prima le parole - dopo la musica!* "First the words, the music after!") and a musician ("*Prima la musica- e - dopo le parole!*" "First the music, the words after!") compete for the love of a countess, but in its heart, it is an extensive dialogue about the relation of form (metaphorically *musica*) and meaning (metaphorically *le parole*). I selected it for a start not only because I deeply adore Strauss but also because it may build a bridge to an important issue of contemporary linguistic theory and in particular the relation between the generative system and its relation with the interfaces with the extra-linguistic world. I will discuss five small sets of data which have been identified between mid-1990 and 2015. These sets of data are remarkable because they are built on apparent paradoxes which look like candidates that demand a general answer, and because this answer may have an important implication for the architecture of the language faculty. Of course, this will bring us back to *Capriccio*.

J. Bayer (✉)
University of Konstanz, Konstanz, Germany
e-mail: josef.bayer@uni-konstanz.de

G. Sengupta et al. (eds.), *Perspectives on the Architecture and Acquisition of Syntax*, DOI 10.1007/978-981-10-4295-9_10

German Indefinites and Lexical Case

German is a Case-marking language in which four Cases can be distinguished: nominative, genitive, dative, and accusative. Due to far-reaching loss of nominal Case-inflection, the language has many nominals that do not show any Case morphology. Indefinites such as *was* ("what"), *etwas* ("something"), and *nichts* ("nothing") are an example, but also feminine substance nouns such as *Hitze* ("heat"), *Kälte* ("coldness"), *Freude* ("joy"), *Wut* ("rage"). As Gallmann (1996) and Bayer et al. (2001) observe, these nominals can appear in their bare form in contexts in which they are assigned (or check) structural Case (nominative, accusative) but not in contexts in which lexical Case (dative or genitive) is required.[1]

(1) a. Nichts ist schiefgegangen NOM
nothing is wrong.gone
'Nothing went wrong'

b. Wir haben nichts erlebt ACC
we have nothing experienced
'We haven't experienced anything'

---

[1] (i) Die Feuchtigkeit hat kein-em Haus geschadet
the humidity has no-DAT house harmed
(ii) Der Kanzler konnte sich de-r Überweisung erinnern
the chancellor could REF the-GEN transfer remember

are grammatical because the quantifier in (i) bears overt dative Case, and the determiner in (ii) bears overt genitive Case. There is another use of *nichts* by which (1c) would be ok. This use is irrelevant here. For discussion, see Bayer (2009). Readers familiar with German may wonder why P-governed dative is fine. Consider the preposition *mit*, which requires dative case on its complement.

(iii) a. Der Chef war mit nichts zufrieden
the boss was with nothing content
'The boss wasn't satisfied with anything'
b. Man muss mit Kälte rechnen
one must with cold reckon
'One needs to be prepared for cold temperatures'

My answer to this is that P is not an assigner of dative Case but rather the *exponent* of dative Case. The true Case-relevant structure is N(P) + P. See Bayer et al. (2001) but in particular Bayer and Bader (2007).

c. *Die Feuchtigkeit hat nichts geschadet[2] DAT
the humidity has nothing harmed
'The humidity didn't harm anything'

d. *Der Kanzler konnte sich nichts erinnern GEN
the chancellor could REFL nothing remember
'The chancellor could not remember anything'

(2) a. Kälte stört mich nicht NOM
cold disturbs me not
'Coldness doesn't disturb me'

b. Ich kann Kälte gut ertragen ACC
I can cold well bear
'I can well tolerate coldness'

c. *Du darfst diese Pflanzen nicht Kälte aussetzen DAT
you must these plants not cold expose-to
'You must not expose these plants to coldness'

d. *Ich kann mich Kälte lebhaft erinnern GEN
I can REFL cold vividly remember
'I have vivid recollections of coldness'

Insertion of the definite determiner yields the expected semantic effect of a definite reading.

---

[2]Manfred Bierwisch (p.c.) observes the following datum which could pose a counterexample. e.g.

(i) Der Versuch nützt nichts und niemand-em
the attempt serves nothing and nobody-DAT
'The attempts neither serves anything nor anyone'

The verb *nützen* requires dative Case but only the second nominal, *niemandem* is overtly Dative-marked. Working with this example reveals interesting aspects. In (ii), we simply permute the two parts of the conjunctive phrase, and the result is ungrammatical:

(ii) *Der Versuch nützt niemandem und nichts.

Similarly, if the conjunction phrase gets disrupted by extraposition, which is otherwise fine:

(iii) Ich glaube, dass der Versuch niemand-em genützt hat (*und nichts)
I believe that the attempt nobody-DAT served has and nothing
(iv) *Ich glaube, dass der Versuch nichts genützt hat und niemand-em

My preliminary conclusion is unattractive but at this moment justified: The coordinated phrase in (i), *nichts und niemand-em*, is headed by the dative morpheme *–em*, i.e. [[*nichts und niemand*]-*em*], absolutely not typical for an inflection system but perhaps nevertheless worth considering.

(3) a. Die Kälte stört mich nicht NOM
'The (actual atmospheric) cold temperature does not bother me (e.g. because I'm wearing a warm coat)'

b. Ich kann die Kälte gut ertragen ACC
'I can easily bear the (actual atmospheric) cold temperature (e.g. because I'm wearing a warm coat)'

In these examples, the use of the definite determiner has a clear semantic effect. We speak of low temperatures in general or about the specific low temperature of here and now.[3]

Observe now that the deviant cases in (2c, d) are rescued when the definite determiner is used because the determiner is overtly Case-marked. Interestingly, the distinctive semantic effect that is observed between the use and nonuse of the definite determiner is absent when we turn to the lexical Cases.[4] Insertion of the determiner rescues the examples because the determiner bears morphological Case. Simultaneously, the example is ambiguous between the definite and the indefinite/nonspecific interpretation of *die Kälte*.

(4) a. Du darfst diese Pflanzen nicht der Kälte aussetzen DAT
(i) 'You must not expose these plants to the (actual atmospheric) cold temperature' DEFINITE/SPECIFIC
(ii) 'You must never expose these plants to cold temperature' DEFINITE/NON-SPECIFIC

b. Ich kann mich der Kälte lebhaft erinnern GEN
(i) 'I have vivid recollections of the cold weather (e.g. when I went skiing last year in Austria)' DEFINITE/SPECIFIC
(ii) 'I have not forgotten how it feels when it is very cold' DEFINITE/NON-SPECIFIC

---

[3]The definite determiner allows also a generic interpretation as in

(i) Die Kälte ist das größte Hindernis für den Energietransfer
the cold is the biggest handicap for the energy.transfer

Although (i) is hardly distinguishable from a version with the bare noun *Kälte*, there seems to be a difference. The definite description works here as it does in natural kind readings like in *The lion lives in Africa*. Also there we find an interpretive closeness with *Lions lives in Africa*. Once the realm of natural kinds is left, things look differently.

(ii) a. Cuckoo-clocks are made in the Black Forest
b. ??The cuckoo-clock is made in the Black Forest

[4]The example with the genitive yields the same effect but sounds less idiomatic. Speakers would prefer a PP after the verb *sich erinnern*. One should bear in mind that the verb-governed genitive has a fragile status in contemporary German.

The interesting fact is that the nonspecific bare NP-meaning is available in spite of the use of the definite determiner, and that this is the only way to express this meaning.

Could this be a funny accident? One can exclude the possibility that in addition to the regular semantically interpretable determiner D-1, there is a meaningless or heavily underdetermined determiner D-2 which occurs precisely for the purpose of Case-marking in the lexical Cases. There are at least two reasons why an account along these lines would fail. The first is that many varieties of German show a pleonastic definite determiner on proper names, especially on persons' names, e.g., *der Hans* (the John), *der Peter* (the Peter), *die Katharina* (the Catherine), and *die Maria* (the Mary), and that its application is independent of Case. The second and somewhat more intricate reason is that semantic distinctness can be achieved independently of the application of the definite determiner. As soon as lexical Case is spelled out elsewhere, e.g., on a prenominal adjective, interpretive differences were obtained, and the different interpretations map on the presence versus absence of the determiner.

(5) a. In Kalkutta konnte man sich d-er groß-en Kälte nicht erinnern
the-GEN big-GEN cold
'In Calcutta, no one could remember the particularly low temperature that held at a particular time in history' DEFINITE/SPECIFIC

b. In Kalkutta konnte man sich groß-er Kälte nicht erinnern
big-GEN cold
'In Calcutta, one could not remember any particularly low temperature in history' INDEFINITE/NON-SPECIFIC

In conclusion, one can be quite sure that the definite determiner is semantically interpreted wherever it distinguishes between two (or more) interpretations.[5] Our interest will be what happens when this is not the case. Before we turn to this, let us take a look at another case in point.

Specificity in Turkish

The following example shows that a very similar situation holds in Turkish, a language which is unrelated to German. Like many languages that provide examples of Differential Object Marking (DOM), Turkish shows an interpretive effect

[5]Application of the definite determiner to proper names is semantically vacuous because proper names are rigid designators (see Kripke 1972) and therefore automatically definite. Thus, the definite determiner is pleonastic, and one can wonder what its motivation is. The usual answer is that it makes Case explicit.

that comes along with Case morphology. According to general wisdom, the morpheme *-(y)I* in Turkish is not only an accusative Case marker but also a marker of specificity, see Enç 1991.[6] This is made clear by the fact that it can be applied to indefinites.[7]

(6) a. (Ben) bir kitap oku-du-m. INDEFINITE/NON-SPECIFIC
I a book read-PAST-1SG
'I read a book'

b. (Ben) bir kitab-ı oku-du-m. INDEFINITE/SPECIFIC
I a book-ACC read-PAST-1SG
'I read a certain book'

Specificity is rooted in a partitivity relationship. According to von Heusinger and Kornfilt (2005, p. 24,) *the referential index of a specific expression must be in an inclusive relationship to the set of corresponding indices of an established set (established in the discourse or made otherwise salient)*. This could be expected to be the reason for the contrast between (7a) and (7b).

(7) a. Ali kadın -lar -ın iki –sin -i tanı -yor -du
Ali woman-PL-GEN two-AGR [3]-ACC know-PROG-PAST
'Ali knew two of the women' (Enç 1991: ex. 28)

b. *Ali kadın-lar -ın iki -si tanı -yor -du.
Ali woman-PL-GEN two- AGR [3] know- PROG-PAST

(7b) would be deviant because *iki* (two) has to be specific by virtue of denoting a subset of an established set. It has first been noticed by Kornfilt (2001) that this argument does not succeed. Kornfilt as well as von Heusinger and Kornfilt point out that there are contexts in which *-(y)I* is required independently of semantic interpretation. Its absence would yield ungrammaticality. The morpheme *–(s)I(n)* is a nominal agreement marker which has to be followed by the accusative marker in a transitive context.[8] Interestingly, this rule holds no matter what, and *-(y)I* stops

---

[6]Outside concrete examples, we write *I* because the segment is subject to vowel harmony.

[7]One could conclude that *-(y)I* is a definiteness marker like the definite determiner *the* in English.

(i) (Ben) kitab-ı oku –du -m
I book-ACC read-PAST-1SG
'I read the book'

But as other examples show, this cannot be the case.

[8]Von Heusinger and Kornfilt (2005) compare *-(s)I(n)* with *one* in English.

(i) I compared various models and bought the new *(one)

The same can be seen in Bangla where the classifier *-Ta* works like a nominal exponent.

performing its usual job of distinguishing between a +specific and a –specific interpretation. Consider (8).

(8) Kitap-lar-ın iki -sin -i al,
book- PL - GEN two - AGR (3) - ACC buy
geri -sin -i kutu-da bırak.
remainder - AGR (3) - ACC box- LOC leave
'Take (any) two of the books and leave the remainder [of the books] in the box'

Crucially, the accusative-marked subset of books may be interpreted as non-specific. This would be unexpected if *-(y)I* is lexically predetermined as +specific. Von Heusinger and Kornfilt (2005: 37) conclude: *Where the accusative marker is required for formal reasons, it is not a reliable marker for specificity; elsewhere, it is.* The case is on a par with the German definite determiner. We can follow their generalization and say: Where the definite determiner is required for formal reasons, it is not a reliable marker for definiteness (or maybe specificity); elsewhere, it is. Let us now turn to a third case.

Specificity in Bangla

The Bangla object Case marker *-ke* applies to a direct human object (DO); it cannot be applied to nonhumans.[9]

(9) a. ami chele-Ta-ke dekhechi
I boy-CL-DO saw
'I saw the boy'

b. ami dur-Ta (*-ke) dekhechi
I mouse-CL saw
'I saw the mouse'

An indirect object (IO), on the other hand, must be marked with *-ke* no matter what its semantic status is.

(10) a. dilip chele-Ta *(-ke) khabar dilo
dilip boy-CL - IO food gave
'Dilip gave food to the boy'

b. dilip ĩdur-Ta *(-ke) khabar dilo
'Dilip gave food to the mouse'

(ii) ami nana rokom rong-er gaRi dekhechi ebong nil *(-Ta) kinechi
I different color-GEN car seen.have and blue CL bought
'I looked at cars of different color and bought the blue one'

[9]*-Ta* is the neutral classifier; in the cases considered here, it functions as a definiteness marker.

That *-ke* marks specificity can be seen in the following data, provided by Probal Dasgupta (p.c.) in which the numeral quantifier *duTo* quantifies over the set denoted by the common noun.[10] (12) shows that the semantic factor +human is again obsolete.

(11) a. ami du -To chele-ke khũjchilam INDEFINITE/SPECIFIC
I two- CL boy- DO searched
'I was looking for two boys (known to me)'

b. ami du -To chele khũjchilam INDEFINITE/NON-SPECIFIC
'I was looking for two boys (e.g. as opposed to two girls)'

(12) a. dilip du-To chagol-ke khũjche INDEFINITE/SPECIFIC
dilip two- CL goat- DO searches
'Dilip is looking for two goats (e.g. which he had lost before)'

b. dilip du-To chagol khũjche INDEFINITE/NON-SPECIFIC
'Dilip is looking for two goats (e.g. as opposed to sheep)'

Observe now that this difference in specificity can be suspended. As Probal Dasgupta (p.c.) points out, the *-ke* marked DP in (13) is ambiguous between the two relevant interpretations.

(13) khali dilip-i du-To chagol *(-ke) du-To bhERa bhab-te pare
only dilip- FOC two- CL goat -DO two- CL sheep think- INF can
'Only (stupid) Dilip can mistake two goats for two sheep'

chagol-ke can be interpreted as arbitrary goats or particular goats, known to the speaker. The context is exactly one in which *-ke* is required for the reason of exceptional case marking. Once again, we see that the semantic interpretation of the object marker stops or remains ambiguous as soon as it is required for a grammar-immanent formal reason.

So far, the examples were related to objects and their interpretation. Before one may develop the idea that something construction-specific is at work here, let us consider two more cases, the first one from Romanian genitive-marking, the other from the verbal syntax of German.

Genitive in Romanian

Romanian has an enclitic definite determiner, which can be represented by the archimorpheme *-L-*, as seen in *codru-l* (forest-D; 'the forest') or *frate-le* (brother-D; "the brother"). The regular interpretation as a definite determiner is also seen in (14b). *-L-* is required to assign genitive Case. In (14b) it is inherent in *prietna.*

[10]Notice that *-To* is a pure classifier here, without the import of definiteness. I suppose it is, on a par with other forms, a variant of *-Ta*.

(14) a. Băiatu-l înalt a plecat
boy -L tall has left
'The tall boy has left'

b. Prietna băiatu-lui înalt a plecat
friend(F)-L boy -L(GEN) tall has left
'The tall boy's girlfriend has left' Grosu (1994:160)

As Grosu (1994: 147) points out, *-L-* "is the sole assigner of GEN(itive) Case in Romanian, and this, *regardless of whether or not it has Determiner status.*" In the following example, which was provided by Alex Grosu (p.c.), one can see that in the genitive construction *-L-* must appear on the functional preposition *a*, although there is no definite DP in the construction.

(15) Un palat *(a-l) un-ui rege
a palace a-L a-Gen king
'a palace of a king'

Under the natural assumption that the grammar of Romanian employs only one underlying *-L-* morpheme, this could be another example which is of relevance here. As a determiner, *-L-* competes with the indefinite *un-* and therefore exerts its semantic impact. As a default form, it is the only form available to satisfy the requirement of genitive assignment. It has no competitor, and it is therefore free of any definiteness implications.

Satisfying the V2-Constraint in German

The examples considered so far have to do with the referentiality of nominal expressions. To see that semantic lacunae of this kind are independent of this domain of grammar, let us consider yet another example from German, but this time one from the grammar of the verb. Certain dialects and/or registers of German have the possibility of using *tun* ("to do") as the carrier of finiteness morphology. For details see Abraham and Fischer (1998), Eroms (1998) and Schwarz (2004), among others. The data which follows have originally been described in Bayer (2008).

(16) Ich glaube, dass er grade den Müll hinunter tragen tut
I believe that he right.now the garbage down carry does
'I believe that he is right now bringing the garbage down'

(17) Er tut grade den Müll hinunter tragen ~~tut~~
'He is right now bringing the garbage down'

This example shows that German is V-final in its base (see (16)), and that the finite verb moves up to the C-position in the root clause (see (17)). German being a "rigid" V2-language, it would normally be the lexical verb that moves. This is shown in (18), where we use strike-out to signal movement.

(18) Er trägt grade den Müll hinunter ~~trägt~~
he brings just the garbage down
'He is right now bringing the garbage down'

Unlike English *do*, which has developed a purely auxiliary sidetrack, the German verb *tun* is up to now a regular open class lexical verb,[11] which retains its lexical semantics throughout. As a consequence, *tun* is only compatible with VPs that denote an event which is under the control of an agent. In terms of *Aktionsart*, this includes states as long as these are under the control of an agent. The VP *auf dem Sofa liegen* ("to lie on the sofa bed") in (19) is a stage-level predicate (SLP), see Carlson (1980).

(19) Der Hund tut schon wieder auf dem Sofa liegen ~~tut~~
the dog does already again on the couch lie
'The dog is once again lying on the couch'

Although "lying on the couch" denotes a state, this state is conceptualized as a bounded event which is under the control of some agent, even if the agent is only a dog. Thus, *tun* can combine with this VP without provoking a semantic crash.

Quasi-eternal properties, individual-level predicate (ILP), such as *own, resemble, and lie on a lake* are semantically incompatible with *tun*. They are nonvolitional and can therefore not be agentive in any sense. They are incompatible with *tun*.

(20) *Er tut einen guten Charakter besitzen
he does a good character own
Intended: 'He has a good character'

(21) *Er tut seinem Vater ziemlich ähneln
he does his father much resemble
Intended: 'He much resembles his father'

(22) *Konstanz tut am Bodensee liegen
Konstanz does at.the Bodensee lie
Intended: 'Constance lies at the Bodensee (=Lake Constance)'

Throughout, the verb *tun* originates in clause-final position and moves to the C-position. As such it displays its semantic effects which may be compatible with the predicate as in (16) through (19), or not, as in (20) through (22). Notice now that the semantics of *tun* can be deactivated, and that this is precisely the case when the

[11]Nevertheless, Eroms (1998) points out interesting areas of erosion in Bavarian in which *tun* can be shown to be on a grammaticalization path along the lines of English *do* but only centuries later.

predicate itself or a projection of it has been moved to SpecCP. The following variants of (20) through (22) are spotless. No semantic in congruency obtains.

(23) [Einen guten Charakter besitzen] tut er auf alle Fälle
a good character own does he in any case
'A good character he has for sure'

(24) [Seinem Vater ähneln] tut nur ER
his father resemble does only he
'Resemble his father only HE does'

(25) [Am Bodensee liegen] tut Stuttgart zum Glück nicht
at.the Lake.Constance lie does Stuttgart luckily not
'Luckily, Stuttgart does not lie at Lake Constance'

In these cases, the finite form of *tun* cannot have been merged like any other lexical verb in VP. It must have been base-generated in C. If it had been merged in clause-final position, it would have left a V-copy, and this copy would give rise to the semantic clash described above. Obviously, *tun* is the "default" form that is selected as the carrier of the relevant features (phi-features and T) of the finite verb.[12] The interesting aspect of this is in the present argumentation that the semantics of *tun* is switched off precisely when no alternative exists to rescue the derivation of the sentence. The finite form of *tun* "rescues" the V2-construction. Its insertion is an act of repair. This puts the present case on a par with the four previous cases. It goes without saying that postulation of a second meaningless *tun* (tun-2) next to the regular *tun* (tun-1) would be nothing but a restatement of the facts.[13]

---

[12]Yiddish and various German dialects show that another choice is a finite copy of the topicalized nonfinite lexical verb. See Cable (2004), Fleischer (2008), Källgren and Prince (1989).

[13]Yvonne Viesel (p.c.) informs me that there are speakers for who the semantic restriction described above does not hold.

(i) Eine Geschichte, die meiner einigermaßen ähneln tut, möchte ich euch heute mitteilen!
a story which mine somewhat resemble does want I you today tell
'Let me tell you today a story which resembles my own story to some degree'
https://www.seniorbook.de/themen/kategorie/fitness-und-gesundheit/artikel/33847/momente-zurueck-holen

Similar ignorance of the semantic restriction can be observed in poetry as in a German folk song where it is important that *-hut* rhymes with *tut*.

(ii) Schön ist ein Zylinderhut, wenn man ihn besitzen tut
nice is a cylinder.hat if one it own does
'A top hat is nice if one owns it'

The core of my argument is not affected by such examples because ALL speakers, including those for who (i) and (ii) are semantically deviant or at best options in poetry, accept examples of the type in (23) through (25); the latter are, in fact, the only choice which the syntax of Standard German offers.

A Generalization

The five cases in point signal that there is a common denominator. What is it? My suggestion is the following. There are formal constraints that supervise the grammar's computational steps. These may be universal constraints as they have been studied extensively in generative grammar but may be also language specific ones. Assume these constraints are rigid and must be observed no matter what. How are these constraints satisfied? Normally, there is a multitude of lexical options. In English, the constraint on determining a singular NP can be satisfied by a choice between different determiners (*the, a*), a quantifier (*some, every*), a *wh*-determiner (*which*), a negative quantifier (*no*), a possessive (*my, her*) etc., and combinations of these (*whose*) etc. The residual V2-constraint as it shows up in subject-aux-inversion can be satisfied by a choice between *do* and a number of auxiliary or modal verbs. All these lexical choices yield distinctive semantic results. Or consider the Case Filter. The set of case-bearing nominals that can satisfy the Case Filter is huge, and the fact that each nominal may be associated with different semantic features and compositions thereof gives rise to an explosion of distinctive meanings. Occasionally, however, there may not be any alternative. In this case, only a single form can be chosen to satisfy the constraint. An example may be expletives. English uses the semantically eroded locative adverb *there*. Selection of the lexical alternative *here* would kill the expletive construction. German uses *es* (it) as in *Es herrschte einst ein Tyrann auf dieser Insel* (it ruled once a tyrant on this island). Selection of an alternative would either kill the construction or change the meaning. Another well-known case is *do*-support in English. The lexical item *do* is a default which as such lacks alternatives. Its selection does not induce a lexical semantic effect. Imagine a situation in which there is only one way to satisfy a constraint. No alternatives. Assuming semantic features for the sake of the argument, can there be meaning without there being alternatives? To draw a comparison with phonology, can there be a phonemic value without there being opposition? If a language employs a vocalic system which lacks front rounded vowels, it is futile to ask for the difference between/y/and/œ/, which in German distinguishes *Düsen* (nozzle-PL) from *dösen* (to doze, to daydream) or *Tüten* (bag-PL) from *töten* (to kill). A language may well have access to a sound like [y], but in the absence of any formal opposition to other candidates like [u] and [œ] and [e], it would not be able to make any symbolic use of it. Extending this old structuralist insight to semantics, one can argue that forms without alternatives lack semantic features and interpretation altogether.[14] The common denominator of the default form considered so far seems to be exactly that they lack semantic alternatives and as a consequence lack meaning altogether. It is, of course, not

---

[14]For example, to grasp the meaning of *here*, one has to grasp the meaning of *there* and what distinguishes the two. Or, to change the example, to compute the meaning of *She is not here* one presumably needs access to the meaning of *She is here*. Work on the processing of negation suggests indeed that negation is initially represented as affirmation and persists as affirmation in memory. See Hasson and Glucksberg 2006. For discussion of the structural notion of semantic space in de Saussure's and in Jakobson's work, see Caton (1987).

easy to determine more precisely what a default form is, and why a form develops this privilege over others. But even with an intuitive understanding of markedness, it should be clear enough what is at issue. This enables us to formulate the following principles.

(26) Constraint satisfaction

Satisfy morphosyntactic constraints rigorously!

(27) Semantic effect of Merge

Merger of a lexical item LI has an effect on the interface with semantics iff LI is chosen from a set of alternatives $\{LI_1, LI_2, \ldots, LI_n\}$.

(28) Default

Due to a markedness convention M, a lexical item LI may be disconnected from its set of alternatives $\{LI_1, LI_2, \ldots, LI_n\}$.

About (26), one can be sure that it is a simplification; let us call it an "idealization." It ignores constraint ranking as in OT or other forms of gradedness. For the present discussion, however, caveats in this direction appear to be less relevant. The background assumption of (27) is that merger of an LI imports, among other properties, semantic features by virtue of semantic alternatives. The background assumption of (28) is that selection of the least marked LI of a set can suspend the competition and therefore semantically isolate the LI.

With this equipment, let us now return to the paradigmatic examples we have introduced in the previous sections. All the forms under consideration are LIs which have alternatives. The German definite article has competitors, the Turkish accusative Case marker has at least the zero form as a competitor, and the German verb *tun* has thousands of verbs as competitors. So to make the argument work, it must be assumed that the constraint satisfiers in question are something like prototypes, and that they have reached their privileged state thanks to this quality.[15] The reasons for this may be manifold, but unmarked status and frequency are plausible conditions. For the actual argumentation, it is important to keep in mind that all these LIs are completely normal words or morphemes in the respective languages but have the potential for default status. Once they kick into the system as defaults, they are outside the system of opposites. Once they are defaults, they are constraint satisfiers with no semantic competitors and, according to our reasoning, semantic impact.

[15]Notice that in the traditional grammar of German the verb is called "*tun*-Wort." Ascribing similar prototype status to the definite determiners *der, die das* as well as to the Turkish accusative morpheme *-(y)I* does not seem to be completely far-fetched.

Consider first the definite article in German. Application of the indefinite determiner *ein* is not admissible in nouns such as *Kälte*, *Hitze*, and *Freude*.[16] The relevant constraint is the Case Filter by which no case-less (lexical) NP/DP can survive. According to Bayer, Bader, and Meng (2001), while structural Case is provided (or rather valued) by the functional syntactic heads *v* and T, lexical Case has to be imported morphologically or otherwise, for instance by a "functional" preposition. The definite determiner can do the job of providing overt morphology as in *d-er Kälte* (the-DAT cold). It is natural to assume that it is the only choice. Other choices like, for instance, *stark-er Kälte* (strong-Dat cold) would solve the overtness problem but import additional semantic material which may be unwanted or may not be in the numeration that is used for the composition of a structure. If, due to the definite determiner's lack of alternatives, its form is incapable of contributing semantic features, the grammar has the freedom of interpreting the lexically Case-marked DP, e.g., *der Kälte*, unrestrictedly, namely as either definite or as indefinite/ ± specific. This is exactly what we observe.

The Turkish example with the accusative marker *-(y)I* works accordingly. Normally, there is the choice between *-(y)I* and zero. Application of *-(y)I* yields the semantics of specificity; nonapplication of *-(y)I* yields the nonspecific reading. According to Kornfilt, (2001) and von Heusinger and Kornfilt (2005), however, the nominal agreement marker *-(s)I(n)* leaves no choice. The accusative Case marker must follow *-(s)I(n)*, or the derivation perishes. In this case, *-(y)I* is the default option, and consequentially, its usual semantic impact is lacking. It is then up to extra-syntactic forces to give the NP a specific or a nonspecific interpretation.

The Bangla example with the object marker *-ke* works accordingly. The specificity effects which are induced by the Case-particle *-ke* are suspended as soon as a formal Case requirement—here ECM—demands marking of overt and distinctive Case. Normally, the choice between *-ke* and zero is an alternative, and the semantics respond to this by assigning specificity to *-ke* while leaving zero for the non-specific interpretation. Under the ECM condition, the rules of the game have changed. Overt case-marking seems to be the stronger requirement. Thus, once the available case-marker *-ke* is selected to do the job of constraint satisfaction, the usual semantic import of *-ke* is suspended.

The Romanian example shows that what is generally the morpheme responsible for a definite description of a DP appears as the sole assigner of genitive Case, and if it appears in this function, its semantic impact as a definiteness marker ceases to exist. Again, there is an alternative in the grammar of Romanian between using *-L-* or *un*. No alternative to *-L-* is around for establishing genitive assignment. The remarkable property is that in this case *-L-* lacks its usual semantic impact.

Coming finally to the satisfaction of the V2-constraint in German, the choice is normally between quasi all the verbs of the language, including the verb *tun*, which, if selected, introduces its agentive semantics. Consider now the special case in

[16]To be sure, I am working here with a simplification that leaves aside special constructions as well as certain dialectal variants.

which, due to V(P)-tropicalization, no finite verb is left over that could be moved up to C for satisfaction of the V2-constraint. In this case, *tun* is chosen as the default form.[17] Being the default form, it has no alternative. According to our reasoning, this is the cause for its not having any meaning. The verb is, so to say, nothing but the morphological carrier of the relevant features (φ and T). Notice that in this situation German *tun* is the same as English *do*. It works on a purely formal basis, with no consideration of semantics. This explains the absence of a semantic clash between the verb *tun* and the semantics of the VP.[18]

The Consequence

Coming back to the question in the title of this article, *Prima la musica, dopo le parole?*, let me take *musica* to refer to a purely formal system without any component of intensional meaning and ergo without the capacity of mapping onto Fregean reference (in German "Bedeutung"). Let me take *le parole* in a very broad sense as descriptions of meaning. We could then venture an affirmative answer to this question. Syntax (including morphology) seems to be a closed system, characterizable as I(internal)-language by Chomsky (1986). It runs on the basis of formal operations characterized in the Minimalist Program as potentially recursively applying *merge* and *agree* operations, and it does so mandatorily and without the influence of external factors of purpose, communication, style, etc. However, unlike the systems of music, which is arguably semantics-free, natural language syntax employs symbols that are most of the time open to semantic interpretation. The semantic system needs and loves alternatives. It looks as if the whole space of alternatives is exploited by semantic interpretation. Non-use would be luxury and is

---

[17]It is unclear to me why it is *tun* (to do). According to my reasoning, it could as well be the equally general verb *machen* (to make).

[18]We assumed so far that in this case a finite form *tun* is base generated in C. There can be no copy in clause-final position because such a copy would declare *tun* to be a lexical part which composes with some VP and yields a complex VP, namely $[_{tunP}\ [_{VP} \ldots]\ tun]$, give rise to regular semantic composition and therefore activate the semantics of *tun*. Notice as a potential problem, however, that *tun* agrees in φ-features with the subject of the clause.

(i) [Den Müll hinunter tragen] tu-**t** **er** nie
the garbage down carry do-3SG he-3SG never
'Bringing the garbage down, he never does'

(ii) [Den Müll hinunter tragen] tu-**st** **du** nie
the garbage down carry do-2SG you-2SG never
'Bring the garbage down, you never do'

The problem is that base-generation of finite *tun* in C would fail to explain how agreement works. Masayuki Oishi (p.c.) suggests that *tun* is base-generated in T, where it agrees with the clausal subject, and then moves to C for satisfaction of the V2-constraint. Since in this case, there is no copy in the VP, and the semantic problem still does not arise. I adopt Oishi's solution.

therefore avoided.[19] There can be no doubts that this is one of the primary sources of linguistic creativity. If we are right, there are however symbols which can be recruited as constraint satisfiers while lacking the property of having alternatives. These are our default candidates. Their role and appearance in *musica*/syntax/I-language is unspectacular. They do whatever grammar dictates them to do. On the way to the semantics interface, however, these elements are identified as not allowing alternatives. As a consequence, the interpretive system circumvents them. One way of circumvention that we have detected is that the constraint satisfier is simply skipped by the semantics.[20] This is clearly the case when *tun* is inserted for no other reason than the satisfaction of the V2-constraint. The other but clearly related way of circumvention that we have detected is to ignore the constraint satisfier by leaving its interpretation open to the semantic system. This is the case if we understand the German and the Turkish cases of indefinite/nonspecific interpretation of formally definite/specific markers as under specification, or more precisely suspended specification.

In Strauss' ingenious opera, the question *Prima la musical, dopo le parole?* remains unanswered because the capricious countess cannot decide who she loves more, the musician or the poet. We may be in a slightly better position than the countess if we can rely on findings like those that have been reported above. These findings speak in favor of the primacy of an encapsulated formal system which is, in a logically independent step, used for semantic interpretation but cannot be identified with it. Semantic interpretation depends on the formal system. An architecture of the language faculty that turns this set-up around would have to show how syntax follows from semantics and ultimately from E-language.[21] As everybody knows, there is a rich functionalist tradition that tried to follow this idea in one form or the other.

An interesting debate about this issue has been opened by Hinzen (2006) and Leiss (2009). Leiss offers a broad critique of the philosophy of language which, according to her, in its history since the medieval tradition but especially at the time of the so-called linguistic turn tried to devaluate language in favor of various language-external extensional, intensional, or pragmatic foundations. In the so-called nominalist conception, according to Hinzen (2012) and Leiss (2009), language is independent of thought; it "is conceived as merely a system of labels, and thought is

[19]One classic observation is that natural languages have more or less no synonyms. Even if German nouns such as *Gesicht, Antlitz, Visage*, and *Fresse* refer to "face," and differences may at times be hard to be pinned down extensionally, they are semantically very different and can normally not be exchanged. Even in notorious cases like *firefly* versus *lightning bug*, there is a difference, albeit only a dialectal/geographical one, see http://www.oldsouthhigh.com/2013/06/10/lightning-bug-or-firefly/.

[20]Following more closely the syntactic *façon de parler*, we may speak of "deletion" before transfer to the C/I-interface.

[21]An extreme position of this belief can be found in Schneider Schneider (1975), where it is not only claimed that semantics must be the foundation of syntax but that the ultimate foundation of both of them must be pragmatics.

structured primarily by logic and has a semantics fixed by relations between concepts and the world unmediated by grammar" (Hinzen 2012:636). This is the reason why logic became the prime formal meta-theory for philosophy. However, as Hinzen argues, there cannot be any *language of thought* (LoT) as proposed by Fodor (1975; 2008) which is epistemologically prior and therefore independent of grammar-based language, and there cannot be any language-independent logical foundation of cognition. Starting out from the pre-Cartesian "modist" tradition of grammar, Hinzen refers to the Sanskrit grammarian Bhartṛhari for the idea that an essential property of thought is to be grammaticalized, and that it is the novel linguistic form which generates a novel thought, and not the other way round. Conceptualization and rational thoughts are the results of the specific form that grammar offers.

Above I referred to Chomsky's concept of an *I-language*. Within the minimalist program, the notion of I-language has acquired a highly restrictive interpretation. Much of what was in the core of syntax in the *Principles and Parameters Theory* of Chomsky (1981) is now considered to be a matter of "externalization." I-language as a LoT, albeit distinct from a Fodorian one, is characterized by the recursive operations of *merge* and *move* while parameterization and other forms of variation are a matter of externalization and are excluded from core syntax. As Berwick and Chomsky (2016: 70) put it, *provided with conceptual atoms of the lexicon, the operation Merge, iterated without bound, yields an infinity of digital, hierarchically structured expressions.* "If these expressions can be systematically interpreted at the interface with the conceptual system, this provides an internal "language of thought"." According to Noam Chomsky (p.c.) the atoms are radically different in character from any known animal system, and their evolutionary origin remains a mystery. Chomsky suggests that some of them may have been there before LoT was externalized—and in fact, before it could even be internalized, modeled after actor-action schemata and other cognitive structures. It is assumed that the lexicon of atoms for generating LoT includes functional as well as substantive categories, externalized at some stage of the history of homo sapiens. So LoT appears to be pretty much like any natural language, albeit without the ingredients that are now ascribed to externalization. It is not always clear what exactly belongs to externalization, but as Berwick and Chomsky (2016: 11) point out, "externalization includes much more than just vocal/motoric learning and production, encompassing at least aspects of language such as word formation (morphology) and its relationship to language's sound systems (phonology and phonetics), readjustment in output to ease memory load during production, and prosody". Almost certainly, Case would be another aspect of language that is assigned to externalization. The danger I see here is that even the Chomskyan version of LoT could boil down to a semantic language with cognitive priority over the form that language and languages take. How would mismatches between meaning and form arise in the first place? What we found in the present study is evidence for a priority of form that offers itself to conceptual semantic interpretation. Of course, the core grammar's operations of merge and move are first of all formal operations, but there is a lot more in language than *merge* and *move* that determines interpretable structure. Case is one such factor, as our consideration of German datives in section "German Indefinites and Lexical Case" has shown. If form, including Case, takes priority over semantic interpretation, the form-meaning mismatch and the corresponding semantic lacunae find a systematic answer. But then, of course, Case is more central to core grammar than suggested in the maximally restrictive conceptualization of I-language.

Of course, the few cases considered in the present study allow only preliminary and somewhat speculative conclusions, and they can certainly address the philosophical debate only indirectly. Nevertheless, the "exceptions" we have encountered would be hard to explain in a model which is based on a concept of grammar as a coding device, a tool to encode some grammar-independently formed message. In such a model, why would grammar entertain the bizarre luxury of leaving small lacunae of interpretive indeterminacy or even interpretive irrelevance in its system? Any system built on intentionality and human rationality would discard a system like this. Speculative as the present conclusion may be, the case studies presented here suggest something different, namely primacy of a pure form of constraint satisfaction. By (26), the grammar is completely uniform. In those cases in which constraint satisfaction can be performed by selection of semantic alternatives from the lexicon, the semantic system takes its chance. In the face of a lack of alternatives, the semantics skips over or leaves interpretation to other extra-syntactic factors. If my interpretation of the facts is on the right track, the question in the title of this chapter may indeed have to be answered affirmatively: *Prima la musica, -e dopo le parole.*

Acknowledgements For discussion and help with data, many thanks to Manfred Bierwisch, Probal Dasgupta, Alex Grosu, Jaklin Kornfilt, Masayuki Oishi, Yvonne Viesel, and Andreas Trotzke. I am particularly indebted to Noam Chomsky for discussing with me some of my questions about his understanding of core syntax and externalization. Any misconceptions and errors are on my side. My research was supported by grant BA 1178/9-1 of the DFG (German Research Foundation).

References

Abraham, Werner and Annette Fischer. 1998. Das grammatische Optimalisierungsszenario von *tun* als Hilfsverb. In *Deutsche Grammatik – Thema in Variationen. Festschrift für Hans-Werner Eroms zum 60. Geburtstag*, ed. Karin Donhauser, and L.M. Eichinger, 35–47. Heidelberg: Winter.

Bayer, Josef. 2009. Nominal negative quantifiers as adjuncts. *The Journal of Comparative Germanic Linguistics* 12: 5–30.

Bayer, Josef. 2008. What is verb-second? Unpublished manuscript. University of Konstanz. http://ling.uni-konstanz.de/pages/home/bayer/pdf/Verb-Second.pdf.

Bayer, Josef and Markus Bader. 2007. On the syntax of prepositional phrases. In *Interface and Interface Conditions*, ed. by Andreas Späth, 157–180. Berlin: de Gruyter.

Bayer, Josef, Markus Bader and Michael Meng. 2001. Morphological underspecification meets oblique case: Syntactic and processing effects in German. *Lingua* 111: 465–514.

Berwick, Robert C. and Noam Chomsky. 2016. *Why Only Us. Language and Evolution.* Cambridge, Massachusetts: MIT Press.

Cable, S. 2004. Predicate Clefts and Base-Generation: Evidence from Yiddish and Brazilian Portuguese. Unpublished manuscript. MIT. http://people.umass.edu/scable/papers/Yiddish-Predicate-Clefts.pdf.

Carlson, Gregory N. 1980. *Reference to Kinds in English.* New York: Garland Publishing.

Caton, Steven C. 1987. Contributions of Roman Jakobson. *Annual Review of Anthropology* 16: 223–260.
Chomsky, Noam A. 1995. *The Minimalist Program*. Cambridge, Massachusetts: MIT Press.
Chomsky, Noam A. 1986. *Knowledge of Language*. New York: Praeger.
Chomsky, Noam A. 1981. *Lectures on Government and Binding*. Dordrecht: Foris.
Enç, Mürvet. 1991. The semantics of specificity. *Linguistic Inquiry* 22: 1–25.
Eroms, Hans Werner. 1998. Periphrastic, tun' in present-day Bavarian and other German dialects. In *DO in English, Dutch and German*, ed. I. Tieken-Boon van Ostade et al., 139–158. Münster.
Fleischer, Jürg. 2008. Zur topikalisierenden Infinitivverdoppelung in deutschen Dialekten: *Trinken trinkt er nich, aber rauchen raucht er* (mit einem Exkurs zum Jiddischen). Dialektgeographie der Zukunft: Akten des 2. Kongresses der Internationalen Gesellschaft für Dialektologie des Deutschen (IGDD) am Institut für Germanistik der Universität Wien, 20. bis 23. September 2006 (Zeitschrift für Dialektologie und Linguistik Beihefte 135) ed. Peter Ernst and Franz Patocka, 243–268. Stuttgart: Steiner.
Fodor, Jerry A. 2008. *LOT 2: The Language of Thought Revisited*. Oxford: Oxford University Press.
Fodor, Jerry A. 1975. *The Language of Thought*. Cambridge, Massachusetts: Harvard University Press.
Gallmann Peter. 1996. Die Steuerung der Flexion in der DP. *Linguistische Berichte* 164: 283–314.
Grosu, Alexander. 1994. *Three Studies in Locality and Case*. London: Routledge.
Hasson, Uri and Sam Glucksberg. 2006. Does understanding negation entail affirmation? An examination of negated metaphors. *Journal of Pragmatics* 38: 1015–1032.
Von Heusinger, Klaus and Jaklin Kornfilt. 2005. The case of the direct object in Turkish: Semantics, syntax and morphology. *Turkic Languages* 9:3–44.
Hinzen, Wolfram. 2012. The philosophical significance of universal grammar. *Language Sciences* 34: 653–649.
Hinzen, Wolfram. 2006. *Mind Design and Minimal Syntax*. Oxford: Oxford University Press.
Källgren, Gunnel, and Ellen Prince. 1989. Swedish VP-topicalisation and Yiddish verb-topicalisation. *Nordic Journal of Linguistics* 12: 47–58.
Kornfilt, Jaklin 2001. Non-specific partitives and the unreliability of specificity markings. Unpublished manuscript. New York: Syracuse University.
Kripke, Saul. 1972. Naming and Necessity. In *Semantics of Natural Language* ed. Gilbert Harman, and Donald Davidson. Dordrecht and Boston: Reidel.
Leiss, Elisabeth. 2009. *Sprachphilosophie*. Berlin: de Gruyter.
Schneider, Hans Julius. 1975. *Pragmatik als Basis von Semantik und Syntax*. Frankfurt: Suhrkamp.
Schwarz, Christian. 2004. *Die tun-Periphrase im Deutschen*. Master thesis: Universität München.

Part IV
Acquisition of Syntax

Chapter 11
The Influence of Visual, Auditory, and Linguistic Cues on Children's Novel Verb Generalization

Bhuvana Narasimhan, Fanyin Cheng, Patricia Davidson, Pui Fong Kan and Madison Wagner

Introduction

Children acquire words at an early age with apparent ease. They are able to map a novel word form onto its referent after only minimal exposure, a process known as "fast-mapping" (Carey and Bartlett 1978; Golinkoff et al. 1994). A rich and rapidly burgeoning literature has evolved to account for the factors that influence children's patterns of verb learning and categorization including perceptual features, conceptual factors, functional information, linguistic context, and speaker intention, among others (Smith et al. 1992; Imai et al. 1994; Kemler-Nelson 1995; Tomasello 1995; Booth and Waxman 2002; Scott and Fisher 2009). Learning the different factors that shape the meaning of a word beyond the initial stage of fast-mapping involves a protracted process during which the child learns to identify the appropriate range of referents to which the word applies in adult language. Based on limited prior experience with the word's use across situational and linguistic contexts, the child must learn to appropriately extend the use of the word to novel situations that have not been previously encountered. That children are engaged in the generalization process early in development is attested by their attempts to

We gratefully acknowledge the cooperation of the Tiny Minders Preschool, Louisville Public Library, and Gateway Amusement Park in allowing us to recruit children to participate in our research, as well as the many children and parents who took part in our study at the Language, Development, and Cognition Lab.

B. Narasimhan (✉) · F. Cheng · P.F. Kan
University of Colorado Boulder, Boulder, CO, USA
e-mail: bhuvana.narasimhan@colorado.edu

P. Davidson
Syracuse University, Syracuse, NY, USA

M. Wagner
Scripps College, Claremont, CA, USA

G. Sengupta et al. (eds.), *Perspectives on the Architecture and Acquisition of Syntax*, DOI 10.1007/978-981-10-4295-9_11

extend word use beyond familiar contexts, leading to a range of overgeneralization errors. For instance, the word *ball* might be "first applied to balls, then to apples, grapes, squash, bell-clapper, or anything round" (Clark 2004: 475). Patterns of (over)extensions can indicate attention to a number of properties including shape, texture, size, sound, and motion, as well as function (Clark 2004).

Despite this rich and extensive literature, however, we still know relatively little about how different types of multimodal cues interact in influencing children's word extension patterns. For instance, research on word learning suggests that children initially attend to a coalition of different cues, with perceptual cues initially receiving greater weight than either linguistic cues or social cues early in development (Golinkoff and Hirsh-Pasek 2007). Similarly, in extending already learned labels, children might also initially prefer to categorize novel referents based on perceptual rather than linguistic commonalities. Such preferences might be exhibited not only in laboratory settings but also in naturalistic contexts where cues occur in isolation as well as in conflict. For instance, in everyday contexts of word learning, children are unlikely to encounter the full constellation of features uniquely associated with a newly acquired verb. Often, it is likely that the child receives only linguistic information without the auditory or visual attributes associated with the referent action, e.g., in responding to questions about future events, they might retrieve the verb labeling an action based on the arguments or adjuncts typically associated with the verb (e.g., *what will you do with the shovel?*). Alternatively, the child might have to retrieve a verb for an action for which only visual information is available (e.g., an action that can be seen but not heard, e.g., a bike being ridden outside the window, or actions depicted in picture books), or in contexts where only auditory information is provided (e.g., the sound of footsteps outside or the closing of a door in a different room). In other situations, the child's task is to categorize ambiguous stimuli with features that belong to more than one preexisting verb category. For instance, consuming soup can involve chewing (e.g., depending on the chunkiness of its ingredients) as well as drinking; hence, either *eat* or *drink* could be used to label a soup-consumption event, whereas one would only *drink* coffee or *eat* stew. The verb that a speaker chooses to produce is likely to depend on a number of factors including the thickness of the soup, whether it is eaten with a spoon, or from a mug versus a bowl, etc.

Thus, the process of verb learning involves the ability to weigh different factors in extending the verb label to situations that are ambiguous or lack one or more of the cues prototypically associated with a verb. In the present study, we ask: what is the relative importance of different types of multimodal cues in influencing children's generalization of verbs to novel actions? Do different kinds of perceptual cues, e.g., auditory and visual cues, play a similar role in influencing verb extension? To what extent does linguistic context, in the form of lexical distributional regularities, compete with perceptual cues? Does the strength of the association of a cue with the verb when it occurs in isolation predict whether it will "win" when placed in competition with another cue? The present study aims to address these questions by investigating how children extend novel verbs to situations in which linguistic, auditory, and visual cues are placed in conflict.

In our study, we adapted a methodology originally used for object labels by Landau and Shipley (2001) and Johanson and Papafragou (2011) in order to examine how perceptual and linguistic cues influence children's extension of verbs to actions they have not yet encountered. Children are first taught nonce verb labels (*wug* and *meek*) for two "action standards" that are associated with different properties. Thus, the standards are "prototypes," each of which is associated with a distinct label and a constellation of visual, auditory, and linguistic features. During the test phase, children are asked to produce one of the labels (*wug* or *meek*) for novel test stimuli. The novel test stimuli consist of (video clips of) actions that either possess only one of the three multimodal features associated with the standard or that are ambiguous, possessing two conflicting features: one feature belonging to one standard (e.g., a visual feature) and the other feature to the other standard (e.g., a linguistic feature). Thus, for instance, the visual cue might be associated with the verb *wug* and the linguistic cue with the verb *meek*. Children's production of either *wug* or *meek* to label the ambiguous action is taken to demonstrate their relative preference for the visual versus the linguistic cue when they are pitted against each other. Children's ability to produce the appropriate verb when each type of cue is presented in isolation is also examined as a baseline measure of the relative strength of association of each of these cues with the verb when they are not in placed in conflict.

Methods

Participants

Participants were recruited through word-of-mouth as well as through local preschools, the town library, or a neighborhood theme park and tested at these locations or at the laboratory. A total of 30 children participated in the study. Data was excluded from 12 children who did not demonstrate the required mastery of the verbs or failed to complete the training or test phase. Data from two additional children who did meet our inclusion criteria of novel verb mastery also had to be excluded since the experimenter erroneously tested more children than mandated by the design of the study (which required the number of participants to be in multiples of 16). Data from the two children was excluded based on considerations of gender in one case (in order to maintain a relatively balanced proportion of males and females in our study) and lower comprehension scores and production scores after learning the two novel verbs in the other case. The participants who were included in the study consisted of a total of 16 children (seven female, nine male) ranging in age between 3;5 and 4;10 years.

Stimuli

The stimuli included video clips and unfamiliar "toys from Mars" designed to help participants learn new words. The toys were constructed using different objects attached together, disguised to be objects that were novel to the children. Each toy consisted of a bucket-shaped object with a spring attached to one side, and a cylindrical object (a small tape-covered bottle) attached at the base of the object (see Fig. 11.1). Four different versions of the toy were created, all of which had a spring attached to one side and a cylindrical, tape-covered bottle affixed to the base. The toys differed in color, size of the spring, and in the small accessories (colored clips, wooden stamps, colored wrappers) that were attached to them.

The video clips consisted of novel actions performed on the toys by two puppets. The novel actions were labeled by two nonce verbs, *wug* and *meek*. Hand puppets (Marsie, a red puppet "from Mars," and Lionie, a yellow lion puppet "from the zoo") were used to create training videos and testing videos. Both the puppets demonstrated the actions on each of the four toys over the course of the experiment. Their left-right position on the screen was counterbalanced across training and test trials.

The rattly and twangy sounds associated with the actions performed on the toys had minor variations in them. There were also variations in the verb forms used for *wug* and *meek* as well as in the forms of the nominals with which they co-occurred. Both forms were used in the progressive (e.g., *I am meeking the toy with my hand*) or in their bare form (e.g., *Do you want to meek the toy?*) and co-occurred with arguments in the object position that were either full noun phrases or pronouns (e.g., *I am wugging the toy/it carefully*) or were omitted if licensed by prior discourse context (in questions such as *Where is she wugging () carefully?* or in statements such as *She is meeking () with her hand*). The subject arguments were pronouns (e.g., *I, he, she*), or obligatorily null in complement clauses (e.g., *Do you want to meek the toy?*). The videos were created using a tripod-mounted camera, and audio files were recorded using a digital recorder and microphone in a quiet booth. Different sets of audio files were superimposed on the same set of videos using iMovie to create a total of sixteen different versions of the stimuli using Powerpoint.

Fig. 11.1 Example of stimuli used in the experiment

Four versions of the training phase were created. In two of these versions, the verb *wug* labeled the action of rolling and releasing a bottle attached with elastic, while the verb *meek* labeled the action of pulling a spring and letting it snap back into place. The actions were accompanied with auditory cues (a rattly sound for the bottle versus a twangy sound for the spring) and linguistic cues describing the manner or the instrument used (the preposition phrase *with his/her/my/your hand* described pulling and letting go the spring, and the adverb *carefully* described rolling and releasing the bottle). In the other two versions, the labels were switched such that *meek* labeled the action on the bottle (with the associated rattly sound and the adverb *carefully*) and *wug* labeled the action on the spring (with the associated twangy sound and the preposition phrase *with his/her/my/your hand*). For each of these verb-action-sound-adjunct phrase constellations, the order in which the verbs were presented during training was counterbalanced such that *wug* was introduced first followed by *meek* in two versions, and the reverse order was used for the other two versions.

Each of these four training phase videos was combined with a common set of stimuli (described further in the Procedure section) used in a comprehension training section, a comprehension assessment, and a production assessment to create four training video sequences. Each of the four training sequences was then combined with four different sequences of test trials that counterbalanced the order in which questions and audiovisual stimuli within the two blocks of the test phase were presented as well as the order of presentation of the stimuli within these blocks. The test stimuli consisted of twelve pairs of video clips. Six out of the twelve pairs of clips were constructed to assess children's ability to associate each type of cue with the appropriate verb when the cues are presented in isolation: the "simple cue" condition. Each pair consisted of one video clip in which a puppet asks a question that provides a linguistic cue associated with either *wug* or *meek* (*What is she doing carefully? What is she doing with her hand?*) or provides no linguistic cue (*What is she doing?*). The other clip was designed to provide either no perceptual cue (a black mask hid the puppet's action), or one of the perceptual cues associated with each verb: either visual (displaying the puppet's action) or auditory (a black mask covering the puppet's action but the sound accompanying the action was audible). The design of the clips used in the "simple cue" condition is as follows:

(a) Two clips were created by removing the sound and linguistic cues associated with the verb (*wug* or *meek*), and displaying only visual information about the action (either pulling the spring or rolling the bottle);
(b) Two clips were created by removing the sound and visual information about the action, and only providing the linguistic information (e.g., a puppet asking *what is she doing with her hand* or *what is he doing carefully*) in accompaniment to a black screen masking the puppet's action;
(c) Two clips were created by removing the linguistic and visual information about the action, and only providing the sound in accompaniment to a black screen (a rattly sound or a twangy sound).

Each of the sounds, actions, and linguistic phrases associated with each verb during training was used to create the six pairs of clips.

The remaining six pairs of clips were designed to assess children's preference for each type of cue (auditory, visual, or linguistic) when pitted against a cue of a different type: the "cue-competition" condition. Each pair consisted of one video clip in which a puppet asks a question that provides a linguistic cue associated with either *wug* or *meek* (*What is she doing carefully? What is she doing with her hand?*) or provides no linguistic cue (*What is she doing?*). The second clip consisted of the puppet performing the action associated with either verb. The clips were designed to visually display the action corresponding to one verb paired with the linguistic information associated with the other verb, the sound corresponding to one verb paired with the linguistic information corresponding to the other verb, or visual information about the action corresponding to one verb paired with the sound corresponding to the other verb. The design of the clips used in the "cue-competition" condition is as follows:

(a) Two clips combined the auditory cue for one verb with the visual cue for the other verb; for instance, the rattly sound (e.g., associated with *wug*) was shown in conjunction with the pulling of the spring (e.g., associated with *meek*). No linguistic cue was provided.
(b) Two clips combined the auditory cue for one verb with the linguistic cue for the other verb; for instance, the twangy sound (e.g., associated with *meek*) was heard in conjunction with the adverb *carefully* (e.g., associated with *wug*) in accompaniment to a blank screen such that no visual cue was provided.
(c) Two clips combined the visual cue for one verb with the linguistic cue for the other verb; for instance, the rolling of the bottle (e.g., associated with *wug*) was heard in conjunction with the adverb *with his/her/my/your hand* (e.g., associated with *meek*) with no auditory cue provided.

All possible pairs of combinations of sounds, actions, and linguistic phrases were used to create the six pairs of video clips for the "cue-competition" condition. The order of the clips in each pair of clips was counterbalanced. The video clip with the puppet asking the question preceded the video clip with the other puppet performing the action in half the clips, or followed it in the other half (in all phases except in the initial training phase and the comprehension assessment of the experiment, see below).

Procedure

After a brief warm-up in which the child or adult participant was engaged in conversation, consent was obtained from the parent. Verbal assent was also obtained from the child before the experiment was initiated. The procedure consisted of a training phase, a comprehension and production assessment, and the test phase.

The stimuli were displayed using Powerpoint. The Peabody Picture Vocabulary Test (PPVT) was administered after the experiment depending on time constraints and willingness on the part of the child. The data from the PPVT is not, however, further analyzed for this study.

Basic Training During the training phase, children were engaged in an interactive game in which they viewed a puppet from Mars who taught them two nonce words for novel actions from his language. The puppet introduced *meek* and *wug* to the viewer by sequentially performing the actions associated with each of the novel verbs with their corresponding sounds and linguistic cues using different variants of the same toy. For instance, the puppet might pull and release the bottle, which created a rattly sound. The puppet then introduced the nonce verb with the associated linguistic information, e.g., *I am meeking the toy* <u>*with my hand*</u>. The child was then given the same toy shown on the screen and asked to reproduce the action on the toy and label the action, with feedback provided if the child did not spontaneously provide the appropriate verb. In this way, the child was introduced to the characteristic visual information (pulling and releasing the bottle), the auditory information (rattly sound), and the linguistic information (*with my hand*) associated with the verb *meek* (in half the training conditions, the verb *wug* was associated with these features). A similar procedure was followed to introduce the child to the characteristic visual information (pulling and letting the spring snap back), the auditory information (twangy sound), and the linguistic information (*carefully*) associated with the verb *wug* (or the verb *meek* in half the training conditions). A second puppet (Lionie, from the zoo) appeared after each verb was introduced and asked the child to produce the label for the action demonstrated by the puppet from Mars. Feedback was provided if the child gave an incorrect response.

The initial training procedure was followed by a series of videos that the child was instructed to simply watch as the puppets demonstrated the actions with their associated sounds and linguistic information along with the appropriate verb label. In half the videos, the linguistic description was provided by one puppet first (e.g., *he/she is wugging () carefully*) before the action was performed by the second puppet, and this order was reversed in the rest of the videos. The two puppets alternated in demonstrating the actions on different toys and provided the linguistic descriptions.

Comprehension After a break, four comprehension videos were shown. The puppet first asked the child to point to the video demonstrating *meek* or *wug* (e.g., *Where is he meeking () with his hand? Where is she wugging () carefully?*). Participants were then shown two videos playing concurrently in which the second puppet demonstrated the action corresponding to either *wugging* or *meeking* on the same toy. Feedback was provided about the correctness of the child's responses.

Production In this phase, the child was shown an action and asked by a puppet to describe the action as either *meek* or *wug* (e.g., *what is she doing, wugging or meeking?*). Both puppets asked the question and both demonstrated the action on all four toys. In half of the videos, the question preceded the action; in the other half, the order was reversed. The experimenter provided the correct label whenever the child failed to do so.

Test Phase The experimenter then introduced the final test phase to the child by explaining that a new puppet (Naughty Piggy) had messed up some of the videos. Therefore, in some videos, the child might not be able to see and/or hear the puppets as they performed the actions corresponding to the verbs. However, the child was asked to try their best to identify what the action might be for each slide, either *meeking* or *wugging*. To encourage the child to answer throughout this section, the experimenter brought in a stuffed animal (Big Bird or Elmo) who asked for the child's help in learning the novel verbs. After the child responded to each video, the experimenter simply repeated the child's response in a neutral tone without providing any corrective feedback. In addition to video clips containing

Table 11.1 Overview of the different phases of the experiment

Experimental phase	Procedure
Training	• Two puppets interacted with the child on the computer. Two novel actions were demonstrated and labeled with a nonce verb (*wug*, *meek*), and the child performed each action on a real toy and labeled the action. • Then the child watched eight pairs of video clips in which a puppet described each of the two actions and the other puppet enacted it.
Comprehension assessment	• The child was shown four pairs of video clips. In each pair, a puppet asked the child to point to the action corresponding to *wug* or *meek*. • Then two video clips were played side-by-side and feedback was provided after the child provided a pointing response.
Production assessment	• The child was shown eight pairs of video clips. In each pair, a puppet asked the child to label the action performed by the other puppet (e.g., *what is she doing carefully/with her hand, wugging or meeking?*). • A second video clip showed a puppet demonstrating the action, and the child produced a label (*wugging* or *meeking*). Feedback was provided about the accuracy of the child's response.
Test	• The child was shown 16 pairs of video clips, 12 of which consisted of the novel test stimuli. In each pair, a puppet asked the child to label the action performed by the other puppet (e.g., *What is she doing (carefully/with her hand), wugging or meeking?*). • A second video clip showed a puppet demonstrating the action, and the child produced a label (*wugging* or *meeking*). • Six of the 12 clips were "simple cue" test stimuli providing only visual information about the action, only the sound, or only the linguistic information associated with *wugging* or *meeking*. The remaining six "cue-competition" test stimuli either showed the action corresponding to one verb paired with the linguistic information associated with the other verb, the sound corresponding to one verb paired with the linguistic information corresponding to the other verb, or the action corresponding to one verb paired with the sound corresponding to the other verb. • Four "control" clips showed familiar actions from the training session to measure accuracy post-training. • No feedback was provided about the accuracy of the child's response.

missing and conflicting cues, the test phase also included four control clips of the type that the children encountered during training, viz. clips that presented the full set of cues associated with each verb. Table 11.1 provides an overview of the different phases of the experiment.

Results

Data Coding

The data was coded for (a) comprehension accuracy during the training phase (the number of correct pointing responses in the four comprehension trials), (b) production accuracy during the training phase (the number of correctly produced nonce verbs in the eight production trials), (c) production accuracy in the control clips during the testing phase (the number of correctly produced nonce verbs in the four control trials), (d) production accuracy in the six test trials in the "simple cue" condition (the number of correctly produced nonce verbs when an auditory, linguistic, or visual cue was presented in isolation), and (e) production preference in the six test trials in the "cue-competition" condition (the cue associated with the nonce verb that the child produced when an auditory, linguistic, or visual cue for one verb conflicted with an auditory, linguistic, or visual cue for the other verb, as described in the Methods section above).

For our first analysis investigating responses in the "simple cue" condition, responses were scored as "correct" or "incorrect" because there was an unambiguous correct response that could be produced when a single cue was presented in isolation. For the second analysis comparing responses in the "simple cue" and "cue-competition" conditions, we recoded responses in the "simple cue" condition in the following manner: correct responses to the linguistic, visual, and auditory cues were recoded as "linguistic," "visual," and "auditory," respectively, and incorrect responses were coded as "other." We used the same coding categories for the cue-competition condition where an auditory, linguistic, or visual cue associated with one verb was presented in combination with a second cue (auditory, linguistic, or visual cue) associated with the other verb. There was no correct response in this condition as the child could choose either of the two nonce verbs when confronted with hybrid stimuli consisting of the three possible combinations of conflicting cues: auditory-linguistic, auditory-visual, and visual-linguistic. Hence, the responses in this condition were scored in two opposite ways for each of the three cue combinations:

(a) auditory-linguistic:

   i. The responses were scored as "linguistic" if the child produced the verb corresponding to the linguistic cue when it competed with an auditory cue;

if the child produced the verb corresponding to the auditory cue, it was scored as "other."

ii. The responses were scored as "other" if the child produced the verb corresponding to the linguistic cue when it competed with an auditory cue; if the child produced the verb corresponding to the auditory cue, it was scored as "auditory."

(b) auditory-visual:

i. The responses were scored as "auditory" if the child produced the verb corresponding to the auditory cue when it competed with a visual cue; if the child produced the verb corresponding to the visual cue, it was scored as a "other."

ii. The responses were scored as "other" if the child produced the verb corresponding to the auditory cue when it competed with a visual cue; if the child produced the verb corresponding to the visual cue, it was scored as a "visual."

(c) visual-linguistic:

i. The responses were scored as "visual" if the child produced the verb corresponding to the visual cue when it competed with a linguistic cue; if the child produced the verb corresponding to the linguistic cue, it was scored as a "other."

ii. The responses were scored as "other" if the child produced the verb corresponding to the visual cue when it competed with a linguistic cue; if the child produced the verb corresponding to the linguistic cue, it was scored as a "linguistic."

Since we used a forced choice response procedure and there were only two missing responses in the entire dataset, the proportion of responses associated with a specific cue (as coded in (i) above) was almost always the complement to the proportion of responses associated with the competing cue (as coded in (ii) above). Coding the responses in these two different ways in the cue-competition condition facilitated comparison of children's reliance on each cue in three different contexts: when it was presented in isolation (e.g., the linguistic cue alone) and when it was presented in competition with each of two other cues (e.g., linguistic vs. visual and linguistic vs. auditory). For instance, the proportion of "linguistic" responses to the linguistic cue (i.e., production of verbs associated with the linguistic cue) presented in isolation can be compared with the proportion of "linguistic" responses provided to the linguistic cue when placed in conflict with the auditory cue and when placed in conflict with the visual cue. Similarly, the proportion of "visual" responses to the visual cue presented in isolation can be compared with the proportion of "visual" responses provided to the visual cue when it competes with the auditory cue and when it competes with the linguistic cue.

We first summarize children's performance in learning the nonce verbs as assessed by their comprehension and production accuracy. We then present the findings from the analyses of the data obtained during the test phase. The data was analyzed using mixed effects logistic regression with treatment coding for fixed effects and participant and items as random effects. Two separate analyses were conducted to examine (a) the accuracy of children's verb production in response to linguistic, auditory, or visual cues presented in isolation, and (b) the relative degree to which children attended to each cue when it was produced in isolation versus in competition with each of the other cues.

Learning Phase

Accuracy in learning the novel verbs, as measured by comprehension and production tests, is summarized in Table 11.1. Although the comprehension assessment revealed that children had not yet fully learned the two verbs (or had difficulties with the pointing task used to assess comprehension), the subsequent performance in the production task during the training phase was above 50% for all participants. Performance accuracy for the "control" items employed in the test phase was also high because we excluded any participants who failed to reach a criterion of correct performance in 75% of the trials (three out of four items correct) (Table 11.2).

It is likely that more participants had low scores (e.g., 0, 0.25, or 0.5) in the comprehension task versus the production tasks because the comprehension task was administered first, after the training phase. Since children received feedback on erroneous responses during the comprehension task, they were able to improve their performance in the production assessment task and also receive feedback, which in turn boosted their scores on the control items in the test phase.

Table 11.2 Accuracy in the comprehension and production of novel verbs

a. Proportion of correct responses in novel verb comprehension (out of a total of four responses)	**0**	**0.25**	**0.5**	**0.75**	**1**
Number of participants in each scoring category	*2*	*1*	*2*	*6*	*5*
b. Proportion of correct responses in novel verb production (out of a total of eight responses)	**0.625**	**0.75**	**0.875**	**1**	
Number of participants in each scoring category	*2*	*4*	*3*	*7*	
c. Proportion of correct responses in novel verb production for the "control" items in the test phase (out of a total of four responses)	**0.75**	**1**			
Number of participants in each scoring category	*4*	*12*			

Simple Cue Condition

The predictor variable was Cue Type (linguistic, visual, and auditory) and the outcome variable was the binary responses coded as "correct" or "incorrect." As shown in Fig. 11.2, children were significantly more likely to produce the correct nonce verb when they encountered a perceptual cue versus a linguistic cue. The accuracy of responses to the visual cue was significantly higher than accuracy of responses to linguistic cues ($\beta = 1.68$, Z value $= 2.96$, $p < 0.01$). Similarly, responses to the auditory cue were also more accurate than responses to the linguistic cue ($\beta = 2.35$, Z value $= 3.61$, $p < 0.001$). Responses to the auditory and visual cues were directly compared in an analysis that releveled the visual cue variable, which revealed no significant differences in accuracy of participants' responses to the two cues ($\beta = 0.67$, Z value $= 0.98$, $p = 0.33$). Keeping participant and item as random effects with only an intercept, we get an intercept that is significantly different from zero for visual cues ($\beta = 1.27$, Z value $= 2.98$, $p < 0.01$) and auditory cues ($\beta = 1.95$, Z value $= 3.64$, $p < 0.001$), but not for linguistic cues ($\beta = -0.42$, Z value $= -1.04$, $p = 0.3$).

Thus, children are more likely to rely on perceptual versus linguistic cues, and both auditory and visual cues are equally good predictors of accuracy in children's responses. However, their responses are at chance when provided with a linguistic cue in isolation. Using the responses in the "simple cue" condition as a baseline to establish the relative degree of association of linguistic and perceptual cues with the newly learned verbs when presented in isolation, we can proceed to the comparison of responses in the "simple cue" and "cue-competition" conditions. This

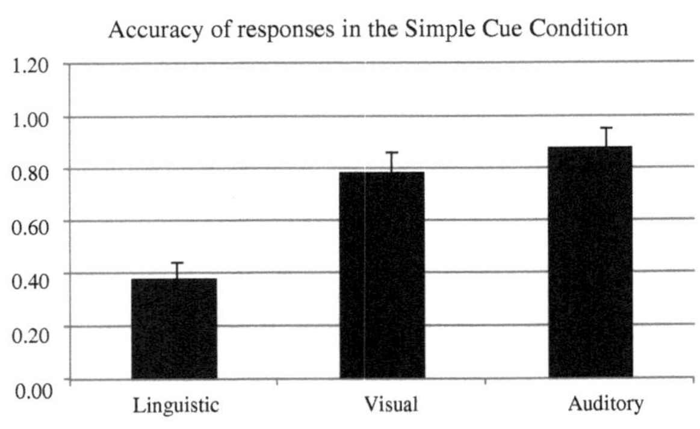

Fig. 11.2 Children's accuracy in producing the appropriate verb in response to linguistic, visual, and auditory cues presented in isolation (with 95% confidence interval error bars)

comparison allows us to examine the change in preference for each cue when placed in conflict with another cue, yielding a hierarchy of relative preferences for the different types of cues, given the baseline patterns of responses to those cues when presented in isolation.

Comparison of Verb Production in the "Simple Cue" and "Cue-Competition" Conditions

Our second analysis compared children's production of verbs in response to different cue types when they occurred in isolation versus when they occurred in conflict with another cue. The analysis involved three separate mixed effects logistic regression analyses corresponding to each cue type: linguistic, visual, and auditory. The first analysis compared how often the appropriate nonce verb was produced in response to linguistic cues presented in isolation, versus in competition with visual and auditory cues. The predictor variable was Condition (Simple-cue, Cue-competition-visual, and Cue-competition-auditory), and the outcome variable was binary responses coded as "linguistic" and "other." The second analysis compared how often the appropriate nonce verb was produced in response to visual cues presented in isolation, and in competition with linguistic and auditory cues. Here, the predictor variable was Condition (Simple-cue, Cue-competition-linguistic, and Cue-competition-auditory), and the outcome variable was binary responses coded as "visual" and "other." The third analysis compared how often the appropriate nonce verb was produced in response to auditory cues presented in isolation, and in competition with visual and linguistic cues. The predictor variable was Condition (Simple-cue, Cue-competition-visual, and Cue-competition-linguistic), and the outcome variable was binary responses coded as "auditory" and "other."

Children's responses to each type of cue, presented in isolation and in competition with each of the other cues, are shown in Fig. 11.3. In situations where cues compete, visual cues always "win" in influencing children's generalization of a verb label to an unfamiliar action. Children are not only highly likely to produce the appropriate verb associated with a visual cue in isolation but also when it competes with other cues. In fact, there is no difference in children's reliance on visual cues in isolation versus in competition with linguistic cues ($\beta = 0.44$, Z value = 0.66, $p = 0.51$) or auditory cues ($\beta = 0.44$, Z value = 0.66, $p = 0.51$).

Correspondingly–when they are in conflict with visual cues—we see a complete reversal in children's reliance on auditory cues relative to when they are presented in isolation ($\beta = -3.63$, Z value = −5.02, $p < 0.001$). Interestingly, there is also a significant decrement in reliance on auditory cues when they compete with

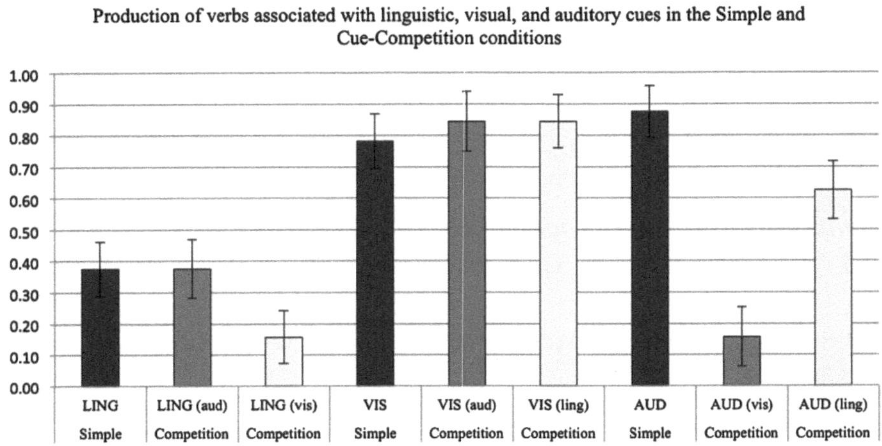

Fig. 11.3 Children's production of the appropriate verb in response to linguistic, visual, or auditory cues presented in isolation (*black bars*) and in competition with a second cue of a different type (*gray* and *white bars*) (with 95% confidence interval error bars)

linguistic cues as compared to when they occur on their own ($\beta = -1.44$, Z value $= -2.22$, $p < 0.05$). An intercept only model keeping participant and item as random effects reveals that–in the presence of a linguistic cue–children's production of a verb corresponding to an auditory cue is not better than chance ($\beta = 0.51$, Z value $= 1.35$, $p = 0.18$). Thus, linguistic cues interfere with the processing of auditory cues even though children respond to linguistic cues only at chance levels in the "simple cue" condition.

As might be expected from the preference for visual cues noted above, there is a significant decrement in reliance on linguistic cues in conflict with visual cues relative to when these cues are presented in isolation ($\beta = -1.28$, Z value $= -2.09$, $p < 0.05$). But there is no significant decrement in the tendency to rely on linguistic cues in the presence of auditory cues versus when they are presented in isolation ($\beta = -0.11$, Z value $= -0.2$, $p = 0.84$). This finding goes in tandem with the absence of a significant preference for auditory cues in competition with linguistic cues.

Conclusions and Discussion

The primary goal of our study was to investigate four-year-old children's relative preferences for linguistic, visual, and auditory cues in influencing their patterns of verb generalization. By comparing children's responses to different cues in the "simple cue" condition (where only one cue is presented) with their responses to the same cues in the "cue-competition" condition (where an additional, conflicting cue is presented), we were able to isolate changes in children's reliance on each type of cue in the context of a competing cue. Thus, we are able to establish a hierarchy of relative preferences for different kinds of cues that guide children's verb extension patterns. Similar to children at the cusp of word learning who favor perceptual cues over other kinds of cues (Hirsh-Pasek and Golinkoff 2007), four-year olds also weight visual cues over linguistic cues in a novel verb generalization context.

But our research shows that there are additional complexities in how the cues interact that go beyond this basic finding. Children have a near-categorical preference for visual cues irrespective of context. Children relied almost exclusively on the visual cue, whether it was presented in isolation, or in competition with an auditory or linguistic cue. Although children respond with a high degree of accuracy to the auditory cue in the "simple cue" condition, the auditory cue does not exert a similar effect in the context of a linguistic cue and plays almost no role in guiding children's verb use when competing with a visual cue. Children attend to linguistic cues in isolation at only chance levels and disregard it almost entirely in the presence of a conflicting visual cue. Contrary to expectation, however, linguistic cues do exert some influence on children's reliance on a competing auditory cue, suggesting that, at some level, children are registering the lexical distributional information that co-occurs with the verb.

Our finding that relative preference for a cue in the cue-competition condition cannot be directly predicted from its relative strength of association with a verb in the simple cue condition is intriguing. For instance, based on the similar levels of accuracy in children's responses to the auditory and visual cues in the "simple cue" condition, one might expect the competition between visual and auditory cues to yield a 50-50 split in responses. Similarly, auditory cues are not preferred over competing linguistic cues, despite the relatively poor accuracy in children's responses to the linguistic cues versus their high accuracy in response to auditory cues in the "simple cue" condition. Such effects might arise owing to processing factors that have to do with how cues compete within versus across modalities, how words are retrieved, and how attention is allocated when cues compete versus when they occur on their own.

Children's overall poor performance in providing the appropriate verb when presented with linguistic cues is surprising given their relatively advanced age; we know that children as young as two years are able to attend to linguistic context as a source of information to distinguish verbs that differ in event types (Scott and Fisher 2009). One possible reason for lack of reliance on linguistic cues may have to do with the fact that the two nonce verbs were distinguished by adjunct phrases (the prepositional phrase *with his/her/your/my hand* versus the adverb *carefully*) rather than core arguments, which are less central to the meaning of the verb. Both phrases could also be used felicitously to describe the manner and instrument used in both actions. Further, they occurred in questions or declarative sentences that were uttered before or after the action was performed. It is possible that lack of temporal overlap with the action may also have reduced the salience of the adjunct phrases that distinguished the two verbs. A production task might also involve greater demands on memory and attention, with concomitant decrements in attention to distributional information in the linguistic input.

Although we know that children's acquisition of verb meaning continues well beyond the initial stages of mapping words to the world, we still have remarkably little knowledge about the nature of this fundamental process as it unfolds over the course of development. Our study demonstrates that investigating the dynamics of cue interactions using a nonce verb generalization task is a promising avenue for future research on patterns of verb categorization. Further research is required to systematically investigate these factors.

References

Booth, A., and S. Waxman. 2002. Word learning is 'smart': Evidence that conceptual information affects preschoolers' extension of novel words. *Cognition* 84: B11–B22.

Carey, S., and E. Bartlett. 1978. Acquiring a single new word. *Papers and Reports on Child Language Development* 15: 17–29.

Clark, E.V. 2004. How language acquisition builds on cognitive development. *Trends in Cognitive Sciences* 8: 472–478.

Colavita, F.B. 1974. Human sensory dominance. *Perception and Psychophysics* 16: 409–412.

Golinkoff, R.M., and K. Hirsh-Pasek. 2007. Language development: The view from the radical middle. [Keynote address.] In *Proceedings of the 31st Annual Boston University Conference on Language Development*, ed. H. Caunt-Nulton, S. Kulatilake, and I. Woo, 1–25. Somerville, MA: Cascadilla Press.

Golinkoff, R.M., C.B. Mervis, and K. Hirsh-Pasek. 1994. Early object labels: The case for a developmental lexical principles framework. *Journal of Child Language* 21: 125–155.

Imai, M., D. Gentner, and N. Uchida. 1994. Children's theories of word meaning: The role of shape similarity in early acquisition. *Cognitive Development* 9: 45–75.

Johanson, M., and A. Papafragou. 2011. Effects of labels on children's category boundaries. In *Proceedings from the 35th Annual Boston University on Language Development*, ed. N. Danis, K. Mesh, and H. Sung, 334–346. Somerville, MA: Cascadilla Press.

Kemler-Nelson, D.G. 1995. Principle-based inferences in young children's categorization: Revisiting the impact of function on the naming of artifacts. *Cognitive Development* 10: 347–380.

Landau, B., and E. Shipley. 2001. Labelling patterns and object naming. *Developmental Psychology* 4: 109–118.

Scott, R.M., and C. Fisher. 2009. 2-year-olds use distributional cues to interpret transitivity-alternating verbs. *Language and Cognitive Processes* 24: 777–803.

Smith, L.B., S.S. Jones, and B. Landau. 1992. Count nouns, adjectives, and perceptual properties in children's novel word interpretations. *Developmental Psychology* 28: 273–286.

Tomasello, M. 1995. Pragmatic contexts for early verb learning. In *Beyond Names for Things: Young Children's Acquisition of Verbs*, ed. M. Tomasello, and W.E. Merriman, 115–146. Hillsdale, NJ: Lawrence Erlbaum Associates.

Chapter 12
On the Child's Role in Syntactic Change

William Snyder

Introduction

A key ingredient in the work presented below is the idea that young children exhibit what I term "Grammatical Conservatism" (GC) as they acquire the syntax of a language. One of the first venues in which I presented this idea to a large audience was the workshop on language acquisition that Raghavachari Amritavalli (Amrit) co-organized in Hyderabad, in conjunction with GLOW in Asia, in 2009. In my efforts to improve on the very rough ideas I presented there, I have been grateful for the astute criticisms, suggestions, and questions that I received from the audience, including Amrit, her students and colleagues at EFLU, and the many scholars from outside India who were brought together for the workshop. I would therefore like to begin by thanking Amrit, not only for her role in that workshop but also for her many other contributions to the field of linguistics.[1]

Here, I will examine the GC thesis in connection with children's role in language change. My starting point will be a 2007 article by David Lightfoot and Marit Westergaard ("L&W"), whose broader goal was to "bring together work on language variation, acquisition, and change, show how these three areas are mutually dependent, and how empirical work in one area may enrich understanding more generally, opening the way to new kinds of empirical work" (2007: 396). This short chapter is an attempt, in my capacity as an acquisitionist, to contribute something to that collaborative effort.

L&W demonstrate that evidence from the history of English, when viewed from the perspective of generative linguistics, leads to what I will refer to as the

[1]I would also like to mention my gratitude to David Lightfoot, Marit Westergaard, Russell Richie, Ian Roberts, Peter Svenonius, Aaron Ecay, and Tony Kroch, for helpful conversations.

W. Snyder (✉)
Department of Linguistics, University of Connecticut, Storrs, USA
e-mail: william.snyder@uconn.edu

G. Sengupta et al. (eds.), *Perspectives on the Architecture and Acquisition of Syntax*, DOI 10.1007/978-981-10-4295-9_12

"Survival vs. Obsolescence" (SvO) puzzle: "why certain things survive as infrequent or marginal aspects of a language, while other things cease to occur at all" (2007:411). My objectives here will be as follows: (i) to show that the type of historical evidence discussed by L&W indicates the need for a revision to the GC thesis; (ii) to provide a suitably revised version; and (iii) to show that the GC thesis, so revised, offers a possible solution to the SvO puzzle.

The GC Thesis

In Snyder (2011), I made the following proposal, which was a more careful formulation of ideas I had presented in earlier work (Snyder 2002, 2007):

(1) **Grammatical Conservatism (GC)**: Children do not make productive, spontaneous use of a new syntactic structure until they have both determined that the structure is permitted in the adult language and identified the adults' grammatical basis for it

This was, by design, a very strong claim.

Some important clarifications were also laid out. They can be summarized as follows: (i) If in fact children are not GC learners, then by definition there is a period of time when their language production is guided by nontarget grammars, and during that period, they are predicted to combine morphemes, at least some of the time, in ways that are clearly impossible under the target grammar; (ii) the errors of commission that are expected under (i) will be "nonerrors" in some UG-compatible grammar; and (iii) these errors will not be confined to elicited production tasks (where even a GC learner might be compelled to make guesses and consequently produce some errors of commission), but rather should also occur in spontaneous speech, where a GC learner would be expected to use a circumlocution instead, or perhaps change the topic of discussion.

Snyder (2011) summarized studies by other researchers who had tested specific predictions of the GC thesis, as applied to a number of different languages and syntactic structures. In all cases, the predictions were supported: Rather than a steady stream of commission errors, followed eventually by adultlike use of the target structure, the only error-types that occurred with any regularity were omission errors, right up to the point when the fully adultlike structure began to appear, and from that point onward, commission errors remained rare.

Note, however, that to the extent that children are indeed GC learners, the prediction is not that they will make zero errors of commission, but rather that (overall) their commission errors will be substantially less frequent and will belong to a substantially smaller range of types, than would be expected from a non-GC learner. Examples of commission errors that do occur reasonably frequently in children's spontaneous speech include Optional Infinitives (which plausibly have some type of maturational basis) and overregularization errors (which are plausibly due to children's difficulties in quickly retrieving irregular forms from memory). In neither case is there a compelling reason to think the errors result from the child's temporary commitment to an incorrect grammatical hypothesis.

A Challenge from Historical Change

L&W's article (drawing on material from Lightfoot 2006) discusses a number of striking morpho-syntactic changes that occurred during the transition from Late Middle English (LME) to Early Modern English (EME). These historical changes raise doubts about the GC thesis, at least when formulated as in (1). As an example, consider the arrival of *do*-support.

In brief, LME was a V-to-I language. During the EME period, however, there was "the emergence, first in the West Country (perhaps due to contact with Cornish; see McWhorter (2009)), of 'periphrastic' *do* forms as an alternative option for expressing past tense: *John did leave*, *John did not leave*, etc., instead of *John left* and *John left not*" (L&W: 406). While the fine-grained details of what happened are unavailable to us, what seems almost inescapable is that, at least in some cases, children acquired a grammar with a form of *do*-support on the basis of input from adults who did not themselves have such a grammar.

If this is correct, we have a direct counterexample to (1). Moreover, even outside this specific case, it cannot be that a child always waits for incontrovertible evidence about "the adults' grammatical basis," because when a new structural option is first emerging, the adults who pick it up from other adults and begin to use it in their own speech are unlikely to have any UG-compatible grammatical basis whatsoever. If the innovation nonetheless persists in the language as part of the native speakers' grammar, as happened in the case of *do*-support, the child's requirements must be less stringent than (1) asserts.

A New Formulation of GC

A more appropriate formulation of the GC thesis will need to allow for those occasions when the child responds to the parents' input by adopting an option that is not in fact present in the parents' grammar. Yet, it will also need to capture the fact that, at least under normal conditions of intergenerational language transfer, children are extraordinarily good at choosing the same grammatical options that are employed by their parents.

What I believe we need to say, first of all, is that the child comes to the task of language acquisition with a species-uniform set of grammatical options to choose from and a species-uniform way of deciding whether any given option should be adopted. This much should, I believe, allow us to account for the very high degree of grammatical homogeneity within a given language community, despite the numerous differences in the exact input that different children receive.

Additionally, and perhaps more surprisingly, I now propose that the "volume" of evidence that the child requires before committing herself to a given grammatical choice is not, in general, very large. In other words, my current hypothesis is that the child can be swayed by a small number of utterances with very specific properties. One might have imagined, instead, that the way a child manages to achieve such a high degree of confidence about a grammatical choice is by amassing a large volume of evidence and finding a high degree of internal consistency. Yet, the findings from historical change—in particular, the existence of well-documented cases of new syntactic structures (like *do*-support) entering a language relatively quickly—militate against this, for the following reason: It is quite unlikely that people who are already adults, and who incorporate some linguistic innovation or crosslinguistic borrowing into their speech, will immediately use it frequently, consistently, and in a UG-compatible manner.

We might instead picture UG as providing a set of "locks" and the child as looking for keys that fit them. The idea, in other words, is that the learner is searching the input for utterances with certain, highly distinctive characteristics. The learner's confidence that a resulting grammatical choice is correct will come from the high quality of the evidence when viewed in isolation, rather than from the quantity or the internal consistency of the evidence.

One small bit of support (albeit anecdotal) for this view of language acquisition and grammatical change comes from a fairly recent occurrence in North American English. During the second half of the twentieth century, many adults decided that it was no longer acceptable to say, for example, *Every doctor treated <u>his</u> patients*, since by that point in history a doctor could equally well be male or female. A variety of third-person singular gender-avoidance strategies were proposed (including novel pronouns, singular *their*, and disjunctive forms such as *his or her*), and prescriptivists even now seem to favor *his or her*, but I can report that by the 1990s, every preschool child I encountered in the context of my child language research had adopted *their* as the third-person singular possessive pronoun, and I would venture to say that as of 2015, the vast majority of young adults speaking North American English use singular *their*. Moreover, my impression from the literature is that changes in pronominal systems most often involve the extension of an existing pronoun to new uses, rather than the introduction of a novel form, and if so, the choice of singular *their* fits the pattern. The present relevance is that adults were making inconsistent use of multiple forms, and children appear to have responded by making consistent use of the one form that "fit a lock" in UG.

In light of the considerations above, I wish to propose the revised formulation of GC in (2).

(2) **Grammatical Conservatism, revised (GCr)**: Children do not make productive, spontaneous use of a new syntactic structure until they have recognized, in the input, a highly specific hallmark for each of the structure-building options that the structure requires

The proposal in (2) is very close, both in spirit and in detail, to ideas found in L&W and elsewhere in Lightfoot's work. Specifically, the conception behind (2) is that the learner is looking for "hallmarks" of abstract syntactic properties (i.e., something similar in nature to what Lightfoot has called the "expression of cues"), rather than simply comparing strings of words in the input to the weak generative capacity of candidate grammars. (Examples of the latter strategy would include the trigger learning algorithm studied in Gibson and Wexler 1994 and the variational model of language acquisition presented in Yang 2002).

Yet, (2) leaves it open exactly how a child would know what to look for. One procedure with many of the right characteristics is Janet Fodor's (1998) "structural trigger learning" (STL) algorithm. The central assumption in STL is that each point of syntactic variation can be recast as the availability, or unavailability, of a syntactic "treelet" (i.e., a contiguous subgraph of a possible syntactic tree, at the point of spell-out). As Fodor and colleagues have demonstrated, it is possible for a parser to operate in terms of an inventory of permissible (i.e., UG-compatible) treelets. With such a parser, if an utterance in child-directed speech is parsed successfully, and if there was no point in the computation when the parser had more than one option available to it (i.e., there was no point of structural ambiguity), then all the treelets employed in the parse may reasonably be taken as "confirmed" treelets (i.e., correct grammatical choices) in the target language.

Note that STL can, in principle, make appropriate grammatical choices even on the basis of a single confirmatory utterance. In practice, the robustness of the acquisition process to nonzero levels of noise (e.g., when the child receives input from second-language speakers of the target language) suggests that the child's acquisition procedure is probably a bit more cautious. Nonetheless, STL can, at least in theory, draw broad, correct generalizations about the target language from a very limited number of critical examples, each of which meets highly specific criteria.[2]

The SvO Puzzle

As I mentioned at the outset, L&W draw our attention to the "Survival vs. Obsolescence" (SvO) puzzle: Why low input frequency of a syntactic form sometimes leads to survival of that form as a low-frequency or marginal option and at other times leads to complete loss of the form. As L&W discuss, there is no clear dividing line between the two outcomes in terms of the corresponding input frequencies. Each syntactic form seems to need a different minimum input frequency in order to survive.

[2]Another possibility, alongside STL, would be to posit some version of an innately specified "learning path", in the sense developed by Dresher (1999), a follow-up to Dresher and Kaye (1990). For a direct comparison of the "STL" and "learning path" approaches, and discussion of a possible hybrid, please see Snyder (2015).

For example, across the Germanic languages, one finds considerable variation in the contexts that require, allow, or disallow the use of I-to-C movement (V2). Thus, where English always requires V2 in matrix questions, but generally has non-V2 order in declaratives, L&W (p. 409) report that many Norwegian dialects show the opposite pattern. In the Germanic languages more broadly, one reportedly finds independent variation in the V2 status of (at least) declaratives, *yes/no*-questions, *wh*-questions, embedded questions, and exclamatives. Furthermore, drawing on work by Westergaard (2007), L&W cite a variety of Norwegian in which exclamatives constitute only 0.4% of parents' child-directed utterances, yet children acquire the distinctive word-order properties of exclamatives correctly and without any sign of difficulty.

In contrast, when *do*-support entered English (in the EME period, as discussed above), the effect seems to have been to push the already low frequency of unambiguous V-to-I movement in children's input below some minimum threshold, because V-to-I movement ceased to be a grammatical option. Prior to the complete disappearance of V-to-I movement, however, there were authors such as William Shakespeare who seemingly allowed both V-to-I movement and *do*-support in their English: For example, "I **like not** that.//What **dost thou** say?" (consecutive lines in *Othello*, as cited in L&W, p. 406). The side-by-side coexistence of the two structures, seemingly within a single grammar, suggests that V-to-I movement simply became progressively less frequent until, at some point, it fell below the minimum threshold needed for "robustness" in the input. The SvO puzzle, then, is why something like the special word-order properties (e.g., lack of V2) in Norwegian exclamatives can survive, even though exclamatives are vastly outnumbered by other sentence-types in the child's input, while V-to-I movement at some point became not a low-frequency option but simply ungrammatical.

An Approach to the SvO Puzzle: The Learner's Response to Conflict

GCr, the revised version of GC proposed in (2), offers a possible solution to the SvO puzzle. The key difference from GC lies in children's expected response to conflicting data. Recall that the earlier version, GC, requires the learner to "identify the adults' grammatical basis" for a given structure before making productive use of it herself. On occasions when the adults' use of a structure seemingly lacks a UG-compatible analysis altogether, because it conflicts with another form that the adults are also using, I assume that a GC learner would not use either of the conflicting structures productively (although she might still be able to understand them when others used them). If so, GC makes it easy to see how an older syntactic structure could fall out of use. The question is how a novel structure could become grammatical and supersede it.

GCr, in contrast, only requires the learner to recognize the distinctive hallmark of a particular grammatical operation, before she adopts that operation as part of her own grammar. By "recognizing a distinctive hallmark," I mean something along the lines of realizing that the latest input sentence has an unambiguous parse (in the sense of STL) and that this parse required the given operation. If the learner receives unambiguous evidence of this kind, the new structure-building operation becomes available for use in language production.

Crucially, when the learner's input contains conflicting data, the GCr learner can be expected to adopt the grammatical option corresponding to the *first* type of evidence encountered. By adopting that side in the conflict, the learner will presumably be blocked from adopting the alternative choice, whatever it might be. The evidence that reaches the learner first will typically—though not always—correspond to whichever form is used more frequently by the child's caretakers. Hence, it is precisely when two types of sentence are grammatically *incompatible* that the low frequency of one may lead to its obsolescence. We should expect to see a dwindling number of speakers who acquire the earlier type of grammar, but those speakers will genuinely have a grammar of the older type. This situation stands in contrast to one in which the majority of speakers have grammars allowing the obsolescent form, but only as a low-frequency option.

How does this help with the loss of V-to-I movement in English? One further premise is needed, namely that a single grammar cannot sanction both *do*-support and V-to-I movement. Granted there were authors such as Shakespeare who employed both options side-by-side, but this does not necessarily indicate that the author personally employed a single grammar with optionality. Shakespeare, in particular, was probably alternating between the two structures in order to achieve specific metrical and dramatic effects. In other authors, there may have been bidialectalism or diglossia, with two distinct grammars in play. In still others, there may have been a single native grammar, plus semiconscious efforts to imitate other speakers. The most important consideration, however, is the widely held view in generative linguistics that *do*-support is a last-resort mechanism, employed primarily when V-to-I movement is unavailable to bring the main verb close enough to inflectional elements that need to combine with it (e.g., Chomsky 1957; Lasnik 1995; Bobaljik 1995). If this is correct, *do*-support and V-to-I movement would be directly in conflict if they coexisted in a single grammar.

In summary, when we move from GC to GCr, it becomes possible to explain (i) how it is ever possible for the child to acquire a grammar different from her parents', and (ii) why it is that low frequency of critical evidence in the child's input sometimes yields survival of a given form as a low-frequency option and other times yields obsolescence of that form. When the learner is searching for very local evidence of a highly specific type, rather than a sizable body of evidence that is highly consistent, it becomes possible that changes in the speech patterns of adults (as in situations of extended language contact) will yield occasional utterances that "fit one of the locks" provided by UG and thereby cause a new UG option to be deployed in the child's grammar, even though that option is not genuinely present in the grammar of the parents.

It also becomes possible that the speech of a parent to a child will contain conflicting evidence and that the child will respond by selecting whichever of the conflicting options is the first to be presented in an accessible way. In this situation, a difference in frequency or accessibility of the evidence for competing options can lead fairly quickly to obsolescence. In the absence of such a conflict, however, a form that is used infrequently by adults, and that is therefore only rarely presented to the learner in an accessible way, could nonetheless persist for a very long time as a low-frequency option.

References

Bobaljik, JD. 1995. *The syntax of verbal inflection* (Unpublished doctoral dissertation). Cambridge, MA: Massachusetts Institute of Technology.
Chomsky, N. 1957. *Syntactic Structures*. The Hague: Mouton.
Dresher, B.E. 1999. Charting the learning path: Cues to parameter setting. *Linguistic Inquiry* 30 (1): 27–67.
Dresher, B.E., and J.D. Kaye. 1990. A computational learning model for metrical phonology. *Cognition* 34 (2): 137–195.
Fodor, J.D. 1998. Unambiguous triggers. *Linguistic Inquiry* 29 (1): 1–36.
Gibson, E., and K. Wexler. 1994. Triggers. *Linguistic Inquiry* 25 (3): 407–454.
Lasnik, H. 1995. Verbal morphology: Syntactic structures meets the minimalist program. In *Evolution and Revolution in Linguistic Theory*, ed. H. Campos, and P. Kempchinsky, 251–275. Washington, D.C.: Georgetown University Press.
Lightfoot, D. 2006. *How New Languages Emerge*. Cambridge: Cambridge University Press.
Lightfoot, D., and M. Westergaard. 2007. Language acquisition and language change: Inter-relationships. *Language and Linguistics Compass* 1 (5): 396–415.
McWhorter, J.H. 2009. What else happened to english? A brief for the Celtic hypothesis. *English Language and Linguistics* 13:163–191.
Snyder, W. 2015. How to set the compounding parameter. In *Proceedings of the 6th conference on generative approaches to language acquisition–North America (GALANA 2015)*, ed. L. Perkins, R. Dudley, J. Gerard, and K. Hitczenko, 122–130. Somerville, MA: Cascadilla Proceedings Project.
Snyder, W. 2011. Children's grammatical conservatism: Implications for syntactic theory. In *BUCLD 35: Proceedings of the 35th Annual Boston University Conference on Language Development*, vol. I. ed. N. Danis, K. Mesh, and H. Sung, 1–20. Somerville, MA: Cascadilla Press.
Snyder, W. 2007. *Child Language: The Parametric Approach*. Oxford: Oxford University Press.
Snyder, W. 2002. Parameters: The view from child language. In *Proceedings of the third Tokyo Conference on Psycholinguistics*, ed. Y. Otsu 27–44. Tokyo: Hituzi Shobo.
Westergaard, M.R. 2007. Learning and unlearning V2: on the robustness of the triggering experience in a historical perspective. In *Proceedings of the XXXII Incontro di Grammatica Generativa*, ed. M.C. Picchi, and A. Pona, 193–207. Alessandria, Italy: Edizioni dell'Orso.
Yang, C.D. 2002. *Knowledge and Learning in Natural Language*. New York: Oxford University Press.

Chapter 13
Root Infinitive Analogues: Evidence from Tamil, Korean, and Japanese

Keiko Murasugi

Introduction

Children are free to project unattested hypotheses based on their innate knowledge, which is species-specific and species-unique. In the course of language acquisition, there are intriguing cases where children, whatever mother tongue they are acquiring, fail to match their hypothesis to the input of the target language and produce "erroneous" sentences. More interestingly, even the erroneous strings children naturally produce are also associated with common features among languages.

One of the typical verbal "errors" that very young children produce in a lot of languages is well known as the Root Infinitive (RI) phenomenon. Very young children go through a RI (analogue) stage where they do not apparently mark Tense and Aspect on main and auxiliary verbs in the root clause.

In this chapter, we will argue that the longitudinal studies of children acquiring Tamil, Korean, and Japanese will provide a piece of additional evidence for the RI Analogues in Asian languages, thereby supporting the psychological reality of RIs at a very early stage of language acquisition.

Verb Inflection in Child Tamil

Tamil, Korean and Japanese share the morpho-syntactic property of being agglutinative languages with rich Case markers and null arguments. Thomas and Vainikka (1994) argue that the inflection phrase and complementizer phrase are missing in the production of Tamil-speaking children between the ages of 14 and 19 months. Lakshmanan (2006), basically in line with Thomas and Vainikka

K. Murasugi (✉)
Nanzan University, 18 Yamazato, Showa-ku, Nagoya, Japan
e-mail: murasugi@nanzan-u.ac.jp

G. Sengupta et al. (eds.), *Perspectives on the Architecture and Acquisition of Syntax*, DOI 10.1007/978-981-10-4295-9_13

(1994), also finds that in the early stage of acquisition, at least prior to 1;10, Tamil-acquiring children do not produce the verbal inflection associated with finite verb forms, and that such knowledge emerges subsequently. Lakshmanan (2006) also supports Sarma's (1995) finding that Tamil-acquiring children after 25 months have adult-like knowledge of verbal inflection.

According to Lakshmanan's observation (2006), Tamil-acquiring children, prior to the age of 24 months, produced an adult-like imperative form in the imperative context as shown in (1).

(1) vee vee peepa taa (Priyanka, 1;09)
different different paper give
'Give me a different paper'
[asking her mother to give her another sheet of paper so that she can draw on it]

Lakshmanan (2006) also observes that a nonfinite verb form where a finite verb form would be required was used in the very early stage of Tamil acquisition, and the particular "erroneous" verb forms were either a bare verb stem, an infinitive verb form, or a verbal participle form.

(2) Verbal Participle
a. Amma puc-ci (Priyanka, 1;09)
Mother like-Verbal Participle
'(I) like mother'
b. Adult Form: Ammaa-v-ai piDi-kkum
Mother-Acc like-FUT3SN

(3) Verb Stem
a. tuuk
lift (Priyanka, 1;09)
'(I am) lift(ing) (the train)'
b. Adult Form: Treen-ai tuuk-kar-een
train-Acc lift-PRES-1s

(4) Non-finitie Verb Form
a. poTTu va-ccu (Mani, 2;0)
dot keep-Verb Participle
'I have kept a poTTu (for Swami)'
[Prior to producing the utterance, Mani had put a 'poTTu' on the forehead of a 'Swami' (i.e., a deity in a picture.)]
b. Adult Form: poTTu vai-ttu-iru-kkir-een
dot keep-VBP-BE-PRES-IS

As the examples shown above indicate, the very young children's verb forms were different from adult ones, and based on such examples, Lakshmanan (2006) reports that children's very early grammar is fundamentally different from adult grammar.

For the reason why such errors are found in the Tamil-speaking children's early production, Lakshmanan (2006) suggests several possible analyses. One of her analyses is, for example, that the omission of verbal inflectional markings, such as Tense, agreement, and the omission of Aspectual and modal auxiliaries, stems from the performance constraint.

In what follows, we will argue that her findings can be more naturally explained if we take the child production of other languages into consideration. That is, her findings would provide a piece of strong evidence for the psychological reality of the RI Analogues in Asian languages, and that of the RI stage in child language in general.

Root Infinitives

Root Infinitives (RIs) are typically the infinitival verb forms used by children around two years of age in matrix (root) clauses, a position where they cannot appear in adult grammar. Root Infinitives are attested in very young children's speech across a wide variety of languages. Although the use of tense-less verbs in root contexts by very young children is a universal phenomenon, there are morphological variations associated with the different verbal systems in the children's target languages. That is, the form of RIs is not always infinitive (see also Poeppel 1996; Coene et al. 2005). Murasugi et al. (2009) argue that there are three types of RIs in world languages: the infinitive forms (e.g., Dutch, French, German, among others), the bare verbal forms (e.g., English, Chinese, ASL, among others), and the surrogate forms (e.g., Japanese, Korean, Arabic, Turkish, among others).

In some languages with relatively rich morphology such as Dutch (e.g., Haegeman 1995; Blom and Wijnen 2000) and French (e.g., Krämer 1993; Rasetti 2003), among others, children may optionally use the infinitival forms of inflection on the verbs, as shown in (5a) and (5b). In languages which are relatively poor in inflectional morphology such as English, RIs appear in the finite (root) contexts as bare verbs. In adult English, infinitive forms are generally the bare stems, and children acquiring English produce the bare stems at around the age of two as shown in (5c) and (5d). Children speaking a language whose verbs do not constitute a well-formed word if the form is uninflected, e.g., Japanese, Korean and Turkish, choose a default affix, or the surrogate infinitive form. For example, Aljenaie (2000) reports that Kuwaiti Arabic-speaking children at the age of one to two typically produce verbs lacking the marking of present and past Tense, and mark the stem with another inflection. That is, the children choose another default infix, masculine imperative form, or what we call the surrogate infinitive form as shown in (5e).[1]

(5) a. Peter bal pakken. (2;01) (Dutch)
Peter ball get- INF
'Peter (wants to) get the ball' (Blom and Wijnen 2000)

b. Dormir petit bébé. (1;11) (French)
sleep- INF little baby
'A little baby sleeps' (Guasti 1993/1994)

c. Eve sit floor. (1;07) (English) (Brown 1973)

d. That truck fall down. (2;00) (English) (Sano and Hyams 1994)

e. Eh xalis (1;11–2;05) (Kuwaiti Arabic)
yes, finished
'Yes, it is finished' (Aljenaie 2000)

Although the form of the RIs varies across languages, it is well known that there are some salient morpho-syntactic and semantic properties common to RIs, as listed in (6).

(6) a. RIs are tense-less verbs in root contexts.
b. At the RI stage, no T-related/C-related items are found.
c. RIs are produced to describe events in real time, that is, as an ongoing activity in the past, present, or future that the child is involved in.
d. RIs occur in modal contexts (the Modal Reference Effects (MREs)).
e. RIs are restricted to event-denoting predicates (the Eventivity Constraint).
f. Head Merger is not available during the RI Analogue stage.
(Deen 2002, among others.)

The Tense- and Complementizer-related items do not co-occur with RIs, and RIs, for example, are produced as a result of children's intention, desire, or volition, in various irrealis modal contexts. This is termed the Modal Reference Effects (MREs) as shown in (6d) (Hoekstra and Hyams 1998).

[1]Just like in English, very young children speaking Swahili also omit functional elements such as Tense and subject agreement (Deen 2002). An RI phenomenon has also been identified for children acquiring languages that do not have an infinitive construction. In Modern Greek, for example, a bare subjunctive/perfective is reported to be the Root Infinitive Analogue (RIA) (Varlokosta et al. 1996; Hyams 2002).

Table 13.1 Mood morphemes in adult Korean

Declarative	Interrogative	Imperative	Propositive
-ta	*-ni*	*-ia*	*-ca*
-e (-a)			

There are several acquisition studies in Asia reporting that children's early verb forms have these specific properties of RIs.

First, let us take a look at the Korean RI Analogues (see Murasugi and Fuji (2008) for the details). Based on a longitudinal study of a Korean-acquiring child (2;02–2;07), Kim and Phillips (1998) argue that the overuse of default Mood inflection *-e* corresponds to RIs. In Korean, bare verb stems not supported by morphemes are impossible just like in Japanese.

(7) *mek-
'eat'

(8) a. mek-e
eat-Declarative
'I eat'

b. mek-ca
eat-Propositive
'Let's eat'

In adult Korean, according to Kim and Phillips (1998), the Mood marker -*e* functions as a default Mood marker (or "speech style particle"). It freely alternates with more specific Mood markers, as shown in Table 13.1.[2]

Kim and Phillips (1998) find that a Korean-acquiring child used the default Mood marker *-e* (*-a*) in imperative, declarative, and interrogative sentences in the adult way at around the age of two as shown in (9).

(9) a. mul cwu-e (2yrs)
water give-Imperative
'give water'

b. i tak-e (2yrs)
teeth brush-Declarative
'(I'm) brushing the teeth.'

c. enni ka-(a) (2yrs)
sister go-Question
'Did sister go?'

[2] According to Lee (1993) cited by Kim and Phillips (1998), the ratio of *-e* and other Mood morphemes used in the informal discourse in adult Korean was 58:42.

Interestingly enough, the child also used the *-e (a)* form in some ungrammatical contexts at 2;02 through 2;03, as shown in (10).

(10) a. mek-e emma (2 yrs) (adult :*mek-ca* (propositive))
eat -Declarative mommy
'Let's eat, Mommy'

b. ayki pwo-a (2 yrs) (adult: *pwo-l-kkeya* (presumptive))
baby look-Declarative
'Baby (I) will look at it'

In (10), the default Mood marker *-e* (*-a*) is "erroneously" used in the context where the specific propositive marker *-ca* and the presumptive marker *-l-kkeya* should be used in adult Korean.

Kim and Phillips (1998) analyze the V-*e* form as an RI Analogue form, as the sentence containing the verbal form bears some typical RI Analogue properties. First, the V-*e* form is not marked for Tense at a very early stage. In adult Korean, the Tense morpheme *-ess* is obligatory to express the completive events as the contrast between (11a) and (11b) indicates. The Korean-acquiring child from 2;02 through 2;03, however, did not use the past-tense morphemes even in the obligatory contexts, as exemplified in (12).

(11) a. mek-ess-ta (past)
eat-Past-Decl
'I ate'

b. mek-e (present)
eat-Decl
'I eat'

(12) enni ka-φ-(a) (2 yrs)
sister go-(Past)-(Question)
Intended meaning: 'Did sister go?'

Second, the V-*e* form did not co-occur with a nominative Case marker, a tense-related item in the child's utterances.[3] In adult Korean, nominative Case markers can be dropped in discourse-licensing contexts as in (13), while they cannot be dropped in the scrambled sentences as shown in (14).

[3]T- or C-related elements do not co-occur with RIs in a lot of European languages (Rizzi 1993/1994; Wexler 1994).

(13) emma-(ka) pap-ul mek-ess-e (sov)
mom-Nom meal-Acc eat -Past-Decl
'Mommy ate the meal'

(14) pap-ul emma-*(ka) mek-ess-e (osv)
meal-Acc mom-Nom eat-Past-Decl
'Mommy ate the meal'

The child, however, dropped a nominative Case marker even in the scrambled sentence or the obligatory context. According to Kim and Phillips (1998), her mother used the nominative Case marker 50% of the time in the discourse-licensing context and 96% in the grammatically requested context; the child used it only 1% in the discourse-licensing context and 0% in the grammatically requested context.

A lot of European RIs are known to be the "Optional Infinitives" in the sense that both tensed and tense-less verbs optionally appear in the root clause.[4] On the other hand, the Korean-acquiring child used the default Mood marker *–e* (*-a*) 100% of the time in the full range of environments. All the verbs the child produced at the age of 2;02 and 2;03 were associated with the Mood marker *–e* (*-a*), and after the age of 2;04 other Mood markers, such as *-ta* and *-ca*, started to appear. Thus, Kim and Phillips (1998) propose that the overuse of the default Mood marker *-e* (*-a*) corresponds to RIs in other languages.

Kim and Phillips (1998) actually do not precisely examine whether or not the RIs in Korean are associated with the typical properties of RIs listed in (6). However, the properties found in the examples Kim and Phillips (1998) show in their paper, do not contradict those found in typical RIs in other languages. For instance, the verb associated with a Mood marker *-e*, exemplified in (10a), can be interpreted as an example showing the Modal Reference Effects. The verbs are all eventive, and according to their report, tense-related items are not observed at the stage in question. The only property of Korean RI Analogues distinct from European RIs is that the tense-marking is not optional. That is, as we mentioned above, the Korean-acquiring child used the default Mood marker *-e* (*-a*) 100% of the time in the full range of environments. This distinct property, however, actually holds for Japanese RI Analogues (see Murasugi, Fuji and Hashimoto (2007);

[4]While children produce erroneous nonfinite verbs in the matrix clause as in (ia) during the RI stage, they also produce adult-like finite verbs as in (ib) (Wexler 1994) in German.

(i) a. Thorsten das haben[-finite]. (2;1)
T that have-INF
'Thorsten has that'

b. Mein hubsauber had[+finite] tiere din. (2;1)
my helicopter has animals in it
'My helicopter has animals in it'#

Murasugi and Fuji (2008); Murasugi, Nakatani and Fuji (2009), among others for Japanese RIs, and Aksu-Koç and Ketrez (2003) for Turkish RIs).

Root Infinitives in Japanese

Murasugi et al. (2007; 2009), Murasugi and Fuji (2008), Murasugi (2009), Murasugi and Nakatani (2013), among others, based on the corpus analysis of Sumihare (Noji 1973–1977) and longitudinal studies, argue, based on such examples as (15), that (i) there is an RI Analogue stage in Japanese, which corresponds to the RI stage in other languages,[5] (ii) the form in question is the past-tense form V-*ta* and/or mimetics (*-ta/-sita*), (iii) the stage is found much earlier than in European languages, i.e., even at one year of age, and (iv) the properties given in (6) are found in the Japanese RI Analogues.

(15) a. Atti. Atti. Atti i-ta. (S: 1;06) (irrealis/volition) (adult form: *ik-u*, or *ik-e*)
there there there go-Past
'I want to go there / Go there'

b. Tii si-ta. (S:1;07) (irrealis/volition) (adult form: *si-ta-i*)
mimetics (pee) do-Past
'I want to pee'

c. byuuuu, byuuuu. (Y:1;08) (irrealis/volition) (adult form: *si-ta-i*)
mimetics
'You draw a picture for me, please'

Noji (the observer) describes that *i-ta* in (15a) means *ik-u* (go-Pres), while Sumihare used the form *i-ta*, because Sumihare could not say *ik-u* (Noji 1973–1977: 195).[6] Noji also writes important comments for (15b), which convinces us of the Modal Reference Effects at the early stage of Japanese acquisition: Sumihare used *tii-si-ta* when he wanted to pee, or in a volition context. (15c) is an example indicating that a bare onomatopoeia is used as an RI Analogue given in Murasugi and Nakatani (2013).

---

[5]Our results are consistent with Sano (1995) and Kato et al. (2003) with respect that the erroneous nonfinite verbs are not found with the two-year-old Japanese-speaking children.

[6]The context for (15a) is the following: Sumihare's father (Noji, the observer) went out for a walk with Sumihare on his back. Noji, Sumihare's father, tried to get back home, but Sumihare pointed to a different direction and produced a bare adverbial "atti (there)" twice. Then, Sumihare, again, got frustrated and produced the V-ta form, "atti i-ta (there go-Past)" angrily.

Interestingly, in addition to V-*ta* form and mimetics (*-ta/-sita*) given above, Murasugi and Fuji (2008) mention the possibility that, at the stage in question, the modals are expressed with another form, i.e., the Mood morpheme *-na(a),* probably the head of Mood Phrase. The Mood morpheme *-na(a)* is attached to the nominals, bare mimetics, and even to the RI Analogues, to refer Sumihare's declaratives and imperatives (expressing volition) as shown in (16).

(16) a. Buu-naa. (1;05)
light-Mood
'I see the light of sunset'

b. Pan-naa. (1;05)
bread-Mood
'I want a piece of bread'

c. Paan-naa. (1;07)
mimetics-Mood
'Please cut the wrapping paper (newspaper) around the fish cake'

d. Sii si-ta-naa. (1;07)
pee do-Past-Mood
'(I) want to pee'

The Mood marker *-na* in Japanese is, just like the Mood marker *-e* in Korean, productively used at around 1;05 through 1;08 by Sumihare (Noji Corpus) during his RI Analogue stage. For example, recall the RI Analogue form *atti* ***ita*** (there go-Past, "I want to go there") given in (15a). Murasugi et al. (2007) found that children's use of RI Analogue V-*ta* form decreases in number in accordance with the increase of the *-tyoodai* ("please-give-me") expression to make a request. To be more specific, Sumihare's request meaning "I want to go there" is first expressed by the bare adverbial (*atti* (there) 1;04), followed by *atti* ***ita*** (there go-Past, 1;06), *atti* ***naa*** (there *naa*, 1;06), *atti* ***ita na na*** (there go-Past *na na*, 1;07), and *atti-****tyoodai*** (there-please-give-me, 1;09) in that order.

Given the wide variation in productivity of using *-na* form (as well as V-*ta* form and bare mimetics) that appears to be consistently linked with *-tyoodai* (please-give-me) form at a later stage of language acquisition, it can be assumed that the *-na* form indicates the child's request.

(17) a. Taata. (1;01)
shoe
'Please let me wear the shoes'

b. Taata na na. Taata na. (1;07)
shoe shoe
'Please let me wear the shoes'

c. Taata tyoodai. (1;08)
shoe please-give-me
'Pease let me wear the shoes'

(18) a. Ringo. (1;05)
apple
'Please give me an apple'

b. Ringo naa. (1;07)
apple
'Please give me an apple'

c. Ringo tyoodai. (1;08)
apple please-give-me
'Please give me an apple'

(19) a. Rii na na. (1;07)
go-down
'Please let me get down'

b. Rii tyoodai. (1;08)
go-down please-give-me
'Please let me get down'

Thus, the Japanese-acquiring child entertains the three types of RI Analogues: V-*ta* form (past form), mimetics (bare verbs), and -*na* form (Mood form) at the very early stage of language acquisition.

Why is the V-*ta* form chosen as the RI Analogue in Japanese? Needless to say, in a lot of languages, infinitive form and bare verb in a root clause are typically used as imperatives. RIs in Italian, for instance, can be used for imperatives in special contexts (Rizzi 1993/1994).

(20) Partire immediatamente!
go immediately (Rizzi 1993/1994)

Interestingly enough, the three types of RI Analogues form in Japanese, i.e., *-ta* form, the bare mimetics, and *-na* form, are possible imperative forms in adult Japanese as shown in (21).

(21) a. Sassa to kaet-**ta** ! kaet-**ta** !
immediately go back go back
'Go back (somewhere) immediately'

b. Si!
silence (mimetics)
'Silence!'

c. Sassa to kaeri -**na**.
immediately go back
'Why don't you go back immediately?'

d. Sassa to kaere -**na**.
immediately go back
'You go back immediately, OK?'

e. Sassa to kaeru -**na**.
immediately go back-Neg
'Don't go back immediately' Or
immediately go back
'(I am sorry to find that) you go back so soon'

Here, note also that the examples from (21c) through (21e) indicate that *-na* ending imperatives in Japanese are quite ambiguous. The different types of imperatives ending with *-na* (with different meaning) exist in the primary linguistic data children receive. *-Na* in (21c) can be the abbreviated form of *-nasai* (the imperative sentence-ending marker): It attaches to the preverbal form of the verb stem. On the other hand, *-na* in (21d) and (21e) is a sentence-ending marker: It attaches to the full form of the verb. Crucially, the meaning of (21d) and (21e) could be completely the opposite: *kaere-na* (imperative form *-na*) in (21d) is imperative, meaning "You go back (somewhere) immediately, OK?"; in contrast, *kaeru-na* (affirmative form *-na*) in (21e) could have either a negative meaning ("Don't go back (anywhere) (so soon)") or a confirmation ("You surely go back"/"I am sorry to find that you are going back"). That is, *-na* that appears in the sentence-final position in adult Japanese can be either a Mood marker or a negative marker, depending on the verbal form that *-na* attaches to, although the intonation pattern slightly differs among (21c), (21d), and (21e).

Here, a question arises. According to the Truncation Hypothesis (Rizzi 1993/1994), the RIs are truncated, and the child phrase structure is smaller than the adult phrase structure at the RI stage. Suppose that *-na* is located in Mood Phrase. Then, does the fact that the Mood element *-na*, which should reside in the position above the Tense Phrase, coexists with the RI Analogue become a counter evidence to the Truncation Hypothesis?

In fact, the answer seems to be negative. The coexistence of a Mood marker and the RI Analogue does not contradict the proposal that the structure of RIs is truncated, due to the peculiar property of Japanese "sentence-ending" Mood markers.

The Mood marker *-na*, just like the other "sentence-ending" particle *-ne*, does not only appear in the sentence-initial position and/or sentence-final position in Japanese adult grammar. They can also be attached to other smaller syntactic constituents quite freely as shown in (22).

(22) a. Naa, asita -**na**, hikkosite kara-**na**, sooji-si-**na**.
Hey tomorrow moving after clean-do
'Hey, clean (your room) after moving (to the new place) tomorrow'

b. Nee, asita -**ne**, hikkosite kara-**ne**,sooji- suru-**ne**.
Hey tomorrow moving after clean-do
'Hey, I will clean (my room) after moving (to the new place) tomorrow'

Thus, even if *-na* is the finiteness head located in Mood Phrase up above TP, *-na* could still be phonetically realized with the truncated structure (lacking Tense and agreement) and assigns finiteness to the Japanese RI Analogue. To put it in another way, because Japanese is a language that allows Mood/modal markers to be attached not only to the tensed sentences, but also to such tense-less constituents as nominals, postpositional phrases, adverbs, adjectival phrases, quite freely, the *-na* RI Analogue form is produced as the reflex of the presence of Mood in Child Japanese.

However, at the same time, we are led to the conclusion that even during the stage where the structure is truncated, Mood Phrase, the higher part of the phrase structure, plays a role independent of the existence of TP. That is, the upper edge of the phrase structure related to the discourse-syntax interface is acquired very early, much earlier than Tense Phrase. The elements of Mood Phrase, which would select CP later, appear in child production earlier than the verbal conjugation or inflection with Tense and agreement. This is consistent with the acquisition order of particles in Japanese: Mood particles are produced much earlier than Case markers (Okubo 1967, among others). The conclusion obtained here does not contradict the hypothesis of ATOM which states that children in the RI stage omit either AGR (agreement) or TNS (Tense), or both (Wexler 1994).

Children in the RI stage produce a truncated structure smaller than TP. Children, even at the age of one, naturally and voluntarily build up a small structure missing Tense and agreement with the default verbal form of their language to express "imperative." At this stage, the finite or "anchoring" element is not the element that has a temporal interpretation ("Tense"), but Mood, which eventually selects the elements in CP in a top-down fashion.

Where Child Language and Adult Syntax in Tamil, Korean, and Japanese Meet

Although it is not clear whether the typical properties of RIs are also found in Tamil at this point, Lakshmanan's (2006) data at least does not provide any contradictive data against the common properties given in (6). For example, very young children use the adult-like imperatives, and the verb stem or nonfinite verb to express the progressive aspects we saw in (1) and (3), respectively. Furthermore, Lakshmanan (2006: 196) writes an insightful analysis about the reason regarding why verbal participle is erroneously used as the first verbal form by Tamil-acquiring children, as shown below.

(23) …the verbal participle suffix in Tamil is homophonous with the various past-tense allomorphs, to which the enunciative vowel *u* is added…when the contexts in which the different nonfinite verb types occur are examined, the evidence suggest that in past-tense contexts, the verbal participle form tends to be strongly preferred compared to the bare stem form and the infinitive form. It might be the case, therefore, that some of the instances of the verbal participle form, which were categorized as nonfinite forms in child Tamil, may actually be past-tense forms without overt agreement. This suggests that overt marking of Tense may be developmentally prior to overt marking of agreement. It is relevant to mention here that the verbs in Malayalam, which is a Dravidian language that is most closely related to Tamil, inflect for Tense, Aspect, and modality but not agreement. If many of the verbal participle forms are in fact finite forms without agreement, then this suggests that Tamil children initially go through a stage in which they assume that Tamil is like Malayalam with respect to verbal inflection (underlined by the present writer.)

As Lakshmanan's (2006) data contains such cases where a past event is described by the nonfinite verb form as shown in (4), it does not seem to be the case that adult-like Tense system is fully acquired at the time when such "erroneous" verb forms are produced. However, our study presented in this chapter finds her claim quite insightful. The three types of erroneous verb forms she observes are the typical RI (analogue) forms found in the other languages. As the RI (analogue) forms, the children speaking English and Chinese, for example, use the bare verb form, or the well-formed imperative form, and the children speaking Japanese employ the (surrogate) past-tensed form. The empirical fact that there is a stage where overt marking of Tense may be developmentally prior to overt marking of agreement does not contradict with the hypothesis of ATOM for Root Infinitives either. Furthermore, our analysis of the child Korean and child Japanese also indicates that they are like Malayalam, given the syntactic analysis of Amritavalli and Jayaseelan (2005).

Amritavalli and Jayaseelan (2005) propose that in Kannada and Malayalam, what appears to be Tense in the affirmative verb is actually Aspect, and that finiteness is a property of Mood Phrase, which can be occupied by any one of the three elements: AGR (agreement), Neg (negation), or modal. They argue that Dravidian clause structure does not project a Tense Phrase, but finiteness in Kannada and Malayalam is constituted by the presence of a Mood Phrase, based on an analysis of negation in Kannada in which a finiteness head in Mood Phrase assigns finiteness to the Neg element *illa*. The finite or "anchoring" element in Kannada is not the element that has a temporal interpretation ("Tense"), but Mood (see Amritavalli and Jayaseelan (2005) and Ramadoss and Amritavalli (2007) for the adult syntax and child grammar, respectively, for detailed analysis.)

Recall here that there is a stage in child Korean and child Japanese in which the very early verbs are obviously "erroneously" associated by a Mood marker, i.e., *-e* form and *-na* form, respectively. At the stage in question, both the nominative Case marking on the subject and the conjugation with Tense on verbs are absent. Based on the argument presented in Murasugi and Fuji (2008) that Japanese- and Korean-speaking children pass through the RI Analogue stage in a parallel way, we would suggest a possibility that a finiteness head in Mood Phrase assigns finiteness to the child RI Analogues, just like in adult Kannada and adult Malayalam. In this case, the "finiteness" of child RIs would be able to be constituted by the presence of a Mood Phrase, just like adult Malayalam. This would provide supportive evidence for the proposal made by Amritavalli and Jayaseelan (2005), who argue that Dravidian clause structure does not project a Tense Phrase, but finiteness in Dravidian is constituted by the presence of a Mood Phrase.[7]

Traditional grammarians divided verb forms into two major classes: finite forms and nonfinite forms. Finite forms express some grammatical Mood, such as indicative, subjunctive, optative, and imperative. They can carry the person agreement and appear as the main verb of a root clause. On the other hand, nonfinite forms such as infinitive and participles lack the expression of grammatical Mood and the marking of person agreement. They usually appear in subordinate clauses. At the child RI (analogue) stage, the form, finite and nonfinite, both appear, while the finite form is expressed by Mood in some Asian languages. If this analysis is correct, RI (analogues) can be finite, although there are variations in the form, and the tense-related items are optionally missing in RI Analogues then, just like Optional Infinitives in European languages. Although it is not still clear whether or not Tamil-speaking children also mark Mood on verbs in addition to the three

[7]It is also interesting to note that *na* in Japanese behaves like Kannada in the sense that Mood Phrase can be occupied by any one of the three elements AGR (agreement), Neg (negation), or modal (Amritavalli and Jayaseelan 2005). It also reminds us of the analysis of the adult Root Infinitives by Etxepare and Grohmann (2005), which states that the adult Root Infinitives consist of two overtly expressed parts: the root infinitive proper (RI), orthographically indicated by "?!" (evoking a question-like exclamation) such as "John go to the movies?!", and the Coda (a further exclamation that seems to deny the truth value of the RI) such as "I would never do such a thing!" According to Etxepare and Grohmann (2005), the two properties are also found in Spanish as in "Yo ir a esa fiesta?! Jamás! (Me go to that party?! Never!)".

erroneous forms mentioned above, if child Tamil is just like adult Malayalam as Lakshmanan (2006) proposes, a consistent analysis of child Tamil, child Korean, and child Japanese, meets here and glows together.

Conclusion

There is an RI Analogue stage in Asian child languages although the forms are not infinitives, as Kim and Phillips (1998) and the Nanzan Acquisition Project on RIs have proposed. The RI Analogues share the properties of RIs with respect that Tense is underspecified, and the typical Tense features (e.g., nominative Case marker) are not observed, yet the Mood is active.

In this chapter, we extended the proposal given in Murasugi and Fuji (2008) and argued that the obvious Mood element in the RI Analogue is realized with the Mood markers, i.e., *-e (-a)* in Korean (Kim and Phillips 1998), and *-na* in Japanese. That is, the volition, imperative and propositive, or Modal Reference Effects are realized with a Mood particle *-e* in child Korean, and *-na* in child Japanese. Children go through the RI Analogue stage at which they speak a language that is like their target language, but one that is also like Malayalam in allowing the presence of a Mood Phrase to express finiteness.

This chapter further extended the analysis to the acquisition of Tamil. Based on the research of Thomas and Vainikka (1994), Sarma (1995), and Lakshmanan (2006), among others, we have argued that their findings can be recaptured as the RI phenomenon, and Lakshmanan's (2006) insight is consistent with the present proposal analyzed based on the findings of Kim and Phillips (1998), the Nanzan Acquisition Project, and the syntactic analysis given in Amritavalli and Jayaseelan (2005). The RI Analogues share the properties of RIs with respect that Tense is underspecified, and the typical Tense features (e.g., nominative Case marker) are not observed, yet the Mood is active.

In the generative linguistic view, the reason that children, without negative evidence or positive reinforcement, acquire the complex system of language is that they are endowed with innate knowledge of Universal Grammar that guides them to acquire their target grammar (Chomsky 1981, among others). According to the generative linguistic hypothesis, both child and adult grammars are restricted in an innately specified space of grammar. The hypothesis predicts that the ways where the child grammar and the target adult grammar may differ are limited to ways in which different adult languages may differ from each other.

While child grammars may contain processes that are not present in the target grammar, they abide by the same universal constraints as adult grammars, and the intermediate acquisition processes which do not apparently conform to the target language have direct correlates in other possible adult languages. As a consequence, we would expect that the structure of RIs in which their language is like Malayalam with respect to verbal inflection is not only found in child grammar, but could be also found in adult grammar in some languages. If the present analysis that very young children Tamil, Korean and Japanese go through a RI (analogue) stage is on the right track, the nonadult grammatical behavior of very young children would provide supportive evidence for the innateness of Universal Grammar.

References

Aksu-Koç, A., and K.N. Ketrez. 2003. Early verbal morphology in Turkish: Emergence of inflections. In *Development of verb inflection in first language acquisition: A cross linguistic perspective*, ed. W.U. Dressler, D. Bittner, and M. Kilani-Schoch, 27–52. Berlin: Mouton de Gruyter.

Aljenaie, K. 2000. The emergence of tense and agreement in Kuwaiti children speaking Arabic. In *Reading Working Paper in Linguistics*, Vol. 4, eds. R. Ingham and P. Kerswill, 1–24.

Amritavalli, R., and K.A. Jayaseelan. 2005. Finiteness and negation in Dravidian. In *The oxford handbook of comparative syntax 2005*, ed. G. Cinque, and R. Kayne, 178–220. New York: Oxford University Press.

Blom, E., and F. Wijnen. 2000. How Dutch Children's root infinitives become modal. In *Proceedings of the 20th Annual Boston University Conference on Language Development* (BUCLD 24), 128–139.

Coene, M., H. Taelman, L. Avram, and S. Gillis. 2005. Early bare infinitives are universally non-finite…but not always infinitives! Paper presented at 5th International Council for Central and East European Studies, Berlin, July 26, 2005.

Deen, K. U. 2002. *The Omission of Inflection Prefixes in the Acquisition of Nairobi Swahili*. Ph.D. dissertation, UCLA.

Etxepare, R., and K. K. Grohmann. 2005. Towards a grammar of adult root infinitives. In *Proceedings of the 24th West Coast Conference on Formal Linguistics* (WCCFL 24) eds. J. Alderete, C. -H. Han, and A. Kochetov, 129–137.

Haegeman, L. 1995. Root infinitives, tense, and truncated structures in Dutch. *Language Acquisition* 4: 205–255.

Hoekstra, T., and N. Hyams. 1998. Aspects of root infinitives. *Lingua* 106: 91–112.

Hyams, Nina. 2002. Clausal structure in child Greek: A reply to Varlokosta, Vainikka and Rohrbacher and a reanalysis. *The Linguistic Review* 19 (3): 225–269.

Kato, S., Y. Sato, Y. Chikuda, R. Miyoshi, Y. Sakai, and M. Koizumi. 2003. *"Root Infinitives": Nihongo-karano Kensho ["Root Infinitives": From the Perspectives of Japanese], Tohoku University Linguistics Journal 12*. Sendai: Tohoku University.

Kim, M., and C. Phillips. 1998. Complex verb constructions in child Korean: Overt markers of covert functional structure. In *Proceedings of the 20th Annual Boston University Conference on Language Development* (BUCLD 22), 430–441.

Krämer, I. 1993. The licensing of subjects in early child language. *MITWPL #19*:197–212.

Lakshmanan, U. 2006. Assessing linguistic competence: Verbal inflection in child Tamil. *Language Assessment Quarterly*, 3(2): 171–205. http://www.tandfonline.com/doi/abs/10.1207/s15434311laq0302_5.

Lee, C. 1993. The acquisition of mood indicators in Korean. In *Harvard Studies in Korean Linguistics V*, eds. S. Kuno et al., 27–41.

Murasugi, K. 2009. What Japanese-speaking Children's errors tell us about syntax. Paper Presented at GLOW in Asia VII, English and Foreign Languages University, Hyderabad, February 28, 2009.

Murasugi, K., and C. Fuji. 2008. Root infinitives: The parallel routes the Japanese- and Korean-speaking children step in. Paper Presented at Japanese/Korean Linguistic Conference 18, City University of New York, November 13, 2008. (Paper appeared in *Japanese/Korean*

Linguistics, Vol. 19, eds. Ho-Min Sohn et al., 527–541. Stanford: CSLI (Center for the Study of Language and Information) in 2011).

Murasugi, K., C. Fuji, and T. Hashimoto. 2007. What's acquired later in an agglutinative language. Paper Presented at Asian GLOW VI, Chinese University of Hong Kong, December 27, 2007.

Murasugi, K., and T. Nakatani. 2013. Three types of 'Root Infinitives': Theoretical implications from child Japanese. In *Japanese/Korean Linguistics,* vol. 20, eds. Bjarke Frellesvig and Peter Sells, 263–280., Stanford: CSLI (Center for the Study of Language and Information).

Murasugi, K, T. Nakatani, and C. Fuji. 2009. The roots of root infinitive analogues: The surrogate verb forms common in adult and child grammars. Poster Presented at BUCLD 34, Boston University, November 7th. (Paper appeared in the BUCLD 34 Proceedings Online Supplement in 2010).

Noji, J. 1973–1977. *Youji no Gengoseikatu no Zittai* [*The Language Use in Child Age*] *I–IV.* Bunka Hyoron Syuppan, Tokyo. (Also available in CHILDES as NOJI corpus.).

Okubo, A. 1967. *Youji Gengo no Hattatsu [The Development of Child Language].* Tokyo: Tokyodou Shuppan.

Poeppel, D. 1996. Commentary on Chapter 10. In *Towards a genetics of language*, ed. Mabel L. Rice, 291–296. Hillsdale, NJ: Erlbaum.

Ramadoss, D., and R. Amritavalli. 2007. The acquisition of functional categories in Tamil with special reference to negation. *Nanzan Linguistics* 1 (1): 67–84.

Rasetti, L. 2003. *Optional Categories in Early French Syntax: A Developmental Study of Root Infinitives and Null Arguments.* Ph.D. dissertation, Université de Genéve, Switzerland.

Rizzi, L. 1993/1994. Some notes on linguistic theory and language development: The case of root infinitives. *Language Acquisition* 3: 371–393.

Sarma, V. (1995). How many branches to the syntactic tree? Disagreement over agreement [on children's acquisition of Tamil]. In *Proceedings of the North East Linguistic Society 25*, vol. 2, ed. J. N. Beckmanvol, 89–103.

Sano, T. 1995. *Roots in Language Acquisition: A Comparative Study of Japanese and European Languages*. Ph.D. dissertation, UCLA.

Thomas, T., and A. Vainikka (1994). Development of functional projections in Tamil. *Penn Linguistics Review.*

Varlokosta, S., A. Vainikka, and B. Rohrbacher. 1996. Root infinitives without infinitives. In *Proceedings of the 20th Annual Boston University Conference on Language Development* (BUCLD 20), 816–827.

Wexler, K. 1994. Optional infinitives, head movement, and economy of derivation. In *Verb movement*, ed. N. Hornstein, and D. Lightfoot, 305–335. Cambridge, MA: Cambridge University Press.

FSC
www.fsc.org
MIX
Papier | Fördert gute Waldnutzung
FSC® C083411

Kolibri 360 GmbH
Ferdinand-Jühlke-Straße 7
99095 Erfurt, Deutschland
produktsicherheit@kolibri360.de